**SAGE** was founded in 1965 by Sara Miller McCune to support the dissemination of usable knowledge by publishing innovative and high-quality research and teaching content. Today, we publish more than 850 journals, including those of more than 300 learned societies, more than 800 new books per year, and a growing range of library products including archives, data, case studies, reports, conference highlights, and video. SAGE remains majority-owned by our founder, and after Sara's lifetime will become owned by a charitable trust that secures our continued independence.

Los Angeles | London | New Delhi | Singapore | Washington DC

# PSYCHOLOGY
## for **INDIA**

Thank you for choosing a SAGE product!
If you have any comment, observation or feedback,
I would like to personally hear from you.
*Please write to me at* **contactceo@sagepub.in**

**Vivek Mehra,** Managing Director and CEO, SAGE India.

## Bulk Sales

SAGE India offers special discounts
for purchase of books in bulk.
We also make available special imprints
and excerpts from our books on demand.

*For orders and enquiries, write to us at*

Marketing Department
SAGE Publications India Pvt Ltd
B1/I-1, Mohan Cooperative Industrial Area
Mathura Road, Post Bag 7
New Delhi 110044, India

*E-mail us at* **marketing@sagepub.in**

## Get to know more about SAGE

Be invited to SAGE events, get on our mailing list.
*Write today to* **marketing@sagepub.in**

This book is also available as an e-book.

# PSYCHOLOGY for INDIA

## Durganand Sinha

with an 'Introduction' by
Girishwar Misra and Ajit K Dalal

**SAGE** www.sagepublications.com
Los Angeles • London • New Delhi • Singapore • Washington DC

*First published in 2015 by*

**SAGE Publications India Pvt Ltd**
B1/I-1 Mohan Cooperative Industrial Area
Mathura Road, New Delhi 110 044, India
*www.sagepub.in*

**SAGE Publications Inc**
2455 Teller Road
Thousand Oaks, California 91320, USA

**SAGE Publications Ltd**
1 Oliver's Yard, 55 City Road
London EC1Y 1SP, United Kingdom

**SAGE Publications Asia-Pacific Pte Ltd**
3 Church Street
#10-04 Samsung Hub
Singapore 049483

Published by Vivek Mehra for SAGE Publications India Pvt. Ltd, typeset in 10/12pt Times New Roman by Diligent Typesetter, Delhi and printed at Saurabh Printers Pvt Ltd, New Delhi.

**Library of Congress Cataloging-in-Publication Data Available**

**ISBN:** 978-93-515-0367-5 (HB)

**The SAGE Team:** Shambhu Sahu, Alekha Chandra Jena, Anju Saxena and Ritu Chopra

# Contents

# Preface

The psychology community in India is currently celebrating the hundredth anniversary of the formal beginnings of the discipline at Calcutta University in 1915. This special occasion prompted us to introspect and reflect on the territory charted so far, and planning and preparing for the journey ahead. While searching for an anchor in this exercise we thought it pertinent to share about a person and his work which embodies the spirit of scholarship in its fullest sense. The Indian mind often draws inspiration from great souls and considers them as role models to be emulated (महाजनो येन गत: स पन्थाः[1]). So we decided to celebrate the centenary year by bringing out an anthology of select writings of Professor Durganand Sinha—a pioneer of psychology in modern India and a champion of the non-Western and indigenous perspectives. His work characterizes a paradigm shift in the field of psychology and illustrates a life of committed scholar. This introduction to the anthology tries to orient the readers to have a feel of the life and range of the works of Professor Sinha that are vast in scope and still remain unparalleled among Indian psychologists. Accordingly we have titled this volume as *Psychology for India*. The essays included in this volume document Professor Sinha's multifaceted engagement with the themes that importantly figure in psychological discourse and illustrate his passion for the growth of psychology in India. While doing so we have tried to contextualize the contributions of Professor Sinha in the broader academic milieu within which he traded the path and carved out a niche for a new kind of psychology. Capturing and documenting the vast terrain of the works of Professor Sinha is a daunting task and the space limitations too constrain us to be exhaustive. Hence, the treatment here has been selective nevertheless it does allow a peep into the world of work of an academician par excellence and leading voice of twentieth century psychology.

The present selection of the published works of Professor Sinha aims at capturing the diverse domains of academic and research interests pursued

---

[1] Common men follow the path shown by the leaders or great persons.

over a period spanning over more than half of a century. Achieving a representative selection of his works proved difficult on many counts. First, the enormous amount of published works of Professor Sinha (a recent Google search yields over 700 citations of his work!) gave manifold choices and that made it difficult to select a few. Second, the changes that have taken place in the discipline as well as in the society during this period are reflected in his writings and one has to be careful in choosing some over the other. Finally, there are space constraints of the publication which required us to keep the number of pages limited. In our selection we chiefly relied on the criteria of relevance, and creative and generative power of the ideas in the papers.

Professor Sinha's writings were addressed to different audiences and occasions and at times he had to emphasize and reiterate the arguments in different ways. The range of Professor Sinha's concerns with respect to psychology and social science in general were numerous. Also, he was swimming against the current and had to convince many sectors about his conceptual, methodological and applied concerns. All this led to apparent diversity in his writings. However, a close scrutiny of his work makes it amply clear that it is charged by a deep-rooted concern and aspiration for a socially connected psychology ingrained in the meanings and practices of the Indian culture in all its variety, complexity and splendor. This was indeed an uphill task as the aura of Euro-American psychology was very strong. It had established the rules of the game for doing psychology and did not allow much reflexivity embedded in the culture. Instead, it directed to invest the academic resources to maintain a kind of status quo. Against this backdrop a lot of energy of Professor Sinha was directed towards shaking the frozen minds, advocating for changing the mindset, setting the agenda and convincing the colleagues from psychology and sister disciplines as well as policy makers, a case for psychology that goes beyond the individual psyche and is in constant dialogue with the dynamic social reality. To him, a psychology imprisoned in 'individual mind' divorced from the surrounding culture and ecology has no legitimacy.

The above concerns of Professor Sinha were the spirit behind the choice of articles comprising this selection. They have been broadly organized in the three sections, that is, rethinking the psychological paradigm, human development and applied concerns.

Colleagues from the Centre for Advanced Studies in Psychology at Allahabad University have helped in procuring relevant material for his volume. Professor Deepa Punetha, the current Head of Department, has enthusiastically supported the project. SAGE Publications has readily agreed to take up the project for publication to be released in the conference organized to celebrate the hundredth anniversary of modern psychology in India.

**Girishwar Misra**
**Ajit K Dalal**

# Acknowledgements

Permission from the publishers to reprint the following articles is acknowledged:

1. Sinha, D. (1989). Research in Psychology in the Developing World: An Overview. *Psychology and Developing Societies*, 1, 105–126. New Delhi: SAGE Publications.
2. Sinha, D. (1965). Integration of Modern Psychology with Indian Thought. *Journal of Humanistic Psychology*, 5, 6–17. New Delhi: SAGE Publications.
3. Sinha, D. (1994). Indigenization of Psychology in India. *Indian Psychological Abstracts & Reviews*, 1(1), 179–215. New Delhi: ICSSR.
4. Sinha, D. (2002). Culture and Psychology: Perspective of Cross-cultural Psychology. *Psychology and Developing Societies*, 14, 11–25. New Delhi: SAGE Publications.
5. Sinha, D. (1988). The Family Scenario in a Developing Country and Its Implications for Mental Health: The Case of India. In P.R. Dasan, J W Berry and N Sartorius (eds), *Health and Cross-cultural Psychology: Toward Applications* (pp. 48–70). Newbury Park, CA: SAGE Publications.
6. Sinha, D. (1980). Socialization, Family and Psychological Differentiation (with Shalini Bisht). In D. Sinha (ed.), *Socialization of the Indian Child*. New Delhi: Concept.
7. Sinha, D. (1978). The Young and the Old: Ambiguity of the Role Models and Values among Indian Youth. In S. Kakar (ed.), *Identity and Adulthood* (pp. 56–64). New Delhi: Oxford University Press.
8. Sinha, D. (1988). Basic Indian Values and Behaviour Dispositions in the Context of National Development: An Appraisal. In D. Sinha and H.S.R. Kao (eds), *Social Values and Development: Asian Perspectives* (pp. 31–55). New Delhi: SAGE Publications.
9. Sinha, D. (1982). Towards an Ecological Framework of Deprivation. In D. Sinha, R.C. Tripathi and G. Misra (eds), *Deprivation: Its Social Roots and Psychological Consequences*. New Delhi: Concept.

10. Sinha, D. (1990). Intervention for Development out of Poverty. In R.W. Brislin (ed.), *Applied Cross-cultural Psychology* (pp. 77–97). Newbury Park, CA: SAGE Publications.

11. Sinha, D. (1986). Motivational Syndrome of Farmers, Education and Rural Development. *Indian Journal of Current Psychological Research*, 1, 65–72. S.N. Rai Publisher.

12. Sinha, D. (1990). Applied Social Psychology in India. In G. Misra (ed.), *Applied Social Psychology in India.* New Delhi: SAGE Publications.

# Introduction: Life and Works of Durganand Sinha

Professor Durganand Sinha was born on 23 September 1922 to Raja Bahadur Sri Kirtyanand Sinha and Rani Srimati Prabhawati Devi, from the erstwhile ruling family of the princely state of Banaili located in north-eastern region of the Bihar state. He received his early academic training in Bihar. He earned B.A. Honours in 1943 and M.A. degree in Philosophy with specialization in Psychology from Patna University in 1945.

## The Patna Centre of Psychology

It is historically important to note that Patna was the seventh oldest university of India and had the credit of establishing the third Department of Psychology in the pre-independent India in 1946, after Calcutta and Mysore which were established in 1915 and 1924, respectively. The Psychology Department at Patna began along with the Institute of Psychological Research and Services headed by Sri H.P. Maiti. Vocational guidance and counselling services were provided by the department to students and to general public. Since Maiti was trained by Dr Girindra Shekhar Bose at Calcutta University, known as the father of psychoanalysis in India, orientation of the Institute was primarily psychoanalytic and clinical. In a short time, Patna emerged as a major centre for teaching and research in psychology and counselling services. Professor S.M. Mohsin was another important faculty in psychology at Patna. Patna has the distinction of training many distinguished psychologists, such as A.K.P. Sinha, Radhanath Rath, J.P. Das, Ravi N. Kanungo, Amar Kumar Singh and Janak Pandey, who have earned international recognition in their respective fields.

After completing M.A. from Patna, Professor Sinha proceeded to Cambridge University for higher studies where he earned M.Sc. degree in Psychology. He stayed there from 1945 to 1949 and got training with

Sir F.C. Bartlett and R. Davis. On his return from Cambridge in 1949, he joined as a faculty in psychology at Patna University. From there he moved to the Department of Humanities and Social Sciences, at the newly established Indian Institute of Technology (IIT) at Kharagpur, West Bengal, in 1959 where industrial psychology was his main field of research and teaching.

# Establishing Psychology Department at Allahabad

Professor Sinha joined Allahabad University as a Professor of Psychology in 1961 on invitation by the then Vice Chancellor Dr Sri Ranjan. The Department started with Professor Sinha as a single faculty in 1961. Later, C.H.K. Mishra, Prem Sankar, R.K. Mishra and R.C. Tripathi joined as faculty. The Department under the stewardship of Professor Sinha grew in later years with more faculty members, including E.S.K. Ghosh, R.K. Naidu, U.N. Agrawal, Meera Verma and Nisha Dhawan. All of them were from the first generation of students of Allahabad University. In course of time, the Department became a hub for scholars from other universities and institutes in India, as well as from the United States and the United Kingdom. In 1973, Professor Sinha accepted the National Fellowship of the University Grants Commission (UGC) and was on leave from the University for three years. However, as a National Fellow he remained affiliated to the Department. Unfortunately, during this period, while attending the Congress of International Union of Psychological Sciences at Helsinki, Finland, he got heart attack and had to be away from academics for some time. He had to undergo bypass surgery but was back to his academic pursuits after the recovery.

In recognition to the research contribution of Professor Sinha and his colleagues, the Department was elevated to the status of Department of Special Assistance (DSA) in 1977 by the UGC. This led to the faculty expansion and many new faculty members joined the Department. In 1977, Professor Sinha inducted Janak Pandey, Uday Jain, Girishwar Misra and Ajit Dalal, who were trained at other centres of learning. Namita Pandey, Rashmi Kumar, Deepa Punetha, Komila Thapa and Purnima Singh, all trained at Allahabad, also joined as faculty. Professor Sinha brought in research associates Anand Prakash, Shalini Bishta, Arvind Sinha and Yoganand Sinha (Raghoo), all of whom are well placed and doing excellent work at different institutions today. Professor Sinha had insight and understanding to pick up the right people and could bring in the Department strong faculty with diverse interests and expertise. He was the inspiration behind building a strong doctoral programme with course work. He got to the Department an independent unit of Social Psychology of Education with UGC funding and new faculty for 5 years. There were research projects, international collaborations and conferences which brought the Department to newer heights. Many faculty members from the Department went abroad with Fulbright, Commonwealth and other scholarships and many scholars came to teach courses and conduct research projects. A library with a large collection of books and journals was established and is one of the best in India. National-level seminars became regular features of the Department. In 1984, the Department was elevated by the UGC to the status of a Centre of Advanced Study (CAS) in psychology, only second one in the country after the first one in Utkal University at Bhubaneshwar. In 1989, he started a journal *Psychology and Developing Societies* in collaboration with SAGE India and contributed to it as its Editor during its formative years. This journal became an important outlet for the researchers from developing countries. Professor Sinha was also instrumental in the Department's participation in a 7-year-long major international collaboration in the area of disability studies funded by the Canadian International Development Agency (CIDA) located at the Queen's University, Canada.

It was the concerted endeavour of Professor Sinha to establish a world-class institution of higher learning in psychology at Allahabad. He took personal interest in the growth of colleagues and tried to provide a conducive environment to the faculty members and researchers to grow in their chosen areas of interest. The range and quality of publications during Professor Sinha's tenure stand in testimony to his academic leadership. To young faculty, he was like a father-figure who would be critical, teasing, challenging and encouraging to get the best out of them. He would stand by them when need be and would nurture talent in whatever way he could. In faculty selection, it was not enough for him to look for academic record only; for him, right values and ability for team work were equally significant.

Professor Sinha stayed at Allahabad throughout his life, except for a few years towards his retirement when he had moved to Patna (1982–1987) as Director of the A.N. Sinha Institute of Social Studies run with the help of Indian Council of Social Science Research (ICSSR) and Bihar Government. In his 5-year tenure as the Director, he concentrated on improving the academic environment there as well. He initiated many new activities at the Institute; directed socially relevant research projects and training programmes and edited the *Journal of Social and Economic Studies* also published by SAGE.

The contributions of Professor Sinha brought many honours to him. He served the International Association of Cross-Cultural Psychology (IACCP) as its President (1982–1984) and was made its Fellow, the highest honour given by the IACCP. He also served as a member of the Executive Board of the International Union of Psychological Sciences for 16 years (1980–1996). He was also associated with the International Association of Applied Psychology (IAAP). He served as the President of the Indian Psychological Association (1974), and edited its journal *Indian Journal of Psychology* (1976–1978), elected as President of Indian Academy of Applied Psychology (1975–1976) and was President of the Psychology Section of the Indian Science Congress Association in 1965. For a short period, he was the Nehru Chair Professor at the Department of Human Development and Family Studies (HDFS), M.S. University, Baroda, and Visiting Fellow at the University of Delhi. He was a founding member of the National Academy of Psychology (NAOP) established in 1989 and served as its advisor. He was awarded its Fellowship. He chaired or was a member of various policy-making bodies of the Government of India. He was also an ICSSR Council Member and its National Fellow in the 1980s. In 1992, he was awarded Pandit Jawaharlal Nehru National Level Award by the Government of Madhya Pradesh for his contributions to the growth of social sciences in India. He used the award money to form a Trust to promote psychology in India which continues to support the researchers.

After retirement from formal service at Allahabad University, Professor Sinha lived at Allahabad and continued his research and writing work. He was very meticulous and hardworking and expected his colleagues to develop the habit of hard work and commitment. He was always eager to communicate his ideas and considered bringing knowledge in the public domain as a requirement of science and scholarship. He was regularly publishing in India and outside. In his illustrious career, he wrote extensively on a wide range of issues encompassing diverse aspects of academic and societal functioning and published in non-psychology journals too (e.g. *Eastern Anthropologist, Indian Journal of Social Work, Social Change, Indian Journal of Industrial Relations,* and *Indian Journal of Labour Economics*). He passed away on 22 March 1998 in Delhi. In 2012, his wife Mrs Radha Devi also left this world. They are survived by two sons, Sri Premanand and Sri Ravi, both are settled in Delhi. Incidentally, their wives Ms Gita and Ms Mala are teaching psychology.

Professor Sinha's seminal work continues to inspire psychologists in terms of ideas, methodological innovations, social concern and professional commitment.

# The Academic Context of Professor Sinha's Works

During the 1950s, when Professor Sinha started his academic career, psychology was usually taught in the Indian universities as a part of philosophy courses. Most of the university departments used to have a mixed identity and were run under one Head who usually happened to be a philosophy faculty. During that transitional period, carving out a separate identity for psychology was a crucial disciplinary goal and posed an institutional challenge. Professor Sinha responded to this challenge constructively and created a strong teaching and research programme. He developed an active group of scholars and kept nurturing interest in exploring culturally and socially relevant problems of the time. His innovative spirit is visible in selecting new problems, evolving new methods and instruments and engaging with the broader concerns at the intersection of different social science disciplines.

Professor Sinha's passion for an interdisciplinary orientation was reflected in his effort to cross the conventional borders of psychology. His engagements with issues such as rural development, generation gap, social psychology of education, psychology of poverty and social disadvantage, and students' scholastic backwardness, to name a few, lend support to his versatility. As one of the senior professors, he enjoyed an unparalleled reputation and respect in the academic and professional world of Indian social science, particularly in psychology. He contributed to the growth of the discipline by his active participation in national-level committees and professional bodies and voicing his deep concern for a relevant and culturally responsive social science.

# Early Research Interest and Later Shifts

During his studies at Cambridge, Professor Sinha worked in the experimental tradition and investigated the effect of interpolated learning on recall and recognition in two papers published with Davis in 1950.

At Patna, his analysis of rumours in the earthquake-affected south Bihar published in *British Journal of Psychology* in 1952 exemplified his social concern. Issues in industrial psychology also drew his attention (see ICSSR review by Sinha, 1970). He also became interested in the phenomenon of 'manifest anxiety' and its correlates (Sinha, 1962) and his psychometric test to assess manifest anxiety, *Sinha WA Self Analysis of Anxiety*, became very popular (Sinha, 1959, 1960, 1961, 1962, 1963) and was used in training students at many Indian universities. His interest in motivation, cognition, perception, cognitive development and memory continued and first few of his doctoral students pursued that line of investigation (Sinha, 1952; Sinha & Sinha, 1957). A series of studies were done on the problems of union membership and job satisfaction (Sinha & Sharma, 1962; Sinha & Pai, 1963; Sinha, 1960, 1965), absenteeism (Sinha, 1960, 1961; Sinha & Singh, 1961) and determinants of job satisfaction (Sinha, 1965; Sinha & Nair, 1965). Student leadership (Sinha & Kumar, 1965, 1966) and qualities of engineering students (Sinha & Misra, 1961) were other issues explored by him.

A gradual shift is visible in his work since 1960. While still working on the themes from mainstream psychology, Sinha started questioning the domination of Western concepts and theories. He was critically engaged in exploring the possibility of a productive interface of Euro-American theories with the insights from indigenous thought systems of India. His paper in the *Journal of Humanistic Psychology* (Sinha, 1965) offered an analysis of the paradigmatic limitations of the mainstream psychology. He pleaded for blending the two perspectives to develop a more comprehensive understanding of the reality. He anticipated the movement of cross-cultural psychology (CCP) and built ground for it to take off. The cross-cultural orientation became a salient feature of Professor Sinha's academic participation, choice of research themes, social advocacy and training in later years.

It is noteworthy that though educated and trained during the British colonial period, Professor Sinha, unlike his contemporaries, did not emulate the Euro-American tradition of psychology. Instead he constantly strived for a delicate balance between scientific rigour and cultural realities within which the social life is embedded. He was open to the developments in the international arena, perhaps more than any of his peers, but he was ahead of them in terms of cultural sensibility. He consciously and consistently pursued the programme of a culturally appropriate and socially relevant psychology. To this end, he used the strategy of making research an increasingly resonant enterprise that attends to the nuances of social reality. He put emphasis on integration of scientist and professional roles (Sinha, 1977). He was always prepared to try new research methods and techniques suitable to specific problems of research. It was an astounding undertaking at the time when the received view of science was the dominant model of academic practices of psychology. A vast body of research in test development and experimental studies by the Indian psychologists clearly attests it (Mitra, 1972; Pareek, 1980a). We must give credit to Professor Sinha who did not succumb to those influences and persisted to develop culturally rooted psychology in India.

## Concern for the Masses and Village Life

Professor Sinha lived most of his life as a sophisticated urbane elite in a posh area of Allahabad, had regular interaction with peers across the globe and endorsed a cosmopolitan view. However, he also had love for village life that continued to occupy his attention throughout his life. In fact, whenever he got an opportunity to engage with the life and challenges of the village people he responded to that. His study of villagers' motivation was a pioneering work (Sinha, 1969). His plea for macro psychology (Sinha, 1985) at the International Congress of Psychology and contribution in establishing a Division of Psychology of National Development at IAAP (Sinha, 1984) are concrete expressions of his interest in the development of rural people. He voiced this concern as the President of Psychology Section of the Indian Science Congress Association in 1966 at Chandigarh convention. He also considered the problem of motivation, change proneness and rural leadership, and supervised the work of several doctoral students in this area (i.e., Sinha & Chaube, 1972, 1974; Sinha & Prahraj, 1980; Tiwari & Sinha, 1980). He was also involved in a project on rural development with UN Agency at Nagoya, Japan.

## Fostering Cultural Sensibility in Psychological Inquiry

The movement of CCP emerged as a methodological critique of mainstream psychology which had limited empirical base in select population groups, but claimed its universality. CCP acknowledged the role of culture and ecology as antecedents of psychological outcomes. Professor Sinha found the eco-cultural perspective suitable for a culture-inclusive psychology that would allow registering the psychological variations across diverse cultural and sub-cultural groups. He was one of the founder members of the IACCP and continued his association with it throughout his life. Professor Sinha raised concern for developing an indigenous perspective. He strongly believed that the development of psychological science should be in tune with the socio-cultural realities, if it has to be useful for the society. Since the realities change across cultural settings, an alien framework often interferes with representing and interpreting social realities. Professor Sinha maintained a delicate balance between cultural and cross-cultural comparative orientations in his work.

Mapping social reality with preexisting alien categories and concepts is often problematic and allows only a distorted view. Realizing that strict adherence to Western methods and themes ignoring the Indian ethos was neither appropriate nor desirable; Professor Sinha took initiative to develop a psychology that could be applied to a wide range of Indian issues. He urged the Indian psychologists for developing and using theoretical frameworks consonant with Indian culture. He recognized the need of indigenization of Western theories and concepts to suit the Indian reality, as well as emphasized drawing from ancient Indian intellectual resources (Sinha, 1997). In conceptual terms, he opted for a perspective that stressed on the relational or symbiotic orientation and harmony with nature and society as key features of the Indian world view. These initiatives were not in tune with the preferences of hardcore Indian psychologists who, being deeply entrenched in the Western tradition, were convinced of the universality and cumulative nature of psychological knowledge. They were satisfied with test construction, test adaptation and laboratory experimentation on borrowed issues and variables, divorced from the Indian social reality, and continued in the same tradition (see the *First ICSSR Survey of Research in Psychology* by Mitra, 1972).

# The Narrative of Psychology in India

In 1982, Professor Sinha attended the meeting organized by Wolgang Schwedler (UNESCO) and Wayne Holtzman (IUPsyS) on the progress in psychology in developing nations which led to a special issue of the *Journal of International Psychology*, 1984, 19(1,2). His publication in that special issue was followed by more work that culminated in the form of a monograph entitled *Psychology in a Third World Country: The Indian Experience* (SAGE India, 1986). It provided the first comprehensive and critical assessment of the growth of psychology in modern India in a historical perspective. He built this account drawing upon a variety of resources and documented the way the discipline was shaped during the twentieth century. Interestingly enough, the story of psychology unfolded during this period was the one in which he was a player as well as a witness, and this has made the account very authentic. Professor Sinha identified the following four phases of the development of the discipline in India: (i) the Pre-Independence Phase, (ii) the Post-Independence Phase of Expansion, (iii) the Phase of Problem-Oriented Research and (iv) the Phase of Indigenization. The monograph elaborates on these four phases, providing a comprehensive picture of the growth of modern psychology in India up till the early 1980s. In addition, Professor Sinha also wrote on the history of the growth of social psychology in India. A major paper appeared in the inaugural issue of the *Asian Journal of Social Psychology* (1998, 1, 17–31) which traced the growth of social psychology in India from the ancient to the modern period.

# Culture, Human Development and International Collaboration

Professor Sinha's cultural psychological concerns were expressed in theoretical and empirical works which he had undertaken and published in collaboration with fellow scholars from different regions of the world including Witkin, Gastav Jahoda, John Berry, Ype Poortinga and John B. Deregowsky. These collaborations were largely in the areas of methodology, psychological differentiation, socialization, changes in family, perceptual development, health-related issues and cultural adaptation. He was fascinated by Urie Bronfenbrenner's developmental ecology and adapted that for the study of human development in the Indian context (Sinha, 1982). Integrative reviews in the field of human development by him have been succinct and insightful. They showcased the Indian work before an international audience and allowed for dialogue and knowledge sharing (e.g. Sinha, 1979, 1982).

Professor Sinha had considerable interest in understanding psychological functions in human development. The study of development of fear in children (Sinha & Sidana, 1973), aggression in cultural and developmental context (Punetha & Sinha, 1982), development of Indian moral values (Sinha & Varma, 1972), understanding family pattern (Polyandrous vs. paternal) and differentiation (with Shalini Bharat) and language development and child-rearing practices (with Anjali Singh) were unique initiatives. The study of pictorial depth perception with Pushpa Shuka/Mishra, which used the paintings by children, provided a very innovative way to understand developmental changes.

The eco-cultural framework of John Berry was a conceptual tool comprehensive enough to accommodate changes along time and space. Professor Sinha used this as a broad framework for analyzing cultural and environmental influences on various cognitive processes and behaviours including values, pro-social behaviour, and perceptual development. It became a very productive area and led to several important publications and doctoral studies on tribal and non-tribal groups (Ramesh Mishra and Tantreshwar Jha). A large-scale project was also undertaken to focus on the pattern of adaptation under changing ecological conditions in Chota Nagpur area of Bihar. Professor Sinha's book in collaboration with Ramesh C. Mishra and John Berry (1996), *Ecology, Acculturation and Psychological Adaptation* reports the project and illustrates that the study of culture has been at the centre of Professor Sinha's academic concerns. The meanings of culture, however, are quite varied. Going through the works of Professor Sinha, one can easily see that his ideas about culture grew over time. From mere categorization to experiences and practices, to generic label for the totality of symbolic resources of a group, indeed culture has been used and misused. Professor Sinha was familiar with this variety of its meanings but opted for the cross-cultural approach. He noted that culture is a packaged variable and to make it useful in research it has to be unpackaged. In 1993, he came across the paper 'On the Place of Culture in Psychological Science', by Misra and Gergen. Taking cognizance of this work, he wrote an interesting piece entitled 'Culture as the Target and Culture as the Source' (Sinha, 1996), and in 1997 his chapter on indigenization of psychology in the second edition of the *Handbook of Cross-cultural Psychology* also got published. He gave keynote address at the Culture-Psychology Seminar at Delhi University in 1997 and the paper was published posthumously in a special issue of *Psychology and Developing Societies* in 2002. He took the position that deployment of culture for psychological knowledge depends on from where we enter into the research process.

Professor Sinha strongly believed that only through the development of local and culturally apt psychologies, an inclusive understanding of human behaviour is attainable. That would not only furnish ways to improve the well-being of the people but also reduce the ethnocentrism prevalent in psychology. Professor Sinha did realize that the pursuit of diverse traditions of psychology in isolation may not be an appropriate goal. That may deprive researchers of the benefits of mutual understanding and exchange. He therefore favoured a synthesis of these two approaches.

# Methodological Pluralism

Historically, psychology has been over-concerned with methodology and that has become the core of disciplinary orientation. This was perhaps an imperative of psychology's movement towards entry to the college of science. Even today, psychologists often fight over the issue of core of psychology and are somewhat unclear about the same. However, they do converge on the centrality of methodology being the discipline's identity signature. The subject matter became increasingly less important than the method. As a result, a kind of method centricity has seized upon creativity and innovation in research. Under scientism, the knowledge claims are method driven and often serve to boost the false pride of a researcher without much substantial gain in so far as understanding is concerned. Professor Sinha was very critical of this tendency particularly of the mindless application of psychological testing and experimental design. His methodological concern for realism in research was clearly evident in the debate about the nature of experimental social psychology which for some stood for verbal simulation of various experimental treatments/conditions (Sinha, 1982). Professor Sinha had gone for methodological plurality, as social psychological reality manifests itself in different forms and no one method can guarantee to provide right image or reality. His innovations in measurement in village studies, like the use of behavioural observation, happy life test, grain sorting (Chaube & Sinha, 1972; Sinha, 1968, 1969), situational measures (Sinha, 1972), use of painting by children (Shukla & Sinha, 1974) and Story Pictorial EFT (Sinha, 1984) and other measures with R.C. Mishra in studies of adaptation, provide good examples of methodological pluralism. It is obvious from Professor Sinha's work that he was open to ideas from the local and indigenous sources, and preferred simpler and naturalistic measures as against artificial measures. He held the phenomenon more important than the method.

# Making Psychology Relevant to the Contemporary Realities

Professor Sinha tried to foster a vision of psychology informed by the contemporary realities of the developing Indian nation, engaged in the gigantic task of socio-economic transformation (Sinha, 1966). He advocated enlarging the research agenda of psychology to include the problems of social change. He worked hard to create the Centre for the Study of Social Change and National Development at the Department and insistently worked on the diverse challenges of social change. The turn of gaze from psychology laboratory to the unstructured, unpredictable and dynamic village life presented a stark contrast to the relatively stable, organized and structured environment of a psychology laboratory where 'control' was the keyword. The challenge involved changing the mindset, developing sensitivity to the cultural nuances and creatively engaging with diverse aspects of reality. He developed newer ways of looking at the psychological processes and concepts appropriate for the villagers. His analysis was published in *Indian Villages in Transition* (1969) and *Motivation and Rural Development* (1974) and opened a new field of interdisciplinary research. Similarly Professor Sinha also became interested in the analysis of changes in value orientation across generations and role models in the youth (1974; 1979). Instead of shying away from confronting the social reality, Professor Sinha endeavoured to bring psychology and its toolkit closer to the reality and if required readily prepared it to engage meaningfully with the demands of reality.

# Psychology of Poverty and Social Disadvantage

The field experience during village studies was critical to the shaping of Professor Sinha's societal concerns as a psychologist. From his work and publications post-village studies, a marked change in the approach and academic engagements of Professor Sinha can be seen. A close connection can easily be seen between village studies and his changed perspective on the issues of indigenization, development of problem-oriented psychology and macro-level analysis which characterized his deliberations for quite some time in future. One of the major changes in his research agenda was a programmatic study of poverty and deprivation. His focus was on the developmental implications of poverty.

Extending Bronfenbrenner's (1977) ecological model, Sinha advanced the ecology of poverty and social disadvantage in the Indian context. He thought of two concentric layers of ecology—the immediate and the surrounding—and looked at them as constraints and affordances that promote and sustain certain cognitive (Sinha, 1977), motivational (Sinha & Misra, 1982) and behavioural patterns. He organized a national seminar and brought out an edited volume entitled *Deprivation: Its Social Roots and Psychological Consequences* (Sinha, Tripathi & Misra, 1982) which became a classic. A series of doctoral studies and research projects were launched by Sinha and his colleagues, including R.C. Tripathi, Janak Pandey, and Girishwar Misra at Allahabad. This theme dominated the academic scene for a decade and the links of poverty and disadvantage with education (Namita Pandey, Rajiv Sharma), attribution and political affiliation (Yoganand Sinha, Tripathi), and well-being and coping (Saroj Kakar, Pandey & Singh, 1980) were published (see for review Misra and Tripathi, 2004). In 1990, Professor Sinha integrated these studies and came out with a model for intervention to grow out of poverty (Sinha, 1990) and drew attention to the mediating role of psychological processes in poverty, emphasizing the key role that psychologists can play in poverty alleviation.

# Consolidating the Cultural Orientation

The significance of 'culture' in psychological research and theorization came in sharper focus with the movement from a generic treatment to cross-cultural comparison to indigenization. The CCP was mainly interested in the testing of Western psychological theories and constructs in non-Western cultural contexts and thus empirically targeted at extending the range of Western psychological theories. Taking a step further, the move towards indigenization was pregnant with the possibility of drawing the concepts, theories and methods from a given culture. Professor Sinha presented the case of India in his chapter 'Indigenous Psychologies', in the volume edited by Uichol Kim and John W. Berry (1993). Subsequently he wrote a full length chapter on indigenization of psychology across the globe for the 2nd Edition of the *Handbook of Cross-Cultural Psychology* (Berry, Poortinga & Pandey, 1997). This chapter presents a new ground for developing an authentic psychology by arguing for paradigmatic indigenization from within. He was indeed a champion of indigenization of psychology.

Engaged in dialogue with colleagues from different cultural backgrounds, Professor Sinha remained creative and to some extent proactive in his work. His decade-long collaboration with Henry S.R. Kao of the University of Hong Kong was very productive and yielded three significant publications that documented the applications of culturally relevant psychology. The first two related to social and organizational contexts in different regions: *Social Values and Development: Asian Perspectives* (by SAGE, 1988) and *Effective Organizations and Social Values* (by SAGE, 1994). The third one titled *Asian Perspectives on Psychology* (by SAGE, 1997) argued for building psychology through indigenous psychological resources from Asia. His interest and commitment to link psychological theory and practice with the cultural context became a dominant concern in his subsequent work. In order to vent his concerns through an academic forum for reflection and discourse, Professor Sinha used his edited journal *Psychology and Developing Societies*.

# Building the Relational Model of Man–Environment Transaction

At a conceptual or paradigmatic level, Professor Sinha was trying to build and extend the relational or symbiotic model of the man–environment transaction. He had applied this to the study of socialization (Sinha, 1980, 1988), morality (Sinha, 1984) and health (Sinha, 1990). He offered an insightful analysis of the notion of hierarchically organized and multilayered self from the classical Indian texts (Sinha & Naidu, 1994). The Western mind often operates through dichotomous categories. Accordingly we find specifications of conceptual categories such as internal vs. external, independent vs. interdependent, introvert vs. extrovert and individualism vs. collectivism. Such binary categorizations do not hold true in the case of Indian thinking which is characterized as context dependent and combines the opposites (e.g. Ardhanarishwar). After a thorough analysis of diverse Indian sources indicating the presence of (tolerance of) dissonance and keeping seemingly inconsistent elements in a broader frame, Professor Sinha made effort to empirically examine how in the Indian self, elements of individualism and collectivism are represented. It was observed that in Indian self-conceptualizations, the opposites coexist (Sinha & Tripathi, 1994).

Professor Sinha realized that the developing countries have their own problems, particularly in the field of managing social change in the era of globalization. Professor Sinha along with Diaz-Guerrero, Henry Kao, H.C. Kelman, Çigdem Kagitçibasi, Michel Duro Jayiye, Uichol Kim, Serpell and V.G. Enriquez struggled hard to register the voices from Asia, Latin America and Africa. They worked together to bring out the limitations of Western Academic Scientific Psychology (WASP) and directed their efforts to offer alternative perspectives.

# Institution Building and Mentoring

Professor Sinha, by his initiative, vision and commitment, was able to gauge the changes which were necessary to meet the societal challenges in India. He changed the priority of research by demonstrating and setting examples through the study of changes in values and Indian family system (Sinha, 1988, 1991, 1996). To this end, he also tried to change the ethos of research by advocating a dialogue between the text and context, theory and practice and culture and psychology.

Indeed, Professor Sinha remained active in the professional and disciplinary discourses at national and international levels and remained a central figure of the psychological profession in India throughout his life. He actively participated in and reciprocated to the emerging and contemporary discourses at various forums and encouraged colleagues to engage with contemporary concerns. His academic concerns were wide ranging and the researcher in him was always eager to learn, grow and share his ideas. This resulted in several international collaborations in diverse fields of psychology. With a rare combination of seriousness, dedication and determined inquisitiveness, he pursued a career of academician over a half century. His multifaceted influence is seen not only in terms of numerous articles, psychological tools, books (see the 'Complete Works of Durganand Sinha' at the end of the book) but also by a large number of colleagues, friends, students and admirers in many parts of the world, who in one way or the other are carrying forward his tradition.

Professor Sinha was a Guru, and one of the stalwarts of psychology in modern India and definitely one who is globally known in the psychological fraternity. A unique combination of academic courage, commitment and initiative he took lead in shifting the focus of research and teaching of psychology from a cultural- and laboratory-oriented positivistic tradition to a discipline with cultural sensibility and interest in understanding, explaining and shaping the social reality. He was aware of the irrelevance of an insular and ivory tower view of psychological enterprise and tirelessly worked towards a vibrant psychology *for* India. This speaks about his reflexivity and futuristic vision, which was missing in most of his peers. He transformed psychology in India from its Euro-American moorings aligned with the dictums of a strong positivist tradition. In true sense, Professor Sinha was an institution in himself. His scholarship and administrative acumen provided a constant source of inspiration for his peers, colleagues and students.

Interaction with Professor Sinha was always a pleasure and a learning experience. He was widely travelled and liked visiting new places and interacting with people. Often marked by humour and a touch of parental concern, he loved sharing his wide-ranging experiences and telling stories about people and places. He was fond of music and many eminent musicians performed at his place and we colleagues would be invited to listen to them. An exceptional degree of sensitivity to learn, play with ideas and apply them were the hallmark of his academic endeavours. He loved teaching and invariably taught the first-year undergraduate students. He started his academic career in an era when psychology did not enjoy a strong independent identity and the academia maintained an ambivalent attitude. Allahabad, once famous as 'Oxford of the East', had an exceptionally strong faculty and scholarly traditions in literature, philosophy, history and physical sciences. It was a fairly new subject on the academic scene of this old university founded in 1887. In this backdrop, Professor Sinha's initiatives were often seminal and expanded the scope of this growing discipline.

The editors of this volume had the proud privilege to have a long association with Professor Sinha who was their mentor, and this volume is a tribute to his memory. We sincerely hope that the select works of Professor Sinha which form the main body of this volume would ignite the minds of readers to provide impetus for promotion of a psychology for India.

# Impact on Research and Practice

The lively, creative and scholarly career of Professor Sinha had many facets. He wielded substantial influence on the field of psychology through his active engagement as a researcher, teacher, academic leader and social thinker. This makes it difficult to grasp and assess his diverse influences on psychology in India. As a person, he was open, inquisitive, ingenious and responsive to the societal concerns of a developing nation. His circle of professional colleagues included scholars from South Africa, Australia, USA, Turkey, Philippines, China, Germany, Bangladesh, Pakistan and Nepal. Those who had the privilege to have met him were impressed by the breadth of his academic, social and cultural interests. He remained a leading advocate of the importance of culture and social context within which human lives are embedded (Kim, Park & Park, 2000; Moghaddam, 1987). His initiatives culminated in several research projects dedicated to innovative and interdisciplinary themes, such as perceptual development, cultural adaptation (Mishra, Sinha & Berry, 1996) and environmental issues. He also strengthened collaborations among researchers which led to collective publications on values and national development (Sinha & Kao, 1988), Asian perspectives on psychology (Kao & Sinha, 1997; Pandey, Sinha & Bhawuk, 1996), effective organizations and social values (Kao, Sinha & Sek Hong, 1995) and management and cultural values (Kao, Sinha & Wilpert, 1999). As an institution builder, he encouraged networking with colleagues and forged serious research programmes and actively participated in professional organizations of psychology in India and abroad. He presented a model of collaborative work and a rare example of institutional innovation.

He had strong ties with cross-cultural researchers and he contributed immensely to the evolution of the subfields of cross-cultural and cultural psychology (see Berry, Mishra & Tripathi, 2003). His contributions to the movement towards indigenization of psychology are highly appreciated (Sinha, 1997). As a pioneer pursuing the studies of rural psychology, macro variables and processes and human values, he significantly contributed to these neglected areas. His early research on rumors (Sinha, 1952) had contributed importantly to the developments of cognitive theories in social psychology. Some themes and concerns such as culture, ecology and Indian ethos have reverberated in his subsequent works (Sinha, 1996). Developmental concern in its wide spectrum, covering individual as well as societal level functioning, remained at the core of much of his theorization and research. As a versatile genius and an ardent student of cultural phenomena, he displayed deep commitment to the growth and development of a culturally relevant discipline which finds no parallel in the Indian subcontinent (Moghaddam & Taylor, 1986; Poortinga, 1999).

The scholarly contributions of Professor Sinha, such as the study of Indian villagers, intergenerational differences, ecology of social disadvantage, psychological differentiation and well-being, have wide-ranging implications for psychological and social intervention. In his works, he opted for a functional theory which starts with data and maintains a reciprocal relationship between theory and data. He was concerned with ecological validity and tried to enrich the toolkit of researchers by incorporating newer methods and techniques. He maintained an applied orientation and was very fond of Kurt Lewin's dictum 'there is nothing as practical as a good theory'. His concern for applied orientation was manifested in the research themes that he chose and the work of his students that he supervised. He put Indian contributions on the world map with emphasis on macro psychology and indigenization. His emphasis was on synthesizing theory and research, and was engaged in making empirical work relevant for social change. He played a key role in the transformation of psychology in India to deal with the intricacies of social reality. In this sense, his work appears to be a turning point in the academic history of psychology in India. The collection of writings included in this volume gives a glimpse of Professor Sinha in action. This volume is especially valuable for those who did not have the privilege to know him personally but got inspired by his work and life. He has left a seminal mark on Indian psychologists and paved the way for developing a distinct identity for psychology in India. The post-Sinha psychology is changing with a new set of psycho-social challenges; new idiom and methodologies are changing the contours of research. But the firm foundation of academic psychology laid by Professor Sinha will keep inspiring generations of psychologists.

## The Present Volume

The essays included in this volume are arranged in three thematic parts—rethinking the psychological paradigm, human development and applied concerns. A brief description of these sections seems to be in order.

Part I titled 'Rethinking the Psychological Paradigm' comprises four articles that provide a perspective on the entire discipline and in some way articulate the lifelong agenda as an academic leader of psychology in the developing part of the world. Chapter 1, originally published in 1989, the first year of the new journal *Psychology and Developing Societies* that he had launched from Allahabad, sets the tone for discipline's agenda. In this piece, he integrates much of the earlier work and offers a synoptic picture of the research scenario in developing countries and places that in a historical context. By charting the course adopted by the researchers in developing countries, the analysis presented shows that the research is gradually undergoing major shifts. Professor Sinha identifies the changes in research trends in terms of phases. The initial phase was predominantly characterized by replication of work going on in the Western tradition. The next phase involved recognition of incompatibility with social reality leading to disillusionment with the borrowed theories, concepts and methods. The need to outgrow from this situation was triggered by the demands of social accountability and the need for undertaking relevant research. In the meantime, the spread of democratic processes in erstwhile colonies led to expansion and diversification of research endeavors which in turn paved the way for redirecting the efforts towards problem-oriented research initiatives. A deliberate and conscious move was initiated to relate to the national needs and developing culturally appropriate concepts, theories and tools. These changes are leading to a phase of indigenization of psychology. Interestingly this pattern of change appears to be common to most of the developing countries.

The second chapter is a powerful reminder acknowledging the potential contribution of the traditions of Indian thought. This clarion call dates back to 1965 when 'culture' happened to be a relatively less familiar dimension in the mainstream psychological discourse. Professor Sinha emphatically argued the case *for* Indian psychology in the *Journal of Humanistic Psychology*. He noted that under the impact of Western education, Indian psychologists *utterly failed to utilize the rich heritage of our philosophical thought in formulating problems for research in modern psychology. In their zeal to be scientific, modern Indian psychologists have shut their eyes to the psychologies of their own systems of thought and are being constantly dazzled by the modern scientific psychology of the West.* Sinha dismantles the myth of any monolithic view of psychology and shows how, even within the Western block, the theories and concepts do not freely travel from one country to the other and different psychologies do exist in the different cultural settings. He identifies many issues in the study of personality, emotion, health, human nature, meditation, perception and cognition and calls for drawing hypotheses, ideas, and theories from the rich repertoire of Indian thought; and invites the peers to bring them in the orbit of scientific study and verification.

The next chapter offers an overview of the nature and process of indigenization. This chapter situates the debate over indigenization chiefly in the Indian context and draws attention to the different forms of indigenization and warns about cosmetic (pseudo!) indigenization which may prove inimical to the growth of psychology. He notes that the process of indigenization is pursued at the level of concept/theory and methodology or it can be integrative. The chapter highlights the nuances of the efforts and sets an agenda for indigenization of psychology. In essence, the move towards indigenization brings the issue of culture in a creative relationship with disciplinary engagements.

The fourth chapter deals with ways in which the notion of culture is deployed by psychologists in their research endeavours. Indeed 'culture' happens to be a difficult concept to be handled in psychology. The large variety of ways in which the concept has been used is really astonishing. It ranges from all-encompassing overarching, super organic umbrella-like treatment to treating it equivalent to mere ethnic label or language use or physical features of environment. The problems are complex and make use of culture concept problematic and unmanageable and make some scholars think it redundant. Professor Sinha has analyzed the uses of culture critically and posits the view that culture can be used as a source or target and it largely depends on the researcher's choice for the use of culture in research process. He illustrates this through many research examples.

Part II consists of a set of four chapters focusing on *Human Development*, a theme very close to the heart of Professor Sinha. This part begins with a chapter on significant changes in the Indian family and their implications for healthy human development. This is attempted in the context of ongoing rapid socio-economic transformations taking place in the society. In particular, the chapter focuses on the individual-level changes affected by the modifications occurring in the family. Though the emphasis is on social and cultural change, the effort has been to identify the changes that have occurred due to various kinds of development programmes and the process of 'modernization' in the country. Professor Sinha draws attention to socialization practices and the experience of the individual in the family, which itself is in a state of transition. It isolates factors in the changing family scenario relevant to healthy human development. It is argued that the situation in the Indian family typifies the situation prevailing in other developing countries that are experiencing the whirlpool of rapid socio-economic development. The chapter highlights contemporary changes in the traditional Indian family structure, which is moving towards nucleation to meet the demands of industrialization, urbanization and modernization.

The next chapter tries to analyze how differences in socialization practices as prevailing in a joint or a nuclear family may influence a child's psychological differentiation. Differentiation as a cognitive style is manifested in an articulated way of experiencing the world, an articulated body concept, greater self- and non-self-segregation and structured and specialized defenses. The field independent cognitive style is related to greater differentiation, while the field dependent style is related to lesser differentiation. A review of existing cross-cultural studies is presented and interaction patterns in joint (traditional) and nuclear (modern) Indian families are delineated. Professor Sinha notes that the hierarchy in family set-up, multiplicity of role models, high infant indulgence, authoritarian structure, adherence to conformity, lesser emphasis on separation and limited role of father in parenting is stronger in a joint than in a nuclear family setting. He advanced the proposition that this may result in a lower degree of psychological differentiation in contrast to the nuclear families.

The next chapter deals with the challenges of youth which forms a significant portion of the Indian population. Youth is a cherished period in one's life and often symbolizes vigour and strength. Ideally the youth is expected to prepare for a smooth transition to the adult role but the diverse expectations generate identity crisis, confusion and anxiety. The problems are rising due to rapid change and desire to grow at a faster rate. The situation of temporal compression leads to the experience of 'cacophony'. The generational differences between youth and adults are examined using ingenious methods and measures of contradictions, conflicts, ambiguities and confusions. In particular, people's perception, role models and heroes, perception of events and perception of human qualities are studied. It was noted that the youth evinced value ambiguity and lack of identification with great personalities and hostility towards teachers. This situation suggested a kind of 'role refusal' on the part of the young that got reflected in unrest on the campuses and development of a 'counter culture'. The intergenerational differences created tension in many spheres of social life and complicated the problem of identity formation.

The last chapter of this part is a comprehensive effort, and perhaps first of its kind, to decipher the basic Indian values and dispositions. It tries to address the question: what it means to be an Indian, which still continues to be a knotty problem. The chapter brings together the values, beliefs and behaviour dispositions in two ways. First, it examines the basic *values* and attitudes that are stressed upon as 'Indian' as given in the religious, philosophical and cultural heritage. Second, it identifies the basic dispositions, typical modes of behaviour and interactional patterns fostered by socialization practices, familial experiences and institutional demands. To this effect, Professor Sinha has amassed a variety of sources from diverse disciplines and orientations. He is very cautious in drawing conclusions as textual sources are not enough. We need to know more about values and attitudes that *actually* form part of the Indian psyche, and the extent to which they operate in ordinary life. It is generally held that some basic values, behaviour dispositions and a common outlook define the core of the Indian psyche. Many of the descriptions indicate the presence of the following features: other-worldly outlook, attitude of renunciation, fatalism, passivity, static aspirations, dependence, hierarchical structure, preference for personalized relationships, emphasis on compliance and loyalty, collective orientation along with a lack of consideration, selfishness and distrust. These features of psyche are often treated as dysfunctional for national development. However, there are indications that many of the indigenous values and modes of behaviour can be effectively utilized for secular and developmental goals.

Part III of the present selection focuses on *Applied Concerns* of psychology. The first chapter in this part relates to the ecology of poverty and deprivation. The mere fact that a sizable portion of the Indian population still lives below poverty line makes its study a major challenge before the social sciences. Using this segment of human resource productively and bringing them to the mainstream of society have implications for the well-being of the entire society. It was realized that understanding the effects that poverty incurs on human beings requires a different kind of strategy as psychologists are very fond of using dispositional explanations of phenomena they study. This shifts the attention of researchers from the actual cause and orients the mind to look at the attributes in the person as the causes or antecedents of behaviours. Professor Sinha looked at the problem differently and opted to attend to the environmental–ecological features that impoverish the growing child and render her ineffective and incapable of solving life problems and meeting the challenges. He departed from the existing tradition by attending to the context and avoided the error of blaming the victim. The preference for an ecological approach was extended to the studies of perceptual development, motivation and coping processes. The chapter describes the ecological model of development, relating to significant developmental outcomes. In this discussion, the term 'social disadvantage' is preferred over poverty or deprivation. In doing so, the intention has been to bring home the point that the hierarchical social structure makes a low-caste person less resourceful on account of the membership of a group or community and resulting iniquitous distribution of resources.

The next chapter relates to integrating psychological approaches to address the challenge of poverty alleviation. It starts with the argument that while economic and structural variables are central, poverty does yield social and personal effects and people's ways of coping. Drawn on the evidence from India and American and Latin American countries, it is argued that understanding these processes is useful in devising strategies and programmes for persons and groups to develop out of poverty and enjoy a life free from unnecessary and avoidable miseries and deprivations. The chapter documents research on the psychological impact of poverty and its concomitants. It is emphasized that the detrimental effects of poverty are mediated by several intervening processes at cognitive, motivational, social and familial levels. The negative consequences of poverty become worse in the unfavorable proximal environment. Therefore, intervention strategies have to aim not only on specific cognitive, linguistic or motivational drawbacks but also on the family setting and educational environment of the disadvantaged children. Poverty appears to interfere with the acquisition of certain skills. Therefore, remedial attention to learning disabilities and incompetencies is required as early as possible.

The next chapter highlights the role of farmers' education in rural development. Indian farmers regard education important and vital for their children in getting government job but not with reference to the rural needs. Regarding motivational aspect, reluctance to take risk, stagnant aspiration and strong fear of failure have been characterized as being typical of Indian farmers. Various rural development programmes have failed in inculcating a new urge and aspiration of better living. A comparison of farmers between highly developed and underdeveloped villages has set out that farmers from highly developed villages have higher level of aspiration, high positive goal discrepancy index and greater flexibility in adjusting their level of aspiration to their performance. The chapter recommends that some amount of education closely integrated with rural needs and inculcating certain skills that are useful in development is likely to have the right kind of impact.

The last chapter focuses on applied social psychology in India. It is observed that while psychology is committed to the study of human nature, its 'approach to break reality into bits and pieces' and distort the same often leads to trivialities, so that insight and understanding are sacrificed for methodological sophistication. The researches often lack external validity. Shunning away from the complexities of social reality and playing about with micro variables seem to be done more for the sake of convenience rather than for gaining insight. The studies reflecting the move to understand reality and education changing the same are illustrated. It is observed that relevant research requires widening the horizon and going for a multidisciplinary and macro orientation. The researchers should undertake research that is useful to the society on whose resources they exist.

*Note:* The references cited in this text appear at the end of the volume. Professor Sinha's all references are included in the section 'Complete Works of Durganand Sinha' at the end.

# Part I

# Rethinking the Psychological Paradigm

# 1

# Research in Psychology in the Developing World: An Overview*

Making generalizations about such a vast tract of land mass scattered over three continents and comprising almost three-fourths of the world population is fraught with certain inherent dangers. The classificatory labels themselves—developed and the developing; first, second, and the third world; the North and the South and the like—are arbitrary and unscientific. Within what is usually designated as the developing world itself, countries are characterized by enormous variations in terms of economic development, scientific advancement, level of education, climatic conditions, geographical features, demography, population, religion, nature of society, and cultural variations. At one end of the spectrum, it comprises countries with the most adverse indices of life expectancy, mortality, morbidity, birth, and death rates, GNP, and other economic indicators and at the other we have those which, on various counts, have developed to such an extent that it is a misnomer to group them any more with the industrially, economically, and educationally backward countries. New classificatory labels have already been coined like the NICs (newly industrialized countries). We have in the grouping countries where a couple of decades ago it was difficult to find a university graduate and on the other hand we have one which is scientifically and technologically so advanced that it can boast of possessing the third latest scientific and technological manpower in the world. With such heterogeneity and diversity, making any generalizations about the entire developing world even with regard to

* Reproduced, with permission, from Sinha, D. Research in Psychology in the Developing World: An Overview. *Psychology and Developing Societies*, 1, 105–126 (1989). New Delhi: SAGE Publications.

This text has been edited for typographical errors, stylistic consistency and sequential organization in order to make it suitable for inclusion in the book.

the status of research in psychology is risky. In all countries the course of psychology has not followed the same path. The development and trends in research are peculiar to a particular country, and the developing world shows a variegated picture. Further, for reasons of the author's closeness and familiarity with the Indian scene, his observations are inevitably based (and probably biased) on his experiences in a particular historical and socio-cultural context. Therefore, what has been discussed about the trends of research characterizing psychology in the developing world is to be taken with due caution.

# Commonalities of Experience

Despite the heterogeneity and diversity, it is also true that these countries have certain commonalities of experiences in historical, economic, and socio-political terms. As a result, certain uniformities are observed not only on the political and ideological planes but also in the way academic disciplines have developed or are developing. It is reflected by the extent to which concepts, methods, and priority areas of research in psychology bear the imprint of history and social forces operating in the developing world.

The first point to be noted in this context is the colonial domination and economic exploitation by the west of most of the developing world. With independence, in most erstwhile colonial countries there has been an awakening and search for a new national identity. Second, in addition to political and economic subjugation there was academic domination. There was denigration of the indigenous systems of knowledge and their entire replacement by western systems of learning, and science. The case of India is typical. As is well known, India has a rich heritage of knowledge and traditional learning from ancient times not only in philosophy but in physical and medical sciences as well (Seal, 1958). But Lord Macaulay in his famous *Minute* in the early nineteenth century declared in the most derisive vein that "a single shelf of good European library was worth the whole native literature of India and Arabia" and regarded oriental learning as an "encumbrance and blemish" for scholarship. In some countries like the Philippines and in Latin America, the local culture and scholarship were consciously suppressed and indigenous knowledge destroyed. There was no exchange of knowledge but only *one-way transfer* of knowledge. Modern scientific psychology was superimposed upon highly developed views of the nature of human mind, human behavior and social interactions, and belief systems that existed in almost all countries of the developing world. As Turtle (1987, p. 2) has rightly observed in the context of eastern countries, "the techniques and ideology of modern psychology are thus being overlaid, in some cases in considerable haste, upon an ideological background composed variously of Hinduism, Islam, Buddhism, Taoism, Confucianism, Shintoism and Marxism-Leninism, themselves occurring in a range of combinations and combination styles". The rich treasure-house of psychological knowledge which most of these countries had from ancient times was ignored and replaced by materialism, determinism, empiricism, and positivistic tradition of western scientific psychology. This domination was reflected in ridiculing the indigenous psychological systems and the wholesale transplantation of western psychology in its largely unadulterated form, a "ready-made intellectual package" (Nandy, 1974). In any case, the net result was that in most of these countries, two parallel and competing systems of knowledge stood alongside-traditional/ indigenous with modern scientific.

# Western Domination and Its Consequences

The process was not only one of simple imperialist domination on the academic plane but also a self-imposed emulation of foreign models due to obvious advantages accruing from it. As a consequence, psychology that developed was largely Euro-American or Soviet (as in case of the People's Republic of China for a long time) in cognitive and value terms. Scholars— at least the influential ones—were western educated. Recognition/ publication of research in foreign journals received preferential treatment in matters of appointment, promotion, emoluments, and other privileges. Thus, the generation of scholars that grew up were virtual second editions of western gentlemen, not only in matters of dress, manners, behaviors, and way of life but also in their thinking and scholarly pursuits. What developed was a "photo copy of psychology as it existed in western countries during the early years of this century" (Ramalingaswami, 1980). Western psychological ethos was so deeply absorbed in academic circles that there was a large element of "foreignness" in research pursuits. It led to a shift in the local scholar's focus of attention away from his own country and its problems (Warwick, 1980). Western models and ideas distracted them from the core issues, and priorities were distorted so that a problem was taken up for investigation not for its intrinsic theoretical value or practical significance to the needs of the society or the country, but because the theme was popular in the west at that time.

The course taken by psychology has not been identical all over, and there are interesting differences in issues and focus of research relative to the situation in each country. Due to differences in the period of university system of education and tradition of research, availability of scientific personnel and resources, employment opportunity, etc., the pace and nature of development of psychology has not been identical. Despite variations, the operation of similar socio-historical factors outlined earlier has generated certain common trends that seem to be operative in most developing countries. A perusal of the studies on the status of psychology in different Third World countries reveals that in spite of differences in levels and emphasis which are conditioned by the socio-cultural milieu and peculiarities of needs of each country, the broad directions look surprisingly alike. To summarize the trends, in almost all these countries, the indigenous knowledge in psychology was in the first instance suppressed and modern scientific psychology as was flourishing in the west was transplanted almost wholesale. There was no effort to bring together the indigenous and the modern systems so that they could be integrated and assimilated in a unified whole. Since the element introduced was alien to the soil, for a long time its character remained foreign. After a phase of imitative and replicative researches, dissatisfaction or disillusionment with the discipline was expressed in varying degrees and locally important problems began to attract the attention of psychologists. Initially they were researched within the framework provided by western models and theories. Gradually, western concepts, tools and methods of data collection began to be questioned. There developed a distinct trend towards "outgrowing the alien framework" (Sinha, 1980/1987), or what may be termed as "a process of indigenization" (Sinha, 1986a). It seems to have come "as a part of protest against neo-colonialism, against cultural subordination and even contamination" (Turtle, 1987, pp. 13–14).

## Gains of Western Influence

Though many scholars in recent times (e.g., Nandy, 1974; DiazGuerrero, 1984, p. 84; Sinha, 1977, 1986a; Enriquez, 1982; Lagmay, 1984) have been highly critical of the foreign and replicative character of psychological researches in most developing countries, and have dubbed them as "Euro-American product" (Sinha, 1977) and adaptology (Agarwal, 1975), and have pointed to the widespread disillusionment with western theories (Diaz-Guerrero, 1984), the "gains" of western influence should not be ignored. On the positive side, it was due to the western impact that for the first time the tradition of empirical research and scientific analysis was seen in psychology in the countries of the developing world. It helped to raise the discipline from a speculative, esoteric, and intuitive level, which were the features of psychology prevailing in those countries, to the pedestal of a science. Many scholars acquired a high level of sophistication in scientific methodology' and techniques of research, and developed academic links with Europe and the United States where the discipline had been flourishing. It led to the adoption of modern laboratory techniques and instrumentation so that experiments were conducted under rigorous and controlled conditions making possible systematic manipulation of variables. Refined sampling techniques, survey research methods, and systematic observation and field experiments were introduced. With such scientific orientation and sophistication, psychology was soon recognized in universities and in many places it became a part of the curriculum of the faculty of science. Further, quantification and measurement constitute essential elements of modern psychology in the west. The same ethos began to prevail in countries of its adoption. Thus, as has been observed with respect to the situation in India (Sinha, 1986a, p. 35), by adopting the scientific psychological methodology of western psychology, the discipline soon achieved the status of a science.

# Brief Account of Early Development

Though the beginning of scientific psychology in the west can be traced to earlier years, it is customary to date its birth in 1879 with the establishment of the first psychological laboratory in Leipzig by Wundt. It took two to three decades for the subject to be introduced in the countries of the developing world. In Latin America, the first psychological laboratory was established in Argentina in 1898. Though Mexico was the first to have a course in psychology in 1896, it was only in 1916 that a laboratory was established at the National University. However, majority of the laboratories were established in the mid-1960s when there was great expansion of Psychology in Latin American countries.

In Francophone Africa, the discipline was introduced earlier. In the rest of Africa, psychology remained for long an offshoot of the education faculty, social anthropology or sociology. It was only in 1968 that the first fully equipped laboratory was established in Zambia.

In China, the earliest book on modern psychology, a Chinese translation of Hoffding's *Outline of Psychology*, was published in 1907. The first course in psychology was introduced at Peking University in 1917, and the first department was established in 1920 in Nanking Higher Norrrial School. In the early 1920s, an Institute of Psychology was established under Academia Sinica.

In India, modern psychology began almost contemporaneously with Mexico. It was introduced as an independent subject in Calcutta University in 1905, though actual teaching of the subject began 10 years later. A psychological laboratory and a separate department were established in 1916.

The main feature of the initial phase of psychology in the developing countries was that it did not develop independently but as a part of the curricular requirements of philosophy or of teacher's training programme or in medical school. Even when independent courses or departments, were established, the models emulated were Leipzig, Cambridge, London, Edinburgh, Harvard, Cornell, Chicago or Columbia. Early researches were largely replicative, and orientation was Euro-American. Nandy's (1974, p. 3) description of the Indian situation in psychology is applicable in a large measure to most of the developing countries: "innumerable half-hearted replications, unending streams of adaptations and readaptations of western scales and tests". There was a good deal of academic research that was traditional and conventional with little relation to the realities of the contemporary situation (Sinha, 1973, p. 87).

# Post-independence Expansion

In most countries the post-independence period was characterized by rapid expansion in teaching and research with the establishment of new universities and departments of psychology, and centers of psychological research and services even outside the academia. As in Europe and the USA, research activity got ramified in different branches and directions. In China, where psychology had been under the influence of functionalism, behaviorism, and mental testing, the post-revolution (1948) period was marked by a search for independence from western domination, and Marxist dialectical materialism was adopted as its guiding principle. Soviet psychology became the model. Due to common ideological linkages, Chinese psychology of the period had all the characteristics of Soviet psychology, and the areas that were prominent in research amply reflected the same, educational and developmental being the prominent research interests with animal psychology coming in a minor way.

In Latin American countries, in the late 1950s and particularly the 1960s, psychology became one of the most popular fields of study (Ardila, 1985). The main areas of research were experimental analysis of behavior, developmental psychology, comparative psychology, social psychology, political psychology, and the history of psychology. There was in addition great emphasis on the applications of psychological principles to clinical, educational, industrial and organizational problems and to social fields. In some countries like Mexico, personality and cross-cultural studies on growth and development were especially popular. Further, in all the countries, the development and standardization of mental tests and adaptation of foreign measures constituted a major area of research activity.

In Africa, research has been concentrated in the areas of psychological testing and educational psychology. Initially, the need for sound scientific assessment procedures was the main impetus for the development of psychology. It is well exemplified in Zambia, where after independence and the introduction of a new educational policy and the expansion of education, what was needed was a method that could be shown as essentially immune to charges of political influence (Heron, 1975, p. 14). Thus, psychological testing for educational and personnel selection assumed great importance in the effort by many African countries to ensure that suitable candidates were selected for education beyond the primary school level and for training in different occupations (Durojaiye, 1985, p. 135). In most African countries even today, psychologists are either working in schools of education or on problems generally connected with educational expansion.

Other salient areas of research in Africa are developmental studies of various skills, child rearing practices, effects of nutritional and socioeconomic deficiencies on cognitive development, work on reasoning along Piagetian lines, and studies of attitudes, stereotypes, vocational aspiration, and mental health. With the onset of rapid socioeconomic changes, the problem of psychological adjustment to urban life and to industrialization is becoming a major research concern (Durojaiye, 1985, p. 110). Further, collaborative work with western scholars since the late 1950s has provided a strong impetus for the development of cross-cultural psychology.

In the Philippines, the major problem facing Filipino psychologists was the applicability of western measures and concepts to Filipino behavior (Lagmay, 1984, p. 34). As in other parts of the developing world, attainment of independence was marked by an expansion of research activity especially in the fields of psychological testing, socio-psychological research, and application of socio-psychological principles.

In India, the attainment of independence roughly coincided with the end of World War II, a period which was characterized by phenomenal expansion and ramification of research activity in the United States. Besides rapid expansion an effort was also made to link the different elements of western psychology to the Indian situation by studying the variables that were operant on the local setting. Various reviews of studies (e.g., Mitra, 1972, 1973; Sinha, 1986a) show that research activities covered nearly all the branches, with social, industrial, clinical, and personality being the more prominent ones. Themes that were taken up for investigation were the ones that were popular among researchers in the west. Realizing their importance to the Indian situation, studies were replicated to determine whether similar factors were operating in the changed socio-cultural setting of the country (Sinha, 1986a, p. 41). In short, Indian scholars followed the footsteps of their western counterparts. Though the search for relevant and significant topics related to the Indian scene had begun, the general framework of western concepts and theories for understanding reality continued to be employed (J.B.P. Sinha, 1976). The whole enterprise remained foreign (Sinha, 1986a). There were isolated efforts to examine various psychological phenomena from a new angle but no new line of thinking or theory was forthcoming. Moreover, it remained divorced from the traditional Indian psychological concepts. Further, researches were sporadic and not sustained or systematic in certain directions so that though the output was fairly large, it failed to make any lasting impact in the field of psychology as such. Another glaring drawback of the studies conducted was the absence of an adequate theoretical base. Without a theoretical framework they neither contributed to the overall theory nor had much by way of practical utility. Indian researchers were good empiricists but poor theorists. Even when they came very near to discovering significant theories like Prasad (1935) and Sinha (1952) with regard to the theory of cognitive dissonance, and Sinha (1958) with regard to the two factor theory of job satisfaction—they failed to identify them or fought shy of elaborating them.

# New Trends in Developing World

It is, therefore, not surprising that there was dissatisfaction and severe criticism about the state of research in psychology—the studies being imitative and repetitive, foreign, and far removed from reality (ICSSR,

1973, p. 43), a phenomenon characterizing many developing countries. As evident on the Indian scene, psychological research began to take a new turn and the trend has become particularly strong since the 1970s. There has been a noticeable change in the quality and content of research. First, compared with what prevailed two to three decades ago, psychologists of the present generation unlike their senior counterparts are better equipped for psychological research. They have not drifted from either philosophy or education, and have been exposed to a full course in the discipline which usually included compulsory and essential requirement courses on research methodology, survey techniques, and quantitative methods.

Second, scholars began to articulate the need for problem-oriented research, which is, conducting studies which were consciously directed towards contributing to certain problems which the country was facing, and a concern for the application of research findings. J.B.P. Sinha (1973) has aptly characterized the position, problems in India big and real and of all kinds—keep bombarding us into an inescapable position from where we do not have any alternative except to address ourselves to them. In my presidential address to the Section of Psychology and Educational Science of the Indian Science Congress in January 1966 (Sinha, 1966), I emphasized the problems connected with the need and impact of rapid change and development taking place on the national level and considered them as a challenge to psychologists.

A glance at some of the popular topics in research indicates the larger national concern that is goading the activities of many psychologists in the country. Poverty, population, agro-economic development, social prejudices and tensions, national and regional identities, work behavior and effective leadership in community, and organizational settings are a few of the topics that are salient at the current juncture. An idea of the shift in emphasis can be had by the perusal of chapter headings in the second and third surveys of research in psychology in India sponsored by the ICSSR. While in the first survey (Mitra, 1972) covering the period up to 1969–70, researchers were grouped into 10 conventional branches like experimental, developmental, social, clinical, and industrial psychology, in the two volumes of the second survey (Pareek, 1980, 1981) covering the period 1971–76, in addition to conventional headings, topics like psychology of poverty, psychology of inequality, psychology of population, and family planning, dynamics of social change, and relevance: a poser for Indian psychology, were included. This not only reflects tremendous diversification and expansion, but also entry into areas which have tended to remain outside the conventional realm of mainstream psychology.

The third survey of research in psychology by the ICSSR covering the period 1977–82, which has been released in three volumes (Pandey, 1988), bears testimony to the intensification of the trend. Chapter headings like "Dynamics of Rural Development", "Intergroup Relations and Social Tensions in India", and sub-headings like "social action and planned social change", "social exploitation", "women and rural development", "family planning and fertility behavior", "social disadvantages, poverty and deprivation", *yoga* as a facilitator or restorer of health, as well as the quantum of work done in various areas are indicative not only of the tremendous expansion but of the entry of psychology into fields which are closely related to overwhelming socioeconomic and national issues the country is facing, and greater awareness of the socio-cultural context and reality. The purvey includes almost 4,000 references and indicates that on the average 750 research papers are published every year by psychologists in India in various national and international journals. For a developing country, the research output as reflected by these figures along with 1,000 entries every year in the *Indian Psychological Abstracts* may look impressive, but it is meager when compared with approximately 32,000 entries annually in the *American Psychological Abstracts* published by the American Psychological Association. It is to be noted that the message of its (psychology) alleged potential in the cause of national development comes out time and again and loud and clear all over the developing world (Turtle, 1987, p. 13). Moghni (1987, p. 31), for example, in his general presidential address to the first session of Pakistan Psychological Association in Dacca in March 1968 concluded that:

> What I wish to emphasize is that understanding man, his motives and capacities, his relations to physical and social environment and how he organizes them, *is basic to the formulation and execution of any plan of national development; that economic behavior in the final analysis is itself determined by psychological factors; that targets of economic development are much easier to reach if they are understood and treated as goals of purposive behavior of man.* And it is here that we psychologists have some role to play. (Italics in original)

In Thailand too, concern has been expressed about the applications of the findings of psychology to national development. Bhanthumnavin (1987, p. 86) asserts that "local research findings with the help of modern knowledge and technologies can hopefully fill some of the gaps and prevent or solve some of the problems, and will thus inevitably promote national development". In China, in the post-Cultural Revolution era, there has been a spurt in research in different areas of psychology. A general account of the trends indicates that most investigations have been on basic and applied problems in a more or less natural science setting. With the new pragmatic twist and the national emphasis on four modernizations, namely, agriculture, industry, science and technology, and defence, the challenge that Chinese psychology faces is: what can psychology do for four modernizations? It "implies that psychology must be closely tied up with our national aspiration" (Ching, 1984, p. 61). Outlining the five areas to which Chinese psychologists should now direct their efforts, Lee and Petzold (1987, p. 118) conclude that "the overall goal is to ensure that psychology does serve the nation's four modernizations of industry, agriculture, science and technology, and defence".

In Malaysia, there is a similar concern as reflected in the focal theme Psychology and Socio-economic Development adopted for the regional conference of the International Association for Cross-Cultural Psychology held at the National University of Malaysia in 1983. Colleen Ward (1987, p. 216) outlining the areas of applications of psychology in the country emphasizes that "whatever paths Malaysian psychologists choose to follow, it is most important that they share knowledge and skill in the service of the community, that they address themselves to significant Malaysian issues and problems and that they adapt themselves to the needs of this rapidly developing country".

In the Philippines, the trend in this direction is strong with a commitment on the part of many psychologists to the "contextualization of psychology in the Philippine setting" (Enriquez, 1987, p. 276), and a plea for a Filipino Psychology (*Sikolohiyang Pilipino*) which as a perspective demands that "the Filipino psychologist confronts social problems and national issues as part of his responsibility" (p. 278). In Africa, the same trend is visible though in a somewhat restricted way. Psychology being closely associated with education, research activity has chiefly focused on the development of scientific tests and training procedures for government departments and private and public sector organizations. In this context, the role of psychology in national development is perceived as provider of competent teachers, research workers, and supplier of services (Heron, 1975, p. 16). In spite of its emphasis on applications, psychology is likely to be seen as a luxury by developing nations. As Heron (1975) points out, to obtain community and government support the discipline has to demonstrate its potential as a contributor to national development.

In Latin American countries, the main characteristic of psychology is its emphasis on practical aspects and applications to social reality. Ardila (1982, p. 110) points out that it has an important role in national planning programmes. In many respects Mexico typifies the situation as it exists in other Latin American countries. Apart from the usual areas of psychological applications, the discipline has extended itself to action research, educational, and social programme evaluation in rural communities. In Cuba, with the emergence of the new concept of medical care and the emphasis on prevention, and health being regarded as a social phenomenon and the right of every citizen (Averasturi, 1980), psychology has become an integral part of the national public health programme. In Venezuela there is an emphasis on the application of psychology, and psychological knowledge and technology have been used extensively in politics, image building and organizing political campaigns. The discipline received a strong impetus with the emergence in 1979 of the national programme for the development of intelligence: "a group of policies and programmes to encourage the systematic development of human intelligence" (Salazar, 1984, p. 119).

The need for problem-oriented research and psychologists playing a role on the larger national scene is strong all over the developing world. The trend corroborates what Jahoda (1975) pointed out while referring to cross-cultural psychology that "there is a strong indication that the Third World will not indefinitely welcome or even tolerate the activities of researchers without at least some prospects of tangible returns".

With the growing popularity of cross-cultural psychology in the west, scholars in India and other developing countries have been attracted by the new strategy for research not only because of the cultural diversity of the country and the felt need for establishing panhuman verity of psychological principles, but also due to the ease and economy with which comparative data could be obtained which elsewhere involved extensive travel and huge expenditure. Here again, the relationship with western colleagues and collaborators was initially one of subordination and dependence both for ideas and resources, and the themes chosen for studies were the ones popular with western cross-cultural psychologists, namely, comparative studies of perceptual and cognitive processes, Piagetian studies, child rearing and socialization, and impact of industrialization and modernization. Gradually some distinct Indian variables like type of family, socioeconomic and cultural disadvantages arising from caste or tribal status and their impact on cognitive functioning and child rearing have been taken up. In a majority of these researches, the eco-cultural framework has been adopted thereby linking them to the peculiar sociocultural context.

With the entry of psychology in the area of rural development, there was an awareness of the need for suitable tests for the clinician dealing mostly with rural clientele, and problems of using conventional tools for data collection on remote and unsophisticated rural and tribal populations for cross-cultural comparisons, psychologists who had already expressed their dissatisfaction with the techniques and tools of data collection borrowed from the west became more articulate about the inadequacies of the existing methods and the urgent need for forging culturally appropriate techniques (Wig, Pershad & Verma, 1974). Special problems of data collection in social-cultural contexts radically different from the ones in which western tests and scales are developed have been highlighted (Sinha, 1983). It has been suggested that reliability and validity of measures could be replaced by psychometric invariance which examines the possibility of a test measuring different psychological processes in subjects who belong to different developmental and cultural groups (Puhan, 1979, 1982). Further, many culturally appropriate measures such as the level of aspiration (Sinha, 1969), risk taking (Chaubey, 1974), change proneness (Tiwari, 1983), and cognitive style (Sinha, 1978, 1984) have been developed. These measures, while utilizing the basic paradigms and rationales of western tests, have utilized indigenous materials and activities common in the population, thereby making them not only appropriate but also meaningful to the people. Finally, another trend is clearly visible. The introduction of modern psychology in most of the countries of the developing world resulted in the suppression of traditional psychological knowledge. As a reaction, in some countries there has been a kind of revivalism. In India in the 1950s there was a plea for Indian psychology which included almost everything that was psychological in ancient texts from the analysis of perceptual processes and Indian typologies of personality to paranormal perceptions, transmigration of the soul, magic, and supernatural power. Premium was put on the esoteric, and the scientism of modern psychology was derided. But such revivalism was not suited to the empirical and scientific ethos of psychologists trained in modern discipline. However, with the realization of the limitations of modern western approach in understanding problems of "becoming", development, integration of personality, and mental health, scholars are turning to the ancient systems for new conceptualizations and procedures. Publications on Indian psychology as rooted in various systems of Indian philosophy have appeared (Safaya, 1976; Kuppuswamy, 1985). Scholars have started making comparative expositions of Indian and western views on the nature, structure, dynamics and typologies of personality (R.S. Singh, 1972), and relating findings of transactional psychology of perception to early Indian thinking (Prabhu, 1966). A plea for integrating modern psychology with Indian thought has been made for "bridging many of the gaps that are too obvious in modern psychological theory and action and at the same time interpret our philosophical thought in scientific light" (Sinha, 1965/69, p. 278).

To mention only a few highlights, there has been a growing interest in psychological concepts and phenomena such as meditation, *samadhi*, "desireless" action, and *guru* (perceptor) that have their origin in eastern tradition. Systematic theoretical and empirical work is being done in these areas and published in psychological journals all over the world. Analysis of altered states of consciousness (Tart, 1972, 1975; Thapa & Murthy, 1985) has been done using the latest electronic instruments and statistical techniques. The setting of *Karma yoga* has been utilized to increase the efficacy of behavior therapy (Singh & Oberhummer, 1980). Another research trend in this direction has been to operationalize some ancient Indian concepts, develop psychometric measures, and investigate their correlates experimentally. The concept of *nishkama karma* (action without attachment to the outcome) has been elaborated and a test for measuring this has been developed, and differences in stress and strain experienced by individuals high or low on it have been analyzed. Data indicate two distinct clusters of *outcome* and *effort* orientations, the former being positively correlated to strain (Pande & Naidu, 1986).

Recently, there have been distinct efforts not only to analyze the non-western perspectives to psychology (Sinha, 1981) but also to integrate the eastern and western approaches to consciousness. 'Paranjpe's (1984) book *Theoretical Psychology: The Meeting of East and West* is an excellent example of the effort to integrate the two traditions. This synthesis is not only being attempted at the theoretical and conceptual levels but also by subjecting various yogic states, relaxation, and meditation to systematic investigations using sophisticated electronic devices.

An overall view of the situation reveals that one of the most vital issues that has emerged is that of outgrowing the alien frame (J.B.P. Sinha, 1976). Contemporary research provides many instances of genuine ideas, fresh thinking, and new attempts to understand the Indian situation in its own right. Outgrowing the alien framework (Sinha, 1980/87) aptly describes the situation of contemporary research in psychology in many parts of the developing world, and is a trend that is gaining in strength all over.

# Towards Indigenization

Growing disillusionment with the foreign roots of psychology, realization of the non-applicability of its concepts and tools of research in the radically different socio-cultural contexts of the developing world, its "irrelevance" to the vital issues facing the country and failure to make a thrust in the national life (Pareek, 1980, p. ix) are "signs of growing crisis" is psychology. As a result, the process of indigenization has been unleashed, and there is a strong trend towards the development of the discipline suited to the needs and socio-cultural context of the country. The trend is particularly strong in India and in the Philippines where there is a distinct effort to "de-colonize" psychology and Filipino psyche (Enriquez, 1987), and is well exemplified in Enriquez's (1982) work *Towards a Filipino Psychology: Essays and Studies on Language and Culture.*

While indigenization of science is a desirable objective, it is essential to analyze carefully the processes involved in it. Conceptualizing it in biological terms from which the expression has been borrowed and extended to the sphere of knowledge, it means to bring about such transformations as to make knowledge or the discipline natural or applicable to the particular socio-cultural features of the country or the region. Applied to psychology, it implies such transformations in the subject that was transplanted from the west so that it is suited to the socio-cultural milieu of the country concerned. It represents a plea for an alternative culture of psychology. But it is not to be confused with revivalism or mere "cosmetic indigenization" (Sinha, 1986b). It consists of integration and synthesis of modern psychology with indigenous psychological concepts, thinking, and socio-cultural context. As Mukherjee (1980) has observed in the Indian context, "psychology has to go native if it has to be creative and relevant to society". Kumar (1979) has pointed out that there are three processes involved in indigenization: indigenization of structure, content (substantive), and theoretic. Apart from building its own institutional and organizational capabilities for production and diffusion of science, the main thrust is on its own society, people, and economic and political institutions, and in constructing distinctive conceptual frameworks and meta-theories which reflect their world views, social and cultural experiences and perceived goals (Kumar, 1979, pp. 104–105). The second and third aspects are more in evidence. Cultural systems are explored for concepts and models relevant for understanding social reality, which are put to scientific scrutiny. This aspect of the process is clearly seen in psychological researches conducted in India. Second, it involves assimilation of western concepts, models, and tools of research by making them appropriate to the social reality of the country. Third, indigenization also involves a new orientation in teaching, remodelling of the syllabus, and producing case reports, books and monographs incorporating authentic local materials. The University Grants Commission, which is concerned with the maintenance of the standard of teaching and research in the universities and colleges in India, asserts that the "subject matter taught in the class should be personally meaningful and socially relevant" (UGC, 1979, p. 10).

# General Impact of New Orientation

What has been the general impact of this new orientation on psychology in the developing world? The obvious impact is already visible on the content or the substantive level, i.e., on the choice of problems taken up for investigation. These are generally of applied nature and are related to the needs or pressing problems of the country. In other words, research conducted is not only for prestige, but for policy as well. Second, in order to be relevant to basic problems like poverty and inequality, it is essential that the perspective of the subject is altered from a predominantly microcosmic one to a proper blend of microcosmic with macrocosmic. Referring to the Indian scene, it has been observed in the Review Committee Report of the ICSSR (ICSSR, 1973, p. 44) that "most of the researches done in social psychology laid disproportionate stress on narrow aspects of large social problems and in consequence, the information gathered lacked in organization, synthesis, and integration." Social change and developmental processes are large and complex and the parameters of their study should not be confined to microcosmic individual processes but should encompass larger social, structural, and cultural influences. If psychology has to make impact on the larger problems of the developing world it has to adopt a more holistic orientation, a macrocosmic perspective and should incorporate structural variables in the very design of its research. In other words, such researches have to be conceived in terms of what may be called *macro psychology* (Cherns, 1969; Sinha, 1985), that is, building structural and systemic variables into the research design so that the social reality which is I brought under study does not lose its basic character and become mere laboratory trivialities (Sinha, 1986a). Third, since larger social problems related to change and development are not the preserve of any particular discipline but their characteristics are shared by many disciplines, psychology in the developing world is showing greater inter-disciplinary and multidisciplinary interactions particularly with other social sciences. Last, the entire process of indigenization is likely to give the subject a distinctive national character. In the Philippines, there is a strong plea for *Sikolohiyang Filipino* (Filipino Psychology); in India there is pressure to *Indianize* psychology. Even when the cognitive model or theoretical framework is borrowed from the west, the issues are being formulated in the context of a particular society. Such a trend is also observable in the People's Republic of China and in many Latin American countries. In other words, the trend is likely to develop *many indigenous psychologies*, each having certain characteristics distinctive to a country.

The trends that are visible in the developing world point to the fact that the traditional ethos of psychology as reflected in the *ILO Standard Classification of Occupations* (ILO, 1969), which does not include social change and development within its ambit, is being widened. Further, taking cognizance of structural and systemic variables is bound to have an impact on a discipline that is so avowedly microcosmic in orientation. How and in what manner would psychology become more macrocosmic is a matter for the future. But the need is being felt, and it is inevitable that some radical transformation in the basic character of the discipline is underway. So far the flow of knowledge has been from the west to the east, from the developed world to the developing world. It has been a case of one-way transfer. As has been pointed out (Sinha, 1986a, p. 127), a "reverse flow" from the east to the west has already begun. Psychology as it has developed in Europe and the USA has made a tremendous impact on the discipline in the developing world. There has been hardly any *exchange* of knowledge, hardly any dialogue between partners in which both stand to profit. In the ensuing years the situation is likely to change. The trends in research that are noticeable in the developing world are likely at least to expand the conventional boundaries of the discipline and thereby have an impact on the general development of psychology.

# 2

# Integration of Modern Psychology with Indian Thought*

For many years psychology has been tied to the apron-string of philosophy. In many places the string still holds while generally the connection has been severed. With the history of such intimate association between the two disciplines, one would have expected psychology to set up its separate household on attaining maturity, but continue to have close family ties with the parental stem. The separation unfortunately has not been cordial. It has resulted in a kind of rebellious-son attitude causing a hiatus between the two disciplines where everything belonging to the parental stem is ridiculed or ignored. As a result, no attempt of any significance has been made to utilize the rich heritage of our philosophical thought in formulating problems for research in modern psychology. In their zeal to be scientific, modern Indian psychologists have shut their eyes to the psychologies of their own systems of thought and are being constantly dazzled by the modern scientific psychology of the West. In India, this has resulted in the development of psychology without firm roots. Instead of presenting a vigorous scientific psychology rooted in Indian traditions, we have at best been able to develop a pale and insipid edition of American or British psychology. Formulation of proper methodology for the study of concepts in Indian and Buddhistic philosophy in the light of modern experimental psychology is urgently required. In the present chapter, certain peculiarities of what is often called "Indian psychology" and "modern psychology" are

* Reproduced, with permission, from Sinha, D. Integration of Modern Psychology with Indian Thought. *Journal of Humanistic Psychology*, 5, 6–17 (1965). New Delhi: SAGE Publications.

This text has been edited for typographical errors, stylistic consistency and sequential organization in order to make it suitable for inclusion in the book.

discussed and it is pointed out that the gap between them is not difficult to bridge. Certain problems are indicated on which modern psychology could profit by adopting working hypotheses drawn from Indian systems and verifying them by the application of scientific methodology.

One of the interesting features of Indian thought has been that religion, philosophy, and psychology do not stand sundered. This does not mean that development in each did not take place. Each flourished and became in due course differentiated into important disciplines, but maintained intimate ties. In ancient India this differentiation did not amount to a divorce. As Hiriyanna (1951) has rightly pointed out, "when the word 'psychology' is used in Indian philosophy, it should be understood in its original sense as the science or doctrine of the soul ('psyche'), for its teaching, except in one or two cases, is based upon the supposition that the soul exists. This study in India never branched off from philosophy and every system has therefore its own psychology" (p. 66).

Modern psychology in the West largely grew out of the scientific and medical traditions. Though its traces can be discerned in the empirical thoughts of Locke and others, or in the German rationalism of Leibnitz and Kant, the development has been largely independent of philosophy. The influence of the biological and physical sciences has been much more potent. Rather than aiding philosophy in prescribing a course for the attainment of liberation modern psychology in the West has been interested in explaining, understanding, and predicting behavior for its own sake. In its initial stages it grew purely as a science. Being intimately concerned with human behavior, its application was inevitable. But, as we know, applied psychology has been a comparatively recent phenomenon.

This takes us to the second and probably the most important feature of psychology in ancient India. Knowledge was not sought for its own sake, but for *moksa* (liberation). *Tattva-jñāna* was followed by strenuous effort to attain *moksa*. The Indian seer did not stop short at the discovery of truth but strove to realize it in his own experience. Philosophy, or for that matter psychology, in India did not primarily take its rise in wonder or curiosity as it seems to have done in the West; rather it originated under the pressure of a practical need arising from the presence of moral and physical evil in life. The problem of removal of evil ever troubled the Indian thinkers and they developed psychological and philosophical explanations of these evils and suggested ways for their eradication. Liberation is not simply a negative state but a condition characterized by positive factors of bliss, knowledge, and existence. Various aspects of life are not necessarily denied in liberation; as in tantras, it is the acceptance and control of all aspects of worldly existence including drink and sex. Psychological knowledge was utilized for the attainment of this highest state. As Max Muller (1899) has said, philosophy was recommended in India "not for the sake of knowledge, but for the highest purpose that man can strive after in this life," viz. liberation.

Thus, unlike psychology in the West, the science of human thought and behavior as developed in the Indian systems has been intensely and avowedly practical. Psychological knowledge became a way of life, not merely a way of thought. To quote a Jaina maxim, it is "Do not live to know, but know to live." In this context it is well to remember Whitehead's (1926, p. 39) characterization of Buddhism as "the most colossal example in history of applied metaphysics".

Modern psychology in the West has largely a scientific bias and is primarily concerned with explanation and prediction of human behavior, and development of a scientific theory of behavior. Its application in the fields of psychotherapy, education, industry, and other spheres of human activities is only a later development. We can even venture to say, despite the fact that most modern psychology is fast becoming applied, that its primary interest lies in formulation of valid principles of human behavior and it is only secondarily that it is interested in their application. This is one of the main reasons why psychology in the West quickly differentiated itself and developed into an independent branch of knowledge. In contrast, the interests of ancient Indian thinkers were always practical, and if there was any psychology, it was only applied psychology. As Akhilananda (1952) puts it, "Indian psychology is not merely conceptual or theoretical. Its therapeutic value is in its teaching of various methods of mental integration. It prescribes systems of physical and mental discipline which gradually stabilize the mind and integrate the emotions" (p. 20). This was true even of the so-called atheistic schools, which while not always believing in the existence of God or the authority of the Vedas, still prescribed liberation as the ultimate goal of earthly existence.

This dependence on Indian metaphysics and all-pervasiveness of the doctrine of liberation implied as a necessary corollary the existence of the soul. Psychology was understood in its original sense as the science of the soul or "psyche." Based on this implicit supposition of the existence of the soul, theories of perception, memory, thinking, action, and personality were formulated, and a path for obtaining correct knowledge and liberation of the soul was recommended. The solitary exception was Buddhist psychology which gave up the belief in a soul-substance. As against this, the modern Western psychologists have not been tied down to any such supposition. They either ignore such a question or imply that no entity which has an existence independent of the body can be proved or be useful to psychology. In fact, modern psychology has its growth in the scientific and materialistic traditions that swept the Western world in the later part of the 18th and in the 19th centuries. This explains why concepts like ego, ego-development, though quite popular now, are sometimes regarded as unscientific and meaningless by many Western psychologists. It also accounts for the resistance which the findings of para-psychology are meeting in being incorporated into the general framework of psychology, despite the fact that some of them have been subjected to the most rigorous scientific controls and have proofs which are incontrovertible.

Another feature that makes psychological theories in Indian thought appear distinct from modern psychology is the difference in methodology. The methods of investigation used in the latter are largely modeled after those of physics, physiology, and clinical medicine. Rigorous techniques for the collection of information, observation, and experimental controls are employed. In recent times there has been a vast inroad of statistical methodology in psychological researches. This is certainly commendable and has helped psychology to mature as a science. However, this itself implies certain underlying assumptions, postulates, or even "unconscious prejudices," about sources of our knowledge and making of inference. And if facts challenge these, there is a natural tendency first to reject the facts rather than reexamine the assumptions. This common tendency of the scientist to keep his postulates intact accounts for what may be termed as "scientific conservatism." It is a good safeguard against rash conclusions but the limitations of its methodology sometimes retard the progress of science by creating a resistance to fresh ideas and new points of view.

The methodology of Indian psychology is different. In the West, there is a tendency to concretize and convert everything into an "object" which is not only measurable but also capable of doing something useful and practical. The word "objective" has usually implied thing-biased. Any experience which is not amenable to this conversion is labeled as "subjective" and considered unworthy of science. This kind of objectivity is not considered absolutely essential by the Indian thinkers. What is important is freedom from bias and dispassionateness on the part of the observer. As such, the Indian seers who have undergone years of rigorous training and discipline have not fought shy of highly complex and subtle experiences as the basis of their science. Rather than depend only upon strict objective observation and experimentation, Indian psychologists have based their conclusions also upon "spiritual experiences." It would be wrong to dismiss these as uncontrolled and unsystematic data unworthy of a science. Before any reliance was placed on his experience, the seer was expected to undergo a long process of self-discipline. This was a very rigorous "control," but of a different order from what we are usually familiar with in scientific experimentation. After this discipline was attained, the spiritual experiences, intuitions and observations of the seer provided the material on which psychological theory was built. It can, therefore, be said that the method was subjective and intuitive, rather than experimental and object-biased. But these so-called subjective experiences are no less empirical, based on dispassionate observations of seers who experienced them in their own life. The propounder of the theories was called a drasta or "seer," i.e., a person who in his own spiritual experience had actually seen the reality. A modern psychologist, steeped in scientific methodology, is amazed to find familiar topics being discussed in the Indian systems. The usual problems of sleep, dreams, origins of human action, processes of thought, attention, ordinary and extraordinary perception, memory, illusion, emotion, anxiety, and development of personality are met with and the conclusions at times are surprisingly like those arrived at by the modern counterparts. What keeps the modern psychologists from this storehouse of knowledge is the apparent lack of experimental basis, and undue reliance on subjective evidence, intuitive wisdom, logical analysis, and occasional hair-splitting on the part of Indian thinkers.

On the other hand, preoccupation with strict experimental designs, borrowed largely from the physical sciences, often acts as a kind of shackle in the development of modern psychology. Instead of adapting the methodology, or developing new ones, to meet with the diverse and highly complex subject-matter of human behavior, the modern psychologist, in a way, follows the Procrustean-bed policy of forcing every problem into a set scheme, and neglecting those which do not appear to be easily amenable to experimental design. This attitude was particularly noticeable in the early days of modern psychology when it was almost solely concerned with simple processes of sensation, analysis of perception, and reaction-time, and had left out the area of the so-called "higher mental processes" and complex phenomena like personality and human motivation, simply because these did not fit easily into strict "controls" of the laboratory. This attitude of negation, though to a large extent corrected by the recent advances in clinical, social, and industrial psychology, still lingers a little in experimental psychology. Therefore, to an average man who feels that the discipline is concerned with the vital problems of man's life and behavior and expects concrete aids to his happiness, most of the topics hotly debated and investigated by the experimentalists appear elementary, trite and trivial, and a pursuit of the obvious. After examining the present-day science of man one critic, Joseph Wood Krutch (1954), complains that "we have been deluded by the fact that the methods employed for the study of man has been for the most part those originally devised for the study of machines or the study of rats and are capable, therefore, of detecting and measuring only those characteristics which the three do have in common" (p. 32).

On the other hand, Indian psychology has remained closely integrated with philosophy and religion, and, as a consequence, always had in its purview vital problems of man's temptation, nature of pain, liability to err in perception and action, conflict, anxiety, emotions, the unsteady nature of mental processes, and at the same time have prescribed practical courses for their control. Complexity has never frightened Indian thinkers. On the other hand, many Western psychologists have fought shy of the complexity of human behavior. For long, the experimental psychologists confined themselves to the study of simple sensory and motor processes, and even Ebbinghaus who ventured into the realm of the so-called "higher mental processes" remained loyal to the ideal of simplification of stimulus and isolation of response. This ideal is all very well in physical spheres, but is a dangerous one in psychology and the social sciences, which by the very nature of their subject-matter cannot avoid a high degree of complexity. Akhilananda (1952) stresses the religio-practical bent when he says, "Indian psychology has grown out of religious concepts. That is the reason that it basically clarifies the philosophy of life. It not merely gives conceptual knowledge of the different states of mind and their functioning but it also teaches us how the emotions can be unified, redirected, and integrated" (pp. 194–196). Referring to the common feature of religious and psychological thinkers, Mowrer (1952) says, "Traditionally, they, more than any other group, have been concerned with the problem of man's relation to others and to himself, with man's goodness and his happiness. They, especially, have been interested in questions of conscience, guilt, temptation, conflict, and anxiety" (p. xi). It seems, however, a strange coincidence that though modern psychology primarily developed out of "curiosity," and took a different course, in recent times some psychologists and psychotherapists take interest in "stabilizing the mind." Psychological healers and religious healers are finding a common ground. Most modern psychiatrists or psychologists would be reluctant to admit this affinity. But the fact cannot be lightly brushed aside.

It may be added here that the area where Indian psychologists seem to have gone very far ahead is the problem of mental health which was considered a necessary prerequisite for spiritual discipline. As Akhilananda remarks, "So long as mind is disturbed and agitated by conflicting emotions and consequent tension, there is no peace of mind; and when there is no peace of mind there is no joy in life. Neither can restless mind have the possibility for realizing the ultimate truth."

Hence, vital differences in approach, outlook, and methodology have kept modern psychology away from the contributions of Indian thinkers. Most modern psychologists in India at the present time, despite the fact that initially many had been trained also in philosophy, have been jealously scientific in their approach, and in their zeal have completely broken away from their philosophical tradition. Training in psychology has been regarded as incomplete without a trip to England, or preferably to the United States. This wholesale dependence on the West has led to a neglect of psychology embedded in our philosophical and religious texts. Unlike Japan, where many modern psychologists are showing scientific interest in Zen Buddhism and mysticism, modern Indian psychologists look upon older psychological thinking with considerable contempt. There is a complete break from the past. As Loomba (1953) has put it, "Every new researcher tends to take his suggestions and cues from abroad rather than try to continue and carry forward the work that has already been done here" (p. 47). This dependence on Anglo-American psychology has enriched psychological traditions in the two countries but at the same time it has stunted "the further growth of the original native genius in our psychologists" and of an approach inspired by it. It is not a very happy situation that the American psychologists, rather than ourselves, are conscious of the inadequacies of their theories of personality, learning, and emotions, and have started to cast exploring glances at our older systems of thought. This has been responsible for the recent interest which some Americans have been showing in the study of yogic and allied phenomena, wherein they expect to find new light on certain problems, e.g., integration of personality. Instead of the policy of denial and negation which the modern Indian psychologist has been following, a more conducive and fruitful outlook would be to see how much he can learn from older psychologies and integrate into his scientific framework. Rather than keep looking to the West all the time, we can sometimes draw inspiration from our own philosophical traditions and socio-historical settings, and the result is likely to be creative and would put Indian psychology on the map of the world.

No slackening of scientific rigor or sacrificing of scientific methodology is suggested. What is required is to draw hypotheses, ideas, and even theories from the rich heritage of Indian thought, and examine how far they can be made amenable to scientific study and verification. After all, Freud was an intuitive genius. Many of his conclusions had no experimental basis. It would have been a tragedy to dismiss his ideas merely because they lacked a solid factual base. Recent efforts to integrate his concepts with experimental psychology by Sears (1942, p. 17), and others, have marked a definite advance in the science. Can we not try a similar procedure with views and ideas of human behavior embedded in our philosophical writings? These can serve two purposes: first, suggest hypotheses and initiate new lines of experiment, and second, provide a fund of ideas for integrating chaotic findings of modern psychology into a general theory of action. Eminent psychologists like James Conant (1953, pp. 46–47) have stressed the need for using new concepts, and new conceptual schemes that serve as working hypotheses on a grand scale. As he says, "only by the use of new ideas of broad significance has science advanced." Indian thinkers can definitely provide the modern experimentalists with many such new ideas of broad significance.

One way in which integration of Eastern and Western psychologies has been done is by finding parallels between the two on various topics like perception, conflict, personality, and psychotherapy. Bringing out such similarities would be a less fruitful approach, and would keep us on the fringes. This effort implies that there are two distinct psychologies—Indian and modern scientific (Western)—and one takes delight in noticing apparent similarities in conclusions. While reality is admittedly one, there is always the possibility of a multi-faceted approach to it. A distinctly Indian approach to psychology cannot be ruled out. While admitting the factor of cultural relativity, it would be absurd to claim that general principles of motivation, personality, or learning—to mention only a few—are different in each country. To quote a phrase made by Loomba, we have to move "towards a universal psychology." Emerging out of Indian traditional and cultural background, a different attack on these common problems could be useful. Edward Shils (1961) aptly points out, "But intellectual work, whether it be creation or consumption, whether it be scholarly, scientific, literary, publicistic, or artistic, must be concerned with problems which arise from the situation it confronts and it must be carried on within an intellectual tradition; the standards of aspiration and judgment which guide it must likewise be conjoined to the situation and the tradition" (p. 77). Our contribution in this direction can be to apply scientific methodology of modern psychology to ideas derived from Indian thought.

A number of problems can be formulated from the point of view of Indian thought and subjected to experimental attack and scientific verification. A topic on which vast amounts of thinking and researches are being currently conducted is that of motivation and personality. Our knowledge has remained meager. The problem of "Becoming," as Allport (1955) has shown, which is so integral to the understanding of personality, is still eluding the grasp of modern psychologists. Divergence about ideas on integration of personality is enormous. Shaffer and Lazarus (1952) remark, "There is no single personality theory to which all psychologists, even clinical psychologists, will subscribe. As it turns out, there are a great many concepts on the nature of personality. As the student wades through the hundreds of thousands of pages which have been written on the subject, he may wonder whether each of the writers is talking about the same thing. Each new treatise confronts him with a bewildering mass of new and often obscure terminology" (p. 162). This being the picture, will it not be worthwhile developing an Indian personality psychology with a scientific basis?

The techniques of integration of personality are of vital concern to Indian thinkers. It lies in knowing how to handle the emotions properly and how to harmonize and unify the different functions of the total mind—emotion, intellect, and will. Man begins his emotional life like an animal, but rises to the higher plane through human development. This transformation of personality is possible if the individual has the desire to integrate his emotions, and this usually comes by constant association with an integrated person (a spiritual teacher). Second requirement for integration is a higher philosophy of life, which helps to resolve inner tensions, and helps to channelize the basal passions. The third step is directing the emotions to ultimate reality. The next involves the development of an attitude whereby everything is viewed as the manifestation of ultimate reality. Arousal of passion against any object is cooled down if we try to see it in this light. The fifth essential step is the cultivation of feelings opposite of anger, hatred, and other disintegrating urges. Indian psychology never prescribed a negative policy of mere controlling of passions and emotions, but deliberate cultivation of higher qualities which replace the former. The last step is the practice of concentration. For those who do not believe in God a slightly different scheme is prescribed.

We may not agree with the details of this but it implies a definite idea of human motivation, and personality, and their development. It can be used as a framework from which a number of working hypotheses could be derived, and scientifically studied. Here it will be worthwhile looking at Maslow's (1954) theory of motivation and personality, which regards the individual as an integrated organized whole. Such views are not as common in modern psychology as they should be, because understanding and classification of man's motives have not been "human-centered" but have been primarily derived from animal studies. Of particular importance is Maslow's arrangement of basic needs in a hierarchy of prepotency, e.g., the physiological needs, the safety needs, the need for belongingness and love, the need for importance, respect, self-esteem, independence, the need for information, the need for understanding, the need for beauty, and need for self-actualization. Maslow thinks that ordinarily it is only after the gratification of the earlier ones that the higher levels can be reached, and not by their suppression or sublimation. An equally plausible scheme of motivation can be worked out on the basis of Indian thought and tested scientifically.

Maslow's emphasis on need for self-actualization is a further pointer in this direction. Not only he, but other investigators have found sufficient clinical basis for assuming a need for self-actualization. They have, however, limited it by asserting that effective self-actualization can emerge freely only with prior satisfaction of the physiological, safety, love, and esteem needs. But when it has emerged fully it seems to organize, and to some extent to control, other needs. The Indian psychologists' outlook is a little different in that they admit the existence and pressing nature of basic needs, and at the same time feel that for the integration of personality these basic needs should be reduced and reoriented to help the cultivation of higher needs. Hypotheses derived from this conceptual framework can be tested experimentally and through clinical observations.

A related field where psychology in Indian thought can be utilized is in building up an overall view about human nature. Modern psychology has not yet given us a satisfactory answer in this regard. Though there is some experimental and clinical support for it, it is largely a matter of speculation that man is essentially a creature of "unreason" and that he is "irrational." Obviously, the views of man that are in different philosophies do not tally with this. It is just possible that being dependent on results of the studies on animal motivation, and observations of persons suffering from different forms of mental disorders modern psychologists have developed only a partial view of man's nature. This undue dependence on the study of the "abnormal" in propounding theories of motivation and personality has been commented upon by Robert White (1957), Allport, and others.

Only recently, we have come to hear of "achievement motive" in modern psychology (McClelland et al., 1953). Thus, gaps are obvious, and a general view of man and his nature derived from Indian thinkers would be suggestive of many fruitful hypotheses, and also would integrate many of the findings of modern psychology into a unified view of personality. That this will imply a new and different approach to motivation and personality need not frighten the modern scientists. In the areas of learning, perception, personality, or for that matter any topic on which a controversy is raging, it is possible to discern "styles," "preferences," or difference in outlook. Allport (1955) rightly remarks, "Except for a common loyalty to their profession psychologists often seem to agree on little else. Perhaps in a broad sense all may be said to be committed to the use of the scientific method there is dispute as to the legitimate outer boundaries of this method" (pp. 4–5). Allport has shown how the two rival traditions in modern psychology, viz., the Lockean and Leibnitzian, have helped to develop distinct theories of personality. Bertrand Russell (1927) has ironically referred to this situation: "One may say broadly that all the animals that have been carefully observed have behaved so as to confirm the philosophy in which the observer believed before his observations began. Nay, more, they have all displayed the national characteristics of the observer. Animals studied by Americans rush about frantically, with an incredible display of hustle and pep, and at last achieve the desired result by chance. Animals observed by Germans sit still and think and at last evolve the solution out of their inner consciousness" (pp. 32–33).

In fact, in the USA as well as in Germany, psychology is marked by distinctive characteristics because the respective philosophical traditions and national outlook have given peculiar direction to psychological research. Maller (1933) shows that as against American obsession with mental tests, statistics, deficiency, reflexes, learning, the psychophysics, the greater number of German psychological studies deal with special conditions, sleep, dreams, psychical research, criminology, degeneracy, psychology of character and personality, voluntary action, and social functions of the individual. The German approach is more qualitative, and every piece of behavior is regarded as meaningfully related to his total personality rather than just so much trait and so much uncontrollable error. As a result, there is little emphasis on the quantitative validation and making of detailed measurement. That some Americans debunk German psychology does not disturb them. Vernon (1933) summarizes the situation "that 90 per cent of the followers of the typical German schools regard American investigations and themes as futile and that 90 per cent of American psychologists return the compliment." Thus, one should not fight shy of developing an approach to psychology peculiar to our traditions. There is a definite scope for freely drawing material from Indian thinkers for scientific investigation and, if required, developing a distinct scientific methodology for investigation rather than being trammeled by pet postulates and the techniques of modern psychology.

Another area where modern psychology can profit by the drawing of working hypotheses and conceptual framework is in perception, and psychotherapy. Further, one of the special features of Indian systems is the prescription of ascetic discipline. This involves regulation of body and mind by different practices both physical and mental. Use of highly sensitive modern psychological and physiological measuring techniques will not only throw light on the nature of meditation, yogic trance, but open windows on a new horizon for modern psychologists. The utilization of the before-and-after test design and the employment of psychometric, behavioral, projective, the EEG, as well as biophysiological tests, would reveal a lot on the nature of mental functioning and personality change as a result of common practices of meditation, trance, oxygen deprivation, and long repetition of mantras. That this is scientifically feasible has been amply demonstrated by psychological studies of effects of drugs like mescalin (Huxley, 1954, 1957). The effects of exercises of concentration and relaxation on adrenal cortical function, plasma, and urinary excretion of hydrocortisone, which is found under stress, would be a fruitful area of research by which psychological phenomena as studied by Indian thinkers can be integrated with the modern scientific psychology. Similarly, the psychology of emotion as contained in Indian musical science (Sangita-Sastra) and aesthetics (Alankara-Sastra), and the psychological effect of different kinds of food and drink discussed in Indian medical and yoga treatises, etc., call for scientific investigation and verification.

To conclude, it is my feeling that there are numerous areas where the two lines can converge and integrate profitably. This would result in bridging many of the gaps that are too obvious in modern psychological theory of action, and at the same time interpret our philosophical thought in scientific light. It is only through such efforts that what we have sometimes called Indian Psychology (and have regarded in a derogatory light) can raise itself to the level of well-established science, and show in what way the East can contribute to the building of a universal psychology of human personality and development. This is possible when we, to quote Conant (1953, p. 36), have as our watchword not "What does the book say about this or that?" but, "Let's try to find out for ourselves" (p. 36).

# 3

# Indigenization of Psychology in India*

Knowledge has its own anchorage in tradition, history, and society. Historical and social forces operate in its production and utilization. As Singh (1986) has observed, production of knowledge is socially conditioned since the categories of science, its tools for the perception of reality, are mediated by social forces, culture, and tradition. The social conditioning of knowledge is revealed by the extent to which the concepts, methods, and priority areas of research have the imprint of history and social forces operative in society (p. ix).

This position has not gone unchallenged. The diehard universalists and absolutists assert that there is no question of cultural relativity about knowledge. With the political and economic dominance which the industrially advanced west gained over the rest of the world, universalism in knowledge came to be equated with the theories, principles, and data generated in the countries of Europe and North America. These were supposed to have panhuman verities and were utilized to explain behaviour not only of the people and societies where they had been generated, but also of other peoples and societies irrespective of the differences in their culture, tradition, and historical antecedents. This position is seriously questioned especially in the social sciences. The socio-cultural context and history are emphasized and the *assumed* universality of the theories and principles developed in the west has begun to be questioned and alternatives are suggested. Just as in general development, the "endogenous" model is

* Reproduced, with permission, from Sinha, D. Indigenization of Psychology in India. *Indian Psychological Abstracts & Reviews*, 1(1), 179–215 (1994). New Delhi: ICSSR.

This text has been edited for typographical errors, stylistic consistency and sequential organization in order to make it suitable for inclusion in the book.

considered more efficacious and desirable than the adoption of western models, in the field of knowledge, servility and dependence on the west is sought to be replaced by "indigenous" knowledge.

Indigenization is a global phenomenon. Neither it is confined to a few countries or regions of the world nor to the social sciences only though in some regions and in certain disciplines, the need for indigenization is greater. In the erstwhile colonial countries which had been for centuries under the domination of the west, there is a strong trend towards *decolonization* of knowledge and a call for "self-rule" in the sciences. Reflections of this trend can be discerned in the powerful intellectual movement for Islamizing knowledge in Pakistan (Al Faruqi, 1982) and other Muslim countries, teaching of Vedic mathematics in some states in India, and popularity in some academic circles of treatises on the physical and positive sciences of ancient Hindus, in many developing countries there is growing scepticism—even outright opposition—to toeing western technological developments. Instead there is a plea for "appropriate" technology. In the Philippines, the trend is most clearly visible in psychology in what has been termed as "decoding the Filipino psyche" (Enriquez, 1987) or the "contextualization of psychology in the Philippine setting" (p. 276) and a plea for a Filipino psychology or *Sikolohiyang Pilipino* (Enriquez, 1982). Even in the west, a distinct European social psychology has become a reality (Moscovici, 1972); and in Canada, social psychology in the Canadian context with a distinct orientation and emphasis has evolved (Berry, 1974; Berry & Wilde, 1972).

As expected, the trend towards indigenization is clearly visible and strongest in the social sciences. In particular, modern psychology being the most "foreign" of the social sciences, the need for indigenization is expressed loudly. The inapplicability of psychological concepts and tools forged in the western context is frequently emphasized and their wholesale transfer/transplantation to countries of Africa, Asia, and Latin America is questioned. It is contended that psychological knowledge should be based on culturally derived categories and appropriate instruments of data collection, and should concern itself with problems that really matter rather than with those derived from a perusal of western research literature or those that are in fashion in the west. It is, however, to be noted that this does not apply to those areas of psychology that deal mainly with the biological and physiological aspects of behaviour in which culture specific factors play but a very minor role. Thus, in fields like physiological psychology and ergonomics, universality of principles and theories is seldom questioned. On the other hand, in fields like social psychology, organizational behaviour, personality, clinical, and developmental psychology where culture and sociogenic variables operate as significant determinants, indigenization is viewed not only as desirable but also inevitable. Even in certain aspects of perception and cognition, characteristic habits of information processing seem to be inculcated by culture (Cole, Gay & Glick, 1968; Das & Molloy, 1975); and the emphasis on cultural variables and indigenization is believed to be necessary. As Berry, Poortinga, Segall, and Desan (1992) have concluded, "not all perceptual variables are equally likely to show cultural differences. On basic sensory functions, equal level of performance is to be expected for all cultural groups. But at higher levels of stimulus complexity the pattern of findings changes" (p. 160). In the case of the latter, the indigenous approach appears fruitful if the goal of universal verity of psychological principles is to be attained rather than merely assumed.

# "Why" of Indigenization

Before delving into the nature of indigenization, factors that have led to the adoption of an indigenous approach to psychology in India are discussed. In order to provide the necessary perspective, its historical background is outlined. In India, the roots of psychology go deep into the vast storehouse of knowledge embodied in ancient religious and philosophical treatises, in epics and in folklores. They contain valuable materials concerning the nature of man, his personality, and social and interpersonal interactions. But the psychological knowledge contained therein is based on speculations and intuitions of seers and can hardly be regarded as "scientific" in the strict sense of the term. Thus, as a part of general transfer of knowledge, when modern scientific psychology, based on positivistic, materialistic, mechanistic, and empirical orientations of the west, was transplanted to India during the second decade of the century, it was imported as a "ready-made intellectual package" (Nandy, 1974, p. 7). It swept away psychology enshrined in Indian tradition and ancient texts and along with that there was an uncritical acceptance of concepts, theories, and techniques used in the west. Shanmugam (1972) who reviewed the study of personality researches for the first ICSSR Survey, rightly concluded that "when we look for significant contributions from Indian psychologists, we are disappointed, since most of the studies reported are based on western models" (p. 302). This was true of almost all the branches, and of concepts, theories, and psychological instruments used for data collection. Whatever constructs and principles became popular at a particular time in the west, psychologists in India readily adopted them without re-defining them or examining their applicability (Sinha, 1984b, p. 199). In fact, they worked with them for years—long after they had gone out of fashion in the country of their origin. As Diaz-Guerrero (1977) has rightly observed in the context of the developing countries, such borrowing had done precious little to stimulate the development of local instruments that would at least measure socio-cultural characteristics of the country and had been completely blind to measures sensitive to idiosyncratic cultural and personality dynamics. The outcome was proliferation of psychological literature and tests that were frequently irrelevant in our cultural context. They lacked creativity, and were imitative and replicative. It is, therefore, not surprising that modern psychology in India is often called a "Euro-American product" (Campbell, 1968; Sinha, 1977, 1984a) with very little concern for the social reality as it prevailed in the country (Sinha, 1988/1993, p. 78).

Mohanty (1988) has content-analyzed papers published during 1984 and 1985 in one of the few research journals in psychology in the country that is published regularly, viz., *Psychological Studies*, and observed that in 85.68 per cent of the cases, the main source was an American journal or dissertation; in 8.14 per cent it was a non-American (European or Japanese) international journal; and in 6.16 per cent of the papers no definite source could be determined. An analysis of originality of the research idea contained in the papers revealed that 83.67 per cent were replications or near-replications of works of their overseas (almost always American) colleagues. Within these, 26.53 per cent were exact replications with no appreciable change from the source, and 57.14 per cent with conscious modification of some of the variables. Only 8.16 per cent reported a genuine critical study and another 8.16 per cent were considered original and were based on some typically Indian context. Naturally, the author regards the average Indian psychologist as "only an uncritical, delayed, but faithful reflection of his American counterpart" (Mohanty, 1988, p. 1). As a result, the psychology that he created seemed to be composed of not-so-mindful, not-so-original and aimless scribblings of ideas picked up from North American psychology outdated by at least a decade—thus earning him the ephitet—Yankee Doodler (p. 1). Most psychologists in India—a large number of them being trained in the west—derived their inspiration from outside which hampered the healthy growth of the subject in the country. References cited in their studies, as the analysis by J.B.P. Sinha (1976) of four books on industrial occupational psychology pertaining to the 1960s has shown, were mostly foreign and an insignificant number, if any, were of their compatriots. Therefore, it is not surprising that the subject remained for long at best a pale carbon copy of western and largely American psychology with very little concern for the social reality in the country. This subservience sometimes went to the ridiculous length of conceptualizing Indian social phenomena in American terms, for example, caste as if it were race, communalism as anti-semitism, and the untouchables as the American blacks, as Nandy (1974, p. 8) has pointed out.

The "foreignness" of the studies divorced the subject both from the traditional system of psychology and the rich storehouse of concepts and ideas which could have provided strong cultural roots as well as linked them to the Indian social reality. Very rightly, the Standing Committee for Psychology of the ICSSR voiced its "concerns about foreignness of social science research in India—in the field of psychology in particular" (ICSSR, 1973, p. 43). Such studies were neither theoretically sound, nor had relevance to the problems of the country.

Indian psychologists looking to the west, especially the USA, for academic recognition and patronage—because they were conducive factors in their career advancement and promotion—naturally adopted the prevailing disciplinary fashion. They accepted the salience and priorities prevailing in western psychology at the time without bothering to examine them in the light of the needs of the country. As Sinha (1986, p. 111) has observed, "the western models and ideas took Indian researchers away from such ideas that might have struck roots in the Indian soil." It frequently led to a shift in the focus of the local scholar away from his own country and its problems, and distracted him from core issues. This was the state of psychology especially during the pre-independence phase and during the decade or so of post-independence expansion.

Immediately after independence, there was a growth of national pride and a gradual awareness of a distinct identity among scholars who began to feel the need for "outgrowing the alien framework" (Sinha, 1980/1987). Initially, though there was an effort to study variables operating in the Indian situation, the topics continued to remain those which were current in the west and the theoretical framework utilized was also western (J.B.P. Sinha, 1976). The 1960s marked the phase of problem-oriented research during which relating psychological research to problems arising from rapid socio-economic development and change, and those that were vital to the country were articulated. Topics like psychological dimensions of poverty, agro-economic development, health and family welfare, diffusion of innovation—to mention only a few—started to attract increasing attention. But the existing psychological theories and principles proved inadequate. Being the products of a specific milieu of the west with parameters like university, impersonality, stability, literacy and a host of shared beliefs and attitudes which were not available in the developing countries, their application for understanding and predicting social behaviour was very limited (Jahoda, 1973). Jahoda (1980/1983, p. 30) has rightly asserted that social psychology is still very weak as regards theories relevant to studies in developing countries.

It was, therefore, inevitable that some Indian scholars began to question the appropriateness of the theories developed in the west, based entirely on western data, and articulated the need for developing the subject rooted in the socio-cultural context of the country. Thus, not only was there an urge to make the subject relevant to meet the needs of a changing society, but also for appropriate theoretical framework and tools of research suited to the situation prevailing in the country (Sinha, 1986, p. 63).

In this context, it should be noted that modern psychology, which with considerable justification is equated with psychology that has developed and flourished in the United States, is regarded by many as an "indigenous psychology of the West" (Rudmin, 1987, p. 1). Even in the USA psychologists are becoming increasingly aware of the "monoculture" nature of North American psychology (Kennedy, Scheirer & Rogers, 1984). It has been observed that Canada, the Philippines and some countries in Europe have shown trends towards developing a psychology in their own cultural context.

In India, growing disillusionment with the foreign roots of psychology, realization of the non-applicability of its concepts and tools for research in the radically different socio-cultural contexts, its "irrelevance to vital issues facing the country and failure to make a thrust in the national life (Pareek, 1980b, p. ix) were indicative of signs of growing crisis in psychology". As a result, the process of indigenization has been unleashed, and since the mid-1970s, there has been a strong trend towards the development of the discipline suited to the needs and socio-cultural context of the country. Pareek (1981) has indicated that there has been an effort to contribute both to the development of theory and to provide effective solutions to social problems. Moghaddam (1987) has rightly observed that "probably the most important factor shaping indigenous third world psychology is the demand that it contributes directly to the development effort of third-world societies" (p. 918).

# Definition and Nature of Indigenization

Before discussing indigenization of psychology in India, it is necessary to clarify the concept. Though it is quite frequently used in social science literature, the expression "indigenization" does not occur in any standard dictionary. Since it is derived from the term "indigenous", we begin with its import. According to the *Concise Oxford Dictionary*, "indigenous" refers to flora and fauna and means "produced naturally in a region; belonging naturally to the soil". Extending its biological meaning to the sphere of epistemology, it would refer to those elements of knowledge that have been generated in a country or culture, and have developed therein as against those that are imported or borrowed from elsewhere. According to this view, concepts, ideas, materials, methods, and techniques that have their origin in the region or have traditional roots and constitute the cultural creations would be regarded as indigenous. Second, due to contact and communication with other cultures, countries or regions, many concepts, theories, and methods are implanted and borrowed from outside. These usually undergo transformations so that they suit the characteristics of the region. Thus, in its second aspect, it implies the process of changing or modifying the imported elements so that they become adapted, natural, or appropriate to the region. Strictly speaking, "indigenization" refers to the second aspect, which implies the way in which an element of knowledge is transformed so as to make it natural or suited to the special features of the socio-cultural setting of the country or region (Sinha, 1988/1993, p. 81). In the context of psychology, indigenization would mean the transformation of scientific psychology that has been borrowed from the west in such a manner that it takes on a character suited to the social and cultural milieu of the country. Puhan and Sahoo (1991) have equated it with assimilation and gradual adaptation. It is a "route" to what Azuma (1984) has called "appropriate psychology". In other words, it is a kind of *contextualization* of the discipline, i.e., blending of foreign models, theories, and methods with indigenous ones (Adair, 1989) to make them culturally appropriate. As Adair (1992a) has pointed out, "an indigenous psychology gradually develops from blending of an imported discipline with increasing attention to unique elements within that culture" (p. 3). In one of his earlier papers entitled "Integration of modern psychology with Indian thought", Sinha (1965, p. 5) has viewed the process as a "converging of two lines", or systems of psychological knowledge, and as an integrative process.

From the above exposition, it is evident that indigenization has two facets or forms. In its first aspect, it is purely the product of a culture and implies utilization in a particular discipline of concepts and categories that belong to that culture, and those that emanate from the social and cultural milieu itself. In its second aspect, it reflects the interaction of the local or cultural elements with concepts, theories, and methods imported from external sources. In other words, it is a kind of integrative or assimilative process. These two can respectively be designated as "internal indigenization" and "indigenization of the exogenous"—a distinction that corresponds to Enriquez's (1987) "indigenization from within" and "indigenization from without".

If we study the definitions of indigenization advanced by Adair and his colleagues, both aspects of the process are emphasized. But the definition propounded by Adair, Puhan, and Vohra (1993) seems to emphasize only the first aspect: "In the context of social research, indigenisation emanates from, adequately represents, and reflects back the culture in which behaviour is studied, rather than a discipline that is imported from, and primarily addresses Developed World models" (p. 150).

In an earlier definition, however, Adair (1992a, p. 62) has confined it largely to the second aspect of indigenization. It is regarded as a process of taking development from elsewhere (such as US psychology) and introducing modifications to make it fit the new culture. It is obvious that the expression refers to a set of complex processes and phenomena that are interrelated. While dealing with them, however, scholars have not maintained a distinction between the various facets thereby leading to a certain amount of confusion. It is to be noted that though Adair is aware of both the facets of indigenization, his analysis of the process is confined mainly to the second aspect.

# Different Forms of Indigenization

So far as the development of psychology in India is concerned, both kinds of indigenization are evidenced. Before going into the details, some other differentiations of the process will be discussed.

## Structural, Substantive and Theoretical

Krishna Kumar (1979, pp. 104–105) has differentiated between three types of indigenization: structural, substantive, and theoretical. The first is defined with reference to the institutional and organizational capabilities of a nation for the production and development of knowledge that is relevant. As far as psychology is concerned, there are very few departments and institutions in the country with the professed and explicit goal of focusing research on social and national issues that are peculiar to the country or developing psychology based on indigenous concepts and categories. They are largely geared to the mainstream psychology, and generally follow the current priorities and are inspired by the problems that are cogitating their counterparts in the west. There are, of course, a few exceptions. Some departments have linked their research activities to contemporary social and national issues like poverty, intergroup relations, social inequality, social change and national development, and are geared to psychological knowledge that is culturally relevant. Their number is not large, but growing all the same. In any case, the process of structural and institutional reorientation in the direction has begun and is likely to become stronger in years to come.

Substantial indigenization can be conceptualized within the content focus of the discipline. It is advocated that the main thrust of the subject should be on its own society, people, and problems. In this respect, the need to put psychology in the arena of social change and national development, and make it problem-oriented has been strongly advocated by D. Sinha (1966, 1969, 1973a, 1977, 1983a, 1984a, 1986), J.B.P. Sinha (1973), Pareek (1980b), and others. Pareek has rightly pointed out that the "new developments have shown that psychology has to share with other social sciences the task of contributing to the solution of the national problems, both in terms of conceptual and intervention insights" (p. vii). Indigenous issues and content are increasingly emphasized and the "crisis of relevance" is being experienced. The content of the subject is undergoing modifications and the discipline is well on the road towards indigenization. The very fact that bodies like the Indian Council of Social Science Research, and a panel of experts appointed by it have tried to identify some priority areas for research (Sinha, 1973b) is indicative of substantive indigenization that is taking place. Theoretical indigenization, according to Krishna Kumar (1979, p. 105), indicates a condition in which scientists are involved in constructing distinctive conceptual frameworks and metatheories which reflect their world-views, social and cultural experience, and perceived goals. Since concepts and theoretical frameworks are difficult to transfer wholesale from one culture to another, culturally-rooted categories and concepts for analyzing social and psychological phenomena are essential. It is this aspect of indigenization that is largely lacking as far as psychology in India is concerned. It has depended almost entirely on western theories and models, and has often uncritically applied them to Indian social reality without realizing their limited applicability. Psychologists in India so far have not evinced sufficient interest in developing culturally-rooted categories and then-own theories. Theoretical indigenization seems to be the most retarded aspect of the whole process.

## Four Fronts of Indigenization

Atal (1981, p. 193) has observed that in the Asian context indigenization has been pursued on four fronts: (a) the use of local materials and teaching in national and regional languages; (b) research by local scholars; (c) determination of research priorities; and (d) theoretical and methodological reorientation. Indigenization of psychology in India is taking place on all these fronts, but with varying pace and success. It is not possible to deal with them at length, only a few main points are discussed here.

Following independence, there was a move towards replacing English and the adoption of Hindi and regional languages for instruction in universities and colleges. But the implementation of this plan has been beset with many difficulties. Suitable textbooks and research literature in Hindi—what to speak of the regional languages—have not been produced. There is also reluctance on the part of most front rank psychologists in the country to give up English which is the main instrument of their maintaining linkages with their peers in the west and the mainstream psychology.

There is a real fear of being isolated from the world community of psychologists. They have shown more interest in getting recognition in the west, which is regarded as a vital factor in their professional and career advancement, and attendant fringe benefits of foreign collaboration and travel. As such, psychologists have not evinced much interest in indigenous and local materials for teaching or production of psychological literature of quality in national or regional languages. On the other hand, teachers of muffasil colleges and in many of the mushrooming universities lack not only high proficiency in English but are also denied the basic infrastructural facilities by way of laboratories and libraries. They teach in Hindi or in one of the regional languages and have churned out a fairly large number of textbooks which are usually out of date and below standard. Generally, they are veritable and unmindful complications in translation of a few outdated foreign books. They constitute best examples of "translation plagiarism". Their style is discursive and the treatment seldom scientific with greater emphasis on abstract definitions. They are full of quotations, and seldom contain suitable illustrations or discussion and analysis of the local settings and hardly any reference to many good studies conducted in the country. A gap—almost "two cultures"—has developed. It is, therefore, not surprising that it has created a kind of communication crisis between a small and active group of frontrank psychologists in a few elite centres and others who constitute the main body of scholars in the country. As far as teaching in national languages, and the creation and use of local materials are concerned, the process of indigenization, though it has been in operation for more than four decades, has not produced the desired outcome.

A significant step towards indigenization is the promotion of research by "locals" and imposing restrictions on "expatriate" research. The establishment of the ICSSR in the country is a significant step in this direction. It has made funds available to research workers in the country which they lacked earlier. But the research output has been far from satisfactory. As for restricting research by outsiders and encouraging them to have local collaborators, it is justified to some extent. In an alien culture, expatriate researchers do not always possess the requisite sensitivity and insight, and imposing foreign categories often gives a distorted picture of the social reality. But these restrictions have often been guided by political rather than academic considerations which cannot always be justified.

The third dimension of indigenization is the promotion of research on topics and themes that are considered relevant and nationally important. As has already been observed, this has been one of the main considerations that has goaded indigenization of research in psychology. In recent years, emphasis on relevant and problem-oriented research has been strong among psychologists in India (D. Sinha, 1973a, 1986; J.B.P. Sinha, 1973). There has also been an attempt on the part of the ICSSR to lay down some research priorities. A few topics considered highly relevant have been enumerated (Sinha, 1973b). But defining priorities is beset with problems. It is difficult to reach a consensus on priorities, and there are problems in evolving satisfactory criteria. Academically, there is not much to commend rigid priorities and strait jacketing of research activity.

The fourth dimension of indigenization is theoretical and methodological reorientation. In psychology, there is near total domination of models and theories indiscriminately borrowed from the west. While iconoclastic discussion about *alien* theories has little to commend, their appropriateness is always questionable. It is, therefore, not surprising that one of the main directions that indigenization in psychology has taken is a re-examination of many of the theoretical frameworks and models that have been borrowed from the west. For example, the effectiveness of the participatory model of leadership has been questioned, and a more culturally appropriate alternative model called "nurturant task leader" has been proposed (J.B.P. Sinha, 1980). Similarly, Miller, Bersoff, and Harwood (1990) taking the Indian socio-cultural context that hypothesized moral behaviour as an acceptance of social responsibilities towards persons in need, reformulated Kohlberg's theory and suggested that Indian judgement reflected the moral code that tended to give priority to social duties while the judgements of Americans reflected a code that gave priority to individual rights.

This is one of the most significant dimensions of indigenization. But there has not been much effort towards linking these borrowed models to cultural realities and of modifying them suitably. It is noteworthy that psychologists in India have paid little attention to developing their own theories which can serve as alternatives to those implanted from the west. However, the situation seems to be gradually changing in the last decade or so.

# Measurement of Indigenization

Indigenization of psychology in India has been discussed and documented by Sinha (1986) citing examples of indigenous orientation, concepts, culturally suitable methods, conceptual analysis and discussion of the findings of studies conducted since independence. The gradual stages through which the process is unfolding has also been outlined. In contrast, Adair and his colleagues have adopted an empirical approach. They have content-analyzed papers published in some journals over a period of time (1972–1974, 1978–1980 and 1984–1988) and have examined the way in which the process is developing in gradual stages. Indigenization has been operationalized as the extent to which the concepts, problems, hypotheses, methods, and tests: (a) emanate from, (b) adequately represent, and (c) reflect back upon the cultural context in which behaviour is observed (Adair, 1992a; Adair, Puhan & Vohra, 1993, p. 149). In other words, reference to culture in locating and formulating the problems for research, adopting methods for data collection that are appropriate for the local sample, and reference to culture in the interpretation and discussion of the findings are the main features of indigenization. In short, reference to culture is essential. Empirical research was scaled as making increasingly indigenous contributions if (a) differences between India and the west were identified, (b) differences within India or between Indian and non-western cultures were identified, (c) the research attempted to explain behaviours observed in the local culture, or (d) an indigenous theory or concept guided the research or its interpretation (Adair, 1992a). Fundamental to the approach is the belief that indigenousness develops by degrees and that increments can be measured in terms of a change in the content, methods, problem development, hypotheses, and interpretations of published research results (Adair, 1992a, p. 63).

Using these indicators, comparisons of the extent of indigenization in Bangladesh, Canada, and India were made. As far as the Indian situation is concerned, though the percentage of studies making either slight or modest reference to the cultural context were virtually constant over the period, articles with substantial reference to cultural variables noticeably increased in recent times. However, indigenous cultural elements have not yet become the focus of study (Adair, 1992a, p. 65). As far as methodology is concerned, by and large there was continued dependence on psychological tests standardized in western culture "indicative of continuing insensitivity to the special characteristics of Indian sample" (p. 66). As Adair (1992a) has observed, "indigenous methodology appears in many respects to be slower to develop than cultural problem sensitivity and the development of indigenous concepts" (p. 67). The identification of native differences and the development or adaptation of tests into one of the local languages were the most common forms of indigenous contributions. There were a few reported attempts to adopt special methods to meet the needs of local subjects, and such attempts have increased in recent years (Adair, Puhan & Vohra, 1993, p. 160). Further, in the interpretation and discussion of the findings, there was only a slight or modest reference to the cultural context, though it tended to increase over time. However, substantial reference to cultural variables noticeably increased only in the most recent period (p. 67). As for identification or resolution of social problems—an important indicator of indigenization—Indian research was found to be "very poor in its social problem contribution" (pp. 67–68). There did not seem to be a shift towards applied research or towards problems of national concern.

Adair (1992a) has also content-analyzed Indian authored articles published in foreign journals. Compared with articles published in Indian journals, they provide considerable evidence of cultural focus in more meaningful ways. "The research published abroad was of better quality . . . and of a more indigenous or culturally sensitive nature compared to research published in India" (p. 69). The general conclusion that seems to emerge from these studies is that there has been "some slight movement towards an indigenous discipline" (Adair, Puhan & Vohra, 1993, p. 149).

# Some Specific Examples of Indigenization

Space does not permit dealing at length with specific examples of indigenization. Only a few cases are discussed briefly to illustrate different ways in which the process is in operation especially on the level of content and constructs as well as methodological reorientation.

For the purpose of analysis, a distinction between four different levels has been suggested by Berry, Poortinga, Segall, and Dasen (1992). Since western psychological research tends to be ethnocentric at the levels of (a) selection of items and stimuli in an instrument, (b) choice of instruments and procedures, (c) definition of theoretical concepts, and (d) choice of topics for research, it is not surprising that in India an indigenous approach to psychology is visible most clearly on these four levels. For the sake of convenience, we could group the last two under the broad heading of *cognitive indigenization* and the first two under *methodological indigenization*. A few examples of each are described.

## Cognitive Indigenization

As has been stated earlier, the main negative impact of overwhelming dependence on the west for psychological concepts and constructs, and aping the prevailing disciplinary fashion, was that the priorities of Indian psychologists were distorted and they became mere "duplicators" of western research (Sinha, 1986a, p. 111). Western orientation became so deep-rooted that the focus of attention of scholars got shifted from their own country and its problems (Sinha, 1992). Thus, the first and probably the inevitable step towards indigenization was to accept the challenges posed by the national programmes of social change and development, and thereby pursue problem-oriented research (Sinha, 1966). Psychologists began to address themselves increasingly to problems such as agro-economic development (Sinha, 1969), population control, family health and welfare, poverty and inequality, caste and other kinds of tensions, and diffusion of innovations, many of which had remained outside the pale of modern psychology. This change in orientation clearly marked the beginning of the phase of indigenization of psychology in the country (Sinha, 1988/1993, p. 80) in the early 1960s. A comprehensive picture of the shift in the choice of topics for research can be gauged from the second and third surveys of research in psychology conducted by the ICSSR (Pareek, 1980, 1981; Pandey, 1988).

This change in orientation automatically led to the next stage of what has been called the "phase of indigenization" (Sinha, 1986) in the 1970s which has become more articulated since the 1980s. This phase was characterized by a questioning of western theories and models, and their appropriateness in the specific socio-cultural context as well as doubts about the efficacy of tools for data collection developed in the west, especially so far as the unsophisticated rural and tribal populations that constitute the bulk of the country's people were concerned.

This level of indigenization, which can be called *cognitive indigenization*, has taken two main forms, viz., *explanatory* or *interpretations* and *conceptual* or *paradigmatic*. Culture has been utilized first, as a source of psychological explanation and for understanding of the phenomenon, and second, for deriving constructs. Or, as Marriott (1990) has said, it is looking at "India through Hindu categories". *In* the past there has been a tendency to explain and interpret the findings purely in terms of theories and principles developed in the west, and whatever differences were observed were attributed in a sort of blanket fashion to cultural differences. For example, lower need for achievement obtained on tests among Indian subjects was often contrasted with that of American subjects and explained in terms of the absence of Protestant ethic and a different kind of work culture and socialization practices. Of late, the Indian socio-cultural context that emphasizes a relational view of the individual and familial concerns as being more salient than personal achievement has been brought into the picture (Misra & Gergen, 1993, p. 236). Results obtained by Misra and his colleagues (Agarwal & Misra, 1986; Singhal & Misra, 1989) have revealed that social concern (e.g., being a good person, well-being of others, fulfilling one's duty, helping others, getting affection from elders) is a predominant part of the achievement goals of Indian subjects.

The individualism–collectivism dichotomy has also been examined and interpreted in the Indian socio-cultural context. Taking into account the Indian philosophical background, ethical percepts, the dissonant character of the Indian psyche and other facets of culture, Sinha and Tripathi (1991) have questioned the contention that Indians are highly collectivistic and have pointed to strong individualistic strands in different spheres. On the basis of an empirical study, they have concluded that rather than being collectivistic, Indian subjects manifest a blend of the two orientations. They also emphasized the need for adopting a more culture-specific approach.

Another excellent example has been our understanding of the findings on reward allocation, distributive justice, and moral judgement. In the

Indian context need has been considered as more salient than equality (Berman, Murphy-Berman & Singh, 1985) so far as reward allocation is concerned. Moreover, judging moral reasoning in terms of Kohlberg's model has been questioned, and moral behaviour has been regarded as the acceptance of social responsibilities towards persons in need reflecting a moral code that tends to give priority to social duties while the judgements of Americans reflected priority to individual rights (Miller, Bersoff & Harwood, 1990).

This trend reflects the utilization of cultural categories for *explaining* research findings and has inevitably led to two other levels of indigenization, viz., modification of western theories to make them in tune with the Indian social reality, and conceptual/paradigmatic indigenization designing psychological studies. There have been many endeavours in this direction. A few examples are described here.

An excellent study representing the first approach in which a western model *is* sought to be assimilated into the Indian setting through necessary modification is that of J.B.P. Sinha (1980). After analyzing the authority patterns in Indian organizations which seem to be dominated by the parental ideology of authority relations (Kakar, 1971), and the need for drawing upon familial values (Ray, 1970), and the importance attached to establishing mutually supportive relationships (J.B.P. Sinha, 1974), he questioned the applicability of the western model of employee-oriented and participatory leadership. Between the two extremes of authoritarian and democratic styles, a third style of *nurturant task leader* was postulated. It is task-oriented with structured expectations from subordinates and draws upon cultural values like affection, dependency, and need for personalized relationships (De, 1974). It was proposed as an alternative model which was felt to be appropriate and effective in the transitional socio-cultural conditions prevailing in the country.

Of late, there has been a growing interest in analyzing indigenous cultural categories and processes located in Indian traditional sources. These concepts and processes provide a perspective very different from western ones. First, many treatises have appeared dealing with what has been called "Indian psychology" or "Hindu psychology", analyzing Indian psychological constructs and theories (e.g., Akhilananda, 1948; Safaya, 1976; J. Sinha, 1958). The treatment in these books is largely philosophical. However, Dwivedi has published many papers which provide, among others, useful psychological analysis of motivation according to traditional Indian psychology (1982), Indian concepts of anxiety (1986), and *asampramosa* doctrine of memory (1987). Paranjpe

(1988) has presented the Vedantic theory of personality, and Akhilananda (1952) has discussed many psychological processes and Indian practices useful for mental health. Beena (1990), after exhaustively dealing with various personality typologies according to western and ancient Indian approaches, has highlighted the similarities and differences between the two. The fundamental features of the Indian approaches are discussed. However, in spite of an exhaustive account of different systems, there is little effort towards integration or a critical examination of Indian approaches in modern scientific terms. Similarly, Krishnan (1992) has explored at length the traditional Indian concept of justice drawing upon the epics, the Dharmashastras, and other ancient treatises. Not only have the different nuances of the meaning of justice been elaborated upon but also the complexity of the concept has been emphasized. Though Krishnan has observed that these perspectives (not only with regard to justice but other psychological constructs and processes also) have not been utilized in designing psychological studies by Indian researchers, his exposition has opened many possibilities for fruitful investigations.

Some researchers have not merely described and elaborated traditional constructs and processes, they have also undertaken psychological studies using the contemporary research practices thereby integrating two systems of knowledge. Many of these investigations, however, have been sporadic and casual. In any case, there is a growing tendency to pursue systematic programmes of investigations in this direction.

Reference has already been made to the studies by Shweder, Mahapatra, and Miller (1990) on morality in Orissa. Basing it on conceptions of *dharma* (natural law) and justice, rather than on individualism, secularism, and social contract which characterize western conceptualizations of morality, they have proposed the existence of "alternative post conventional moralities". The findings reflect perspective differences rooted in Indian culture rather than differences in the levels of development which most of the Kohlbergean studies seem to indicate.

The elaboration of the concepts of psychosocial well-being taking into account the Indian perspective is another case in point. On the basis of the conceptions of *sukhswarup* (happy life) *and dukhaswarup* (unhappy life) in the ancient Indian medical treatise by Charaka, the holistic approach to health by Sushrut, the ancient proponent of the traditional system of medicine, and the concept of *sama* (avoidance of extremes) and the maintenance of balance or equilibrium in all functioning as enjoined by Sankhya philosophy and the *Bhagvadgita*, Sinha (1990) has formulated the concept of well-being as epitomized in the Indian tradition. Unlike the western perspective which equates it with fulfilment of needs and production of material wealth through control and exploitation of nature, the Indian tradition perceives it as a capacity to develop and maintain harmonious relationships in the environment. The emphasis is on man's harmony with his fellowmen, society, nature and cosmos, and on the unfolding of potentialities of the self. Efforts are being made to develop an appropriate test for coping and adjustment within this perspective. Mohan and Sandhu (1986) have developed a *triguna* (threefold qualities) scale of personality based on the Sankhya theory.

By initiating a programme of systematic psychological investigations on concepts and constructs derived from traditional Indian sources, Naidu and his colleagues (Naidu, Thapa & Das, 1986; Pande & Naidu, 1986, 1992) have taken a significant step in this direction. Studies on *niskamakarma* or nonattachment (action/work without attachment to the outcome) provide an excellent illustration. Delving into the *Bhagvadgita*, they have identified an orientation to work which is very different from the current management practice borrowed from the west, i.e., setting a goal and being obsessed with attaining that goal. It is a kind of process or work orientation, i.e., to perform the work as best as one can and not be over-concerned with the outcome. Excellence in work/activity rather than concern for its outcome has been considered vital. These researchers have operationalized the concept of detachment, developed a scale for measuring it and analyzed its various correlates. Statistical analysis has revealed two distinct clusters indicating process/effort and outcome orientations. In terms of success, groups with the two orientations did not differ significantly. However, those scoring high and low on nonattachment reported more or less the same number of stressful events in their lives. But the "nonattachment" group reported significantly less stress on a standardized measure.

It is to be noted that the different forms of cognitive indigenization referred to above have not necessarily occurred in chronological sequence. They are visible in the various phases of development of psychology in India. However, they can be taken as indicators of different levels of indigenization—from mere seeking of cultural explanations and transforming western theories and models to making them in tune with cultural reality, and ultimately designing studies within the framework of culturally derived concepts and categories.

Another feature of indigenization has been the sudden upsurge of interest in examining indigenous practices and modes of health measures like yogic exercises and meditation. Using sophisticated electronic devices, physiological and psychological character as well as therapeutic values of *samadhi* (Anand, Chhina & Singh, 1969), states of meditation including

TM (Gellhorne & Kiely, 1972; Mishra, Mishra & Murthy, 1974; R.N. Singh, 1975), altered states of consciousness (Thapa & Murthy, 1975), *hatha* yoga (Udupa, Singh & Yadav, 1973), and various techniques of Patanjali like *asana, pranayama, prathyahara, dharana,* and *dhyan* (Vahia, Doongaji, Deshmukh, Vinekar, Parekh & Kapoor, 1972; Vahia, Doongaji, Jeste, Ravindranath, Kapoor & Ardha Purkar, 1973), and of relaxation (Rao & Murthy, 1975) have been investigated. These efforts represent attempts of subjecting Indian traditional practices to experimental and scientific analysis thereby integrating them into modern scientific thought.

## Methodological Indigenization

Methodological indigenization consists of the processes by which tests and procedures for data collection are sought to be made suitable to the special characteristics of the sample. Doubts have often been raised about the utility of western tests and the tools of data collection especially in the case of rural and tribal people who are unsophisticated and preliterate and not used to taking- tests (Wig, Pershad & Verma, 1974; Sinha, 1983b). The development of culturally appropriate measures has especially attracted the attention of Sinha who has devised tests for studying the level of aspiration (Sinha, 1969), and cognitive style (Sinha, 1978). To ensure both equivalence and appropriateness, the original paradigm of the measures has been kept constant, but the materials and activities prevalent in the communities have been utilized.

The development of culturally appropriate measures and tests rooted in indigenous categories has not been a widespread endeavour among psychologists in India. As has been observed earlier, adaptation of foreign tests and forging tests in local languages largely modelled on western measures constituted the commonest form of indigenization in the sphere of psychological assessment (Adair, 1992a). There have not been many instances of developing tests that adequately take into account the special cultural characteristics of the population (Adair, Puhan & Vohra, 1993). Back translation has been sometimes utilized for the purposes. Efforts in the direction have largely consisted of making superficial changes in the test items of borrowed foreign instruments. Diaz-Guerrero's (1977) observation in the context of psychological testing in Third World countries is pertinent. Commenting on the impact of cross-cultural psychology, he has noted that it promoted a great deal of application of instruments developed in the First World. It did precious little to stimulate the development of local instruments that would be sensitive to idiosyncratic cultural and personality dynamics of the developing world. However, unlike what is happening in the Philippines (Enriquez, 1990; Mataragnon, 1988; Ho, 1988), researchers in the country have neither seriously questioned the scientific methodology of modern psychology nor evinced much interest in the potentialities of indigenous techniques and utilizing the peculiar features of social intercourse for data collection available in the culture.

# Pitfalls and Potentials of Indigenization

It is too early to make an exhaustive appraisal of the impact of indigenization on the development of psychology in India. But some portends and prospects, both negative and positive, are already visible. They are discussed briefly.

## Pitfalls of Indigenization

There are certain pitfalls inherent in the process of indigenization which, if not guarded against, are likely to lead to chauvinism and antiscientific tendencies that would be dysfunctional to the development of the discipline.

### Cosmetic Indigenization

A spurious manifestation of the process, which is rapidly becoming "fashionable" and needs to be guarded against, is "cosmetic indigenization" (Sinha, 1988/1993). "As the expression implies, the process is usually one of superficial embellishment, and is resorted to only for the purpose of imparting 'local colour' so that the research or the treatise may *appear* rooted in the Indian soil" (Sinha, 1992a, p. 43). It involves making casual references to certain concepts and formulations from different ancient Indian sources while dealing with the "modern" problem of research. They are cosmetic and meant more for enhancing "appearance" rather than for a better understanding of the phenomenon. There is little effort to go into any depth by expounding these indigenous concepts or examining their relevance and integrating them with the contemporary constructs or the problem under study. As Sinha (1992a, p. 43) has observed, "it is a process that recognizes implicitly the parallelism of two systems of psychological knowledge and neither displays proper appreciation of the ancient, nor is there any effort towards interlinking the two. Such an exercise is futile and has little to commend itself."

## Indigenization as a Bandwagon

It has been observed that indigenization has almost assumed the form of a movement. As it accelerated, "a broader set of investigators have begun to jump on to the bandwagon" (Adair, 1992b). For these second-stage promoters, indigenization has become a slogan and a sort of catchy phrase used in advertising. There is not only confusion about what constitutes an indigenous psychology but also uncertainty about how to make one's own research more indigenous (Adair, 1992b). Even those who do not truly subscribe to its goals and lack the requisite sensitivity to Indian cultural reality have begun to talk glibly about indigenization and undertake research in the area. Inevitably, there is more talk than action, as Naidu (1990) has observed. Instead of clarifying the nature of the process and assessing its impact, there is confusion and lack of understanding about what indigenization of psychology means. A glaring instance is provided by two eminent psychologists (Puhan & Sahoo, 1991) when they state that the researches of Naidu and his colleagues (Naidu, Thapa & Das, 1986; Pande & Naidu, 1986) have been rightly dismissed as "cosmetic indigenization" by Sinha (1988/1993). The fact is that in a number of publications (Sinha, 1986, 1988/1993, 1992a) as well as in this paper, they have been cited as "excellent instances" and illustrative of a more mature level of indigenization.

## Revivalism

Berry (1986) has proposed a model for conceptualizing inter-cultural relations, which is useful in understanding the dynamics of the processes that indigenization has generated. According to the model, the outcome is governed by reactions of people to two different but interacting systems of knowledge—in the present case, traditional/indigenous and modern/western psychology. Of the four possible outcomes, the one called *deculturation* (reactions to both systems are negative and they are both rejected) does not concern us here. The pre-independence period and the one immediately following could be considered as the phase in which imported western psychology was highly valued while traditional psychology was often decried. As we have seen, there was a proliferation of a whole plethora of researches which was imitative and replicative thereby imparting to the subject a look of foreignness and making it irrelevant. The attainment of political independence roused the consciousness of the people to re-assert their identity. One way in which this was done—to follow Berry's model—was to react positively to one's own system and negatively to the imported one. This is exactly what happened in the early 1950s. The inadequacies of the positivistic and mechanistic orientations of modern scientific psychology in understanding complex phenomena like human personality, and mental health were highlighted, and the psychological knowledge enshrined in ancient sources was eulogized uncritically. The outcome was a kind of "revivalism" in psychology which was often known as "Indian psychology". The proponents rightly pointed to the superficiality and weaknesses of modern psychology. They vociferously debunked scientific values without suggesting a satisfactory alternative. At the same time, they talked glibly about all kinds of esoteric phenomena like transmigration of soul, rebirth, and supernatural powers. They culled from ancient sources speculative views about phenomena whose only claim to validity was their ancient origin. For obvious reasons, the trend did not have many supporters among psychologists.

Revivalism is one of the pitfalls of indigenization which in the field of psychology is seen in the form of antiscientism, esoterism, and an attitude that whatever is ancient and traditional is per se good (Sinha, 1992a, p. 42), and whatever is brought from outside is necessarily bad and is to be rejected. Revivalism is one of the distortions of indigenization and can lead to obscuration, outright rejection of scientific values, and "scientific ethnocentrism" in a new guise (Poortinga, 1992). The result is often insipid philosophical discussion of some concepts drawn from ancient sources rather than sound psychological analysis.

## Eastern/Indian vs Western Dichotomy

Another danger that emanates from indigenization is parochialism in knowledge. It also spells a kind of eastern vs western dichotomy. In their zeal to emphasize the distinctive characteristics of psychology in India, many scholars have given the impression that the two systems are irreconcilable. They plead for *Indian* psychology. Such parochialism is ill-conceived. Though scientific enterprise is conditioned by historical and socio-cultural factors, there is no question of knowledge being bound and circumscribed by national and continental boundaries. Science which seeks truth cannot be so compartmentalized by national or continental limits (Sinha, 1992a, p. 42). What has been objected to is the uncritical dependence on the western system for concepts, models, and theories, and viewing non-western cultures and psychological functioning through the lens of western norms. This does not imply "local" psychologies, and dichotomization of Indian and western systems. There is always the possibility of mutual learning and integration which is likely to benefit both the systems. The goal of indigenization is not parochialism in psychology, but the development of *appropriate* psychology. Since indigenization is an essentially cultural approach, it sometimes tends to generate a kind of "radical cultural relativism" (Berry, 1972) in understanding and studying reality. Heelas and Lock (1981, p. 4) have viewed indigenous psychologies as "cultural views, theories, conjectures, classifications, assumptions, and metaphors—together with notions embedded in social institutions—which bear on psychological topics." Culture is seen in terms of its own evaluative system. In its extreme form, it does not encourage comparison between cultures. The emphasis seems to be more on *cultural* rather than on *cross-cultural*. As a result, it is likely to lead to a proliferation of psychologies with every population, each locality, and each village having their own psychologies. This kind of cultural relativism and parochialism has not much to commend, and in the last analysis is inimical to the development of the subject.

## Cultural Parallelism

A related manifestation of indigenization, which has gained popularity, is "cultural parallelism". Here different systems are not dichotomized but parallels between concepts, ideas, and formulations contained in traditional systems with those propounded by modern psychology are highlighted (Sinha, 1992a, p. 43). Many treatises have been produced that offer an excellent analysis of Indian conceptualizations of perception, personality, dreams and the like. Similarities with formulations proposed by psychologists in the west are pointed out. However, very little effort is made to bring together and integrate the two approaches. Such efforts take for granted that two distinct systems of psychology co-exist, and imply that no interface or interaction is necessary. Studies like those of Akhilananda (1948, 1952), and Paranjpe (1984) are excellent in themselves. But in spite of the stance of the "meeting of the East and the West", they seem to take for granted that the Indian and the western systems, because of their vital differences in approach and method of study, cannot be reconciled (Sinha, 1992a, p. 44). Indigenization by its very definition does not imply cultural duality of knowledge, and essentially endeavours to bring about an interface of the two to their mutual advantage.

# Prospects and Potential

In spite of the dangers involved, indigenization has opened a new vista in the development of psychology in India. Scholars entertain new hopes and expectations. As we have seen, it is an integrative process through which a system of psychological knowledge is sought to be made relevant to the socio-cultural milieu of the country. In terms of Berry's (1986) model, it is a position in which people entertain positive valence towards their own traditional system as well as towards the one that has been imported. Though critical of each other, various aspects of both the systems are valued. Interface and interaction between the two is sought to produce an organic synthesis (Sinha, 1992a, p. 44). To use Dr. Radhakrishnan's expression (Gropal, 1989, p. 31), it is a kind of "assimilative synthesis" of the two systems of knowledge in which what is valuable is retained and old knowledge is re-stated in new forms adapted to the present needs. It is, therefore, the development of the subject in consonance with the character and needs of the country. The process enables the retention of the cultural identity of one's own system as well as movement to become an integral part of the larger framework.

The process can be viewed as a "battle for consciousness" as Gopal (1989, p. 61) has expressed, and a challenge to western intellectual domination, and a search for restoring the identity of the people who have lost it. It would be an oversimplification to regard it as an ethnocentric denial of the west, or as a clash between tradition and modernity (Sinha, 1992b). It is not an approach to embrace the past and hold on to it at all cost; nor is the western system accepted or rejected simply because it is foreign and, therefore, good or bad, as the case may be. The best of traditional/ indigenous and modern/scientific are sought, accepted and synthesized, so that the outcome serves as the beacon for the future (Sinha, 1992a, p. 46). The whole process of indigenization in psychology seeks to give the discipline a distinctive character suited to the socio-cultural reality of the country. In this effort to look for its *Indianness* and to understand it in terms of its own idioms, psychology is developing a new identity. Indigenization is a process that conforms to Mukherjee's dictum (1980, p. 93) that "psychology has to go native if it is to be creative and relevant to society".

Indigenization has twofold concerns: the need for roots in the specific cultural setting, and the establishment of universal verities in psychology. This dual aspect of the process is not always appreciated especially by those who are overanxious about maintaining the intellectual dominance of the west. Unwarranted criticisms are often raised against the approach. It is to be noted that indigenization in no way decries universal psychology. What it does, however, is to assert clearly and unambiguously that the road to universal psychology is through the development of indigenous psychologies. Indigenous developments have seriously challenged many of the principles and theories of the mainstream psychology. But it is not negative and destructive in its orientation. It is strongly contended that indigenization is a necessary step towards the establishment of true *universals* in psychology which are proved rather than merely assumed. As Kao (1989, p. 88) has observed, indigenous psychology based on unique behavioural phenomena must of necessity be the foundation upon which cross-cultural comparisons are to be made. Only then true universal psychology is possible.

The trend is new and it is too early to gauge its impact on the development of psychology in India, and on the mainstream psychology. One thing, however, is clear; if scholars steer clear of the dangers inherent in the process and remain firmly committed to science (though its conventional boundaries may have to be extended), it will lead to vigorous and meaningful developments that will not only enrich psychology in the country and make it "relevant", but also extend the conventional boundaries of the discipline itself.

# 4

# Culture and Psychology: Perspective of Cross-cultural Psychology*†

*I am not* going into the intricacies of defining culture nor consider it essential in the present context. What I am going to attempt is to give a brief account of how over the years cross-cultural psychology has increasingly got involved in studying culture. In the process it is hoped that the approaches to the nature of interface between culture and behaviour in psychology would get highlighted.

Starting mainly as a methodological strategy in search of "universals" in psychology, cross-cultural psychology has come to a position where bi-directional nature of culture-behaviour interface is accepted—a position in which the original nomenclature of cross-cultural psychology appears inadequate. It has now acquired a much wider space in culture which deserves to be differently designated as ethnic psychology or culturally-rooted psychology or even cultural psychology—a claim that may be vehemently disputed and resented by some self-appointed proponents who have pre-emptied the expression and jealously guarding it against "intruders", however, legitimate their claims may be.

* This chapter is based on the Delhi University Platinum Jubilee Lecture delivered by the late Professor Sinha on the occasion of the National Seminar on Culture and Psychology held at Delhi University in December 1997. The manuscript was made available by Mala Sinha and edited on the basis of the transcript and notes taken by the editor.

† Reproduced, with permission, from Sinha, D. Culture and Psychology: Perspective of Cross-cultural Psychology. *Psychology and Developing Societies*, 14, 11–25 (2002). New Delhi: SAGE Publications.

This text has been edited for typographical errors, stylistic consistency and sequential organization in order to make it suitable for inclusion in the book.

According to Hindu tradition, to understand behaviour and evaluate the same, it is essential to view it in the context of *desh* (place), *kala* (time) and *patra* (the person or individual). This contextual approach which recognizes the embeddedness of behaviour in culture has been there since ancient times. Therefore, culture-behaviour interface has not posed a serious problem at least to those contemporary psychologists in the country who maintain intellectual links with traditional Indian thinking.

The position, however, is very different with modern scientific psychology, especially what is regarded as the "mainstream psychology"— sometimes dubbed as the WASP (Western Academic Scientific Psychology) to hint at its culture-blind and ethnocentric predilections. Speaking about modern psychology, Wilhelm Wundt (1832–1920), who established in 1879 the first laboratory for experimental psychology as an independent branch of science, recognized two traditions in psychology: *Naturwissenschaften* (the natural science tradition) and *Geiste-swissensch aften* (the cultural science tradition). Appreciating the double destiny of man both as a natural and cultural being, he firmly believed these two approaches to be complementing rather than mutually exclusive (Danziger, 1983). In fact, his unique contribution is the amalgamation of psychological level of analysis with the cultural level of analysis. But the way modern psychology developed, his experimental approach became the defining feature of psychology and the *sine qua non* of psychological research. Wundt was, however, very conscious of the limitations of the natural science approach and the experimental method in psychology. He emphatically pointed out that human behaviour was heavily conditioned by language, custom and myths which were considered by him as the primary area of *Volkerpsychologie* or folk psychology. He regarded the latter as a "most important branch of psychological science which was destined to eclipse experimental psychology" (Danziger, 1983, p. 307). In his 10-volume treatise on *Volkerpsychologie* (1910–20), he devoted himself to examining socio-cultural influences on psychological processes laying thereby the foundation of what are known today as indigenous psychologies.

But the course that mainstream psychology has taken is quite different and Wundt's prophecy did not come about. Experimental psychology more or less eclipsed culture. It was not until the emergence of what is called cross-cultural psychology that culture as a variable came seriously into psychological research and in course of time the study of culture-behaviour interaction became the main concern.

From a historical point of view, psychologists have displayed only a casual interest in the relationship between behaviour and culture. But as already pointed out, Wundt was a notable exception. There have been other "ancestors" of cross-cultural psychology. Edward Burnet Tylor (1832–1917), often regarded as the father of anthropology, is another notable exception. In his famous definition of culture, he in a way suggested the "comparative method" which was remained the main weapon in the armamentarium of cross-cultural psychologists. I would quote his definition:

> Culture or Civilization, taken in the widest ethnographic sense, is that complex whole which includes knowledge, belief, art, morals, law, custom, and any other capabilities and habits acquired by man as a member of society. The condition of culture among the various societies of mankind, in so far as it is capable of being investigated on general principles, is a subject apt for the study of the laws of human thought or action. (Tylor, 1871/1958, p. 1)

The expression "laws of human thought" obviously implies the "universals" in human behaviour, search for which has been the main concern of cross-cultural psychological research. Moreover, reference to "conditions of culture among the various societies" has obvious implication for the "comparative method" which has been the principal instrument in cross-cultural psychological investigations. In this context, it may be mentioned that this method got further impetus by the creation of a massive database of all world cultures in "The Human Relations Area Files" by the American anthropologist Murdock, which has remained the goldmine for comparative cross-cultural research by psychologists, generally called holocultural or hologeistic research.

Francis Galton (1822–1911), a cousin of Charles Darwin, has been another significant influence on the comparative cross-cultural approach. He attempted an assessment of "the comparative worth of different races". He made many assumptions about human abilities and his clarification of human beings according to their natural gifts appears not only naive and simplistic but also ethnocentric from the contemporary point of view. However, during his extensive travels in Africa and other parts of the world, he made many significant observations that have been confirmed by contemporary cross-cultural psychologists. For example, his attribution to Eskimos the ability "to see vast tracts of country mapped out in their heads" has since been confirmed by researches of John Berry (1966), one of the leading cross-cultural psychologists today.

It has been the Cambridge experimental psychologist W.H.R. Rivers (1864–1922) who along with two other famous psychologists of the time, William McDougall and Charles S. Myers, during the Cambridge

Anthropological Expedition to the Torres Straits (New Guinea) in 1898 made the initial but most significant contribution to cross-cultural psychology and brought culture into focus as far as behaviour was concerned. Working under the prevailing bias of social evolutionary theory which held sway at that time, the so-called "primitives" were supposed to expend most of their mental energy on sensory and perceptual processes and did not develop, unlike what was the case with the Europeans who were taken as "civilized" and "superior", the higher mental processes. Rivers made the study of sensory and perceptual processes among Polynesians as the main focus of the research programme and compared them with Europeans. His investigations constitute the first systematic effort to study by psychological techniques the different cultural groups (whom he designated, following the fashion of his time, the "primitives"). Whatever criticisms may be advanced against his biased assumptions, by the extension of experimental methods in the "field", and his conclusions, he displayed a unique methodological sophistication. His checking and validating the findings by the observation of dress, and everyday activities, of the natives (which in modern terminology can be called "unobtrusive methods") have been the inspiration of many contemporary cross-cultural psychologists. It is significant to note that his initial assumption about "superiority" of the "civilized" Europeans over the so-called stupid "savages" in the processing of sensory inputs and thereby being less susceptible to some geometrical optical illusions like the Muller-Lyer, was not borne out by the findings. On the contrary, the simple inhabitants of Torres Straits were *less* deceived by some of the illusions—a finding that seemed to knock the bottom of the assumption about the superiority of the Europeans over the so-called primitives in cognitive functioning. It also provided an inspiration for the extensive work of Segall, Campbell and Herskovits (1966) on what has come to be known as "the carpentered world hypothesis" in their famous book *The Influence of Culture on Visual Perception*—a treatise that highlights the role of culture in behaviour.

Sigmund Freud's involvement with culture and the role that he conceptualized for it in human behaviour are too familiar to require any detailed discussion. The point that is of a particular relevance is his focus on the relationship between culture and the development of personality. The major purpose of culture was considered to be the channelization of impulses of the individual through inhibition and sublimation factors which had their origin in culture. Freud's views on culture had a major influence on Kardiner, Ralph Linton and others constituting what has come to be known as the culture-personality school or approach, and later on as psychological anthropology. In the true anthropological tradition, the relationship was investigated between characteristics of a culture and its bearers (the individuals) by delineating the distinctive psychological characteristics of the culture.

Professor Bartlett (1886–1969), was in more than one respect, not only a precursor of cross-cultural psychology but by orientation, approach and studies, a true cross-cultural psychologist in his own right. This is evidenced in his very first major publication *Psychology and Primitive Culture* (1923), which was a purely theoretical treatise. He forcefully argued against the prevailing ethnocentrism of social scientists of the social evolutionary tradition in studying "other" cultures. In his magnum opus called *Remembering*, Bartlett (1932) provided ample evidence of what one perceived and recalled being conditioned by culture. In my own studies in his laboratory in Cambridge, I observed interesting and distinct differences between the British and Indian students in recalling stories and pictorial materials that were unfamiliar to them and in serial reproductions; differences which were clearly attributable to their respective cultural backgrounds and experiences. Bartlett provides the example of Swazi chiefs during their visit to England, remembering vividly out of so many new things encountered, the image of London policemen regulating the traffic with their up-raised arms because it was very similar to the gesture for welcoming a friendly visitor common among the Swazi tribe. Another revealing example was that of cowherds in South Africa faring poorly on the test of recalling lists of nonsense syllables but exceeding any European settlers in naming and remembering hundreds of cows of their herd and identifying them with uncanny accuracy. These examples highlight the central importance of culture in understanding psychological processes, and the relationship of lifestyle, habitat of and economy in shaping perceptions and cognition. It may *be* mentioned that the study of Allport and Pettigrew (1957), conducted over a couple of decades later, on the cultural influences on the perception of movement (the trapezoidal illusion among the Zulus), belong the same tradition. Living in a habitat that was characterised by "roundness" of huts, fields, windows and so on, the Zulus unlike the European settlers were not susceptible to the "rotating window" illusion. The studies were in the true tradition of cross-cultural psychology and as would be clear later on in my discourse, which by emphasizing the determining role of the nature of habitat, economy and cultural practices in influencing cognitive processes, anticipated the ecological perspective of the maturer phase of cross-cultural psychology. It is significant to note that after his visits to South Africa and encounters with indigenous tribes,

Bartlett (1932) pointed to "a type of field investigation for the psychologist which had been strongly neglected, but which might easily yield results, not only of theoretical, but also of great practical importance" (p. vi). These were prophetic words, for psychology largely ignored for a long time but came into prominence from the mid-1950s, when cross-cultural psychology began to blossom.

Inspite of this heritage of cultural orientation, mainstream psychology accords—if at all it does—only a very peripheral place to culture in behaviour. From my student days before I went to Cambridge and later on teaching various courses in psychology, I remember only two examples from Munn's (1946) textbook on introductory psychology which illustrated the role of culture in perceptual and emotional processes: one was perceiving a visual pattern which though it cast the same retinal image was perceived differently by subjects who gave it a "meaning" that was coloured by collective cultural experiences. A black and white picture of a small object was perceived variously as a bug, an oil lamp and a smudge-pot used in orange groves. But shown to a central Australian, it *was* unhesitatingly perceived, with watering mouth, as a honey-ant—a cherished delicacy for them. Again, Munn gave Klineberg's (1938) excellent comparison between expressional difference among the Chinese and Europeans in emotion. The stereotyped gesture and facial expressions were often indicative of contrary emotions, for example, *surprise* by raising eyebrows and wide-open eyes by Europeans, while Chinese stick out their tongue; scratching behind the ears and cheek being a sign for *embarrassment* with Europeans, while for Chinese they connote *happiness*; and clapping of hands is a sign of *happiness* for Europeans, but of *worry* and *disappointment* for the Chinese. Except for these illustrations and some examples regarding cultural conditioning of memory, there were hardly any references to culture as a factor in various psychological processes. Walter Lonner (1989) in his presidential address to the International Conference of Cross-Cultural Psychology in Newcastle (Australia) in 1988, by analyzing some thirty-five introductory psychology texts pointed out that they lacked in providing interacting and timely examples for explaining cultural variations in behaviour thereby reflecting ignorance about cultural material and geographic myopia. The situation is no better within social psychology, which is largely western-based and western-biased, and to a very great extent *a cultural* in orientation. In fact, in mainstream psychology at least, cultural aspects in general are divorced from behaviour. In experimental and scientific investigations of behaviour, culture is regarded as a "noise" the effect of which has to be controlled and eliminated for the proper understanding of behaviours and the establishment of psychological universals. It is for this deficiency in psychology that cross-cultural psychology, which was "institutionalised during the sixties" (Jahoda & Krewer, 1997, p. 3), is acting as a necessary corrective. It not only rediscovered a more socio-culturally oriented tradition in psychology (Boesch, 1991; Cole, 1995) but also adapted the perspective and took account of "culture-inclusiveness of human psychic development" (Price-Williams, 1980). To these facets of behaviour, psychology had been for long "blind" (culture blind).

Additionally, psychology was also "culture-bound" and ethnocentric in the sense that it has been largely grounded in the study of urban middle class adolescents constituted by the American sophomore population—a trend which we have still to cast off in this country. As a consequence, as Jahoda (1980) points out, most psychological theories and principles, especially dealing with social processes, were the product of a specific social milieu that characterized advanced industrial societies of the West and hence was often designated as an "Anglo-American product". As such, those principles were not applicable to people of underdeveloped and culturally divergent populations of the developing countries. Concern for establishing universal validation of psychological theories was the major over-arching rationale for psychologists venturing to obtain cross-cultural data. Thus, cross-cultural psychology started off primarily as a convenient and useful methodological strategy for "explaining psychology to panhuman populations" (Malpass, 1977, p. 1069). The main concern being the generalizability of current psychological knowledge. It studied diversities and differences (later on also similarities) in human behaviour in different parts of the world, and through comparative analysis with the behaviour of western people tried to establish a link between behaviour and its cultural context as well as isolate what transcended the cultural difference to be considered as "universals" in particular psychological processes. Thus cross-cultural psychology came into being as a particular methodological strategy of mainstream psychology (Brislin, 1983). By focusing on cultural differences in behaviour and through "unwrapping the packaged variable culture" (Whiting, 1976), "universals" in psychology were sought to be established. From a methodological point of view, Segall (1984) discussed "culture" as an intolerably vague entity and proposed substituting a set of variables. Molecular nature of the concept of culture was thus implied. Particular cultural variables rather than culture as such were taken to constitute an explanation of cultural differences (Segall, 1984). The metaphor used for the purpose has been "peeling the onion called culture" (Poortinga et al., 1987). It is to be noted that in a way the model implies eliminating the cultural fact on one layer after another to arrive at the universals in behaviour. In a way, it amounted to de-culturation of psychology by divesting human behaviour of its cultural elements.

A few points have to be noted in this context. First, in the initial phase, cross-cultural studies were largely conducted in the domains of sensation, perception, complex cognitive functions and differences in patterns of socialization and consequent differences in the development of motivation and other personality qualities in individuals belonging to diverse cultures. Entry of social behaviour in a big way on the agenda of cross-cultural psychology radically altered the situation about the role of culture and brought about a kind of "cultural revolution" (Sinha, 1989, p. 28). Social phenomena were so different and complex in character that cross-cultural and cross-national comparisons began to pose very serious problems both at the level of constructs and that of methodology for studying them. Second, particular aspects of culture rather than culture per se, constituted the explanations of observed differences in behaviour. As indicated earlier, specific layers of culture were sought to be isolated and removed to arrive at the "core" constituting the behaviour that was "universal". Focus of interest was not so much on culture but on "eliminating culture" to establish universal applicability of psychological principles. Thus, in a certain way, for cross-cultural psychology, culture was a sort of external element outside the behaving organism to be eliminated for generalizations. Third, culture acted as an influence from outside and not as an integral part of behaviour. This dichotomy between culture and behaviour, with some notable exceptions, has been prominent in cross-cultural psychological research. Culture appeared more like a behaviour-inducing condition rather than a culture-behaviour system having bi-directional influence. Lastly, cross-cultural psychological research was conducted not so much to understand the behaviour-culture interface in particular cultural contexts; rather the data on cultural differences gathered largely in African, Asian and Latin American countries served the need for universal validation of theories of mainstream psychology, which I have already hinted as being the Western Academic Scientific Psychology (WASP). As Campbell and Naroll (1972) pointed out, the developing countries served as "a crucible in which to put to more rigorous test, psychologists' tentative theories and expand western psychology to panhuman propositions". This has been termed as the *transport and test* goal of cross-cultural psychology (Berry & Dasen, 1974) in which psychologists sought to transport their present hypotheses, instruments for investigation and findings to other cultural settings in order to test their applicability in other—and eventually in all groups of human beings. As a result, formulation of psychological questions and measures utilized for testing are not particularly sensitive to discovering psychological phenomena that may be important in other cultures.

In these studies, a single psychological instrument (or even a set of instruments) developed in the West to assess qualities like intelligence, achievement or autonomy are "transported" and administered on the "native" population, and the differences in scores obtained on western samples are analyzed. In this etic approach, as we know, almost insurmountable problems of equivalence and comparability are faced. Transferring tests from one cultural setting to another is difficult. It is more so in the case of concepts. Apart from cultural appropriateness of tests, we are now very familiar with the relativity of concepts like intelligence, achievement and so on. Researches have revealed that whereas in the West intelligence is identified with cognitive and analytic functions, the African intelligence has a strong social component (Dasen et al., 1985; Wober, 1974). Similarly, with regard to the concept of achievement it has been observed (Agarwal & Misra, 1986; Singhal & Misra, 1989) that unlike in the West, familial and social concerns like "well-being of others", "fulfilling one's duties" and "helping others" are a predominant part of the achievement goals of Indian people.

Though the concern for testing cross-cultural generality of theories persists, the realization of western ethnocentric bias involved in the etic approach has generated interests to *explore* other cultures in order to discover psychological variations that are not present in one's own limited cultural experiences which constitutes the second goal of cross-cultural psychology (Berry & Dasen, 1974). This has taken two interrelated forms: analysis of the cultural determinants of behaviour and the study of indigenous psychological concepts and forms of behaviour peculiar to different cultures.

As for the first aspect, cultural influences on cognitive functioning, child rearing and socialization, development of personality, leadership, management of conflict, dispute processing, and organizational functioning, have been extensively studied and constitute topics of high points of contemporary cross-cultural research. Culture here is treated as what has been called the "compositional" factor (Soudijn et al., 1990). In other words, various elements of a culture (for example, child rearing practices and lifestyles) are related to behaviour. This is done either by taking a somewhat global view of culture, like industrially and economically advanced or developing, and trying to interrelate it to the development of topological or Euclidean perception (as Piaget calls it), as we have done (Jahoda et al., 1974) by taking children's sample from Scotland, Hong Kong, India and Africa or by taking specific aspects of "carpenteredness" of the cultural environment as moulding visual perception of space (Segall et al., 1966).

In recent years, a significant development has occurred in the adoption of initially an ecological perspective which has later on been expanded into the *ecocultural perspective* which John Berry popularized. We utilized this perspective for our studies of Birhors, Asurs and Oraons recently published under the title *Ecology, Acculturation and Psychological Adaptation: A Study of Adivasis in Bihar* (Mishra et al., 1996). It is not possible to provide details of this perspective. It would suffice here to say that a long interactive relationship between ecological and socio-cultural contexts is posited leading both to biological and cultural adaptation, which in turn gets reflected in observable behaviours. Background variables that constitute the ecocultural, surround the process variables and their psychological outcomes are sought to be interlinked. Culture is largely taken as a form of "adaptation" of the group to its environment. A similar model has been developed by Super and Harkness (1986) which is very popular in development studies and called the "developmental niche" to understand the interaction between environment and biological factors. It is described as a system in which the physical environment, socio-cultural customs of child-rearing and psychological customs (beliefs and so forth) of caretaker play a role.

A point to be noted is that these approaches are rooted in the positivistic and scientific traditions seeking cultural explanations and causes of behaviour. They view a culture as a determinant or variable/variables rather than a system. These studies have been possible due to the entry of psychologists from Asia, Africa and Latin America, not as veritable data-gatherness of their Western counterparts under some high sounding designations, but as true collaborators and researchers in their own right who helped to provide insight from their cultures in designing the studies and explaining the findings. It is also to be noted that due importance given to the culture is reflected in the careful ethnographic analysis of the group/groups that usually precedes the designing of the investigation. The hypotheses concerning the kind of relationship between certain aspects or configuration of cultural variables and their behaviour outcomes are proposed only after careful ethnography.

Further, many psychologists from developing countries who entered the orbit of cross-cultural research were able to provide inputs from different cultural contexts and emphasized cultural nuances in the meaning of different psychological concepts and processes. They not only helped to evolve culturally appropriate instruments for gathering data but also delved into the culture to re-discover and isolate culturally derived categories and concepts and conducted studies on particular cultural groups. Beginning with comparative studies of psychological phenomena and processes in western and non-western culture, an increasing number of cross-cultural psychologists are now concerned with the study of cultural groups in culturally plural societies.

As would be obvious, this marked a shift from the study of cultural differences in search of "universals" and studying aspects of culture as mere determinants of behaviour to the psychological study of culture as a system. The story is a long one. I would only indicate that these trends have resulted in what is often called indigenizing psychology or the process of indigenization (Sinha, 1997) and the development of indigenous psychologies—a development that is causing worry within mainstream psychology—reflected in the statement of the past president of APA (American Psychological Association) in the Kyoto IAAP (International Association of Applied Psychology) Congress during the symposium on "Unity of Psychology" that all was well within the discipline, except possibly for the threat from the indigenous psychology movement.

Let me now summarize the different aspects of involvement with culture in cross-cultural psychologists' investigation. First, for experimental psychological research, culture is regarded as a "noise" the effects of which have to be eliminated so that culture-free universals in behaviour are established and this has remained the abiding goal of cross-cultural research. Thus, in a way cultural factors are studied and analyzed for the purpose of *de-culturation* of behaviour.

Second, culture occupies the place of a significant determinant of behaviour, i.e., as an antecedent condition or a set of antecedents that provide the explanation of behaviour. Culture is treated as a behaviour inducing condition. It is regarded as a significant *variable*, and *causal* aspects are analyzed. The studies as a result fall within the mould of the positivistic scientific paradigm. In the preceding two orientations, culture-behaviour interface is conceptualized in dualistic terms.

Third, the studies reflect both nomothetic and ideographic (molecular and molar) approaches and accordingly provide both specific and holistic conceptualizations. In fact, there has been a change in orientation from purely etic to emic. Effort has also been made towards the goal of derived etic.

Fourth, there has been a transition from the study of *explanations* to one of *understanding* of behaviour in a culture. This distinction is not always clear and today many large scale cross-cultural psychological investigations contain aspects of both. In any case, culture is no longer simply the target of the study but also the *source* of constructs and ideas (Sinha, 1996). Fifth, following Price-Williams (1980, p. 77), different approaches to culture emerge according to where exactly culture is supposed to enter behaviour. The basic question "where does culture enter" the psychological arena, is very pertinent. Approaches to culture in psychology are different when the entry point of culture in behaviour is conceptualized as "late" or "early" (Table 4.1).

In conclusion, I would observe that viewed from the point of view of the development over the years of what "culturally-rooted psychology" (Sinha, 1996) or the derivatives that have emerged following Wundt's "cultural science tradition", one comes across great diversity in the way culture has been viewed in relation to behaviour. Even if we take the nomenclature, there are many diversities far beyond the level of fruitful exchange of ideas. In fact, I have definitional difficulty in distinguishing between ethnopsychology, folk psychology, psychological anthropology, cultural psychology, societal psychology and indigenous psychology. The situation is best explained on the analogy of a banyan tree and

**Table 4.1**

*Two Approaches to Culture "Where does Culture Enter?"*

| Late Entrance of Culture | Early Entrance of Culture |
| --- | --- |
| Emphasis on *explaining* behavior | Emphasis on *understanding* behaviour |
| One phenomenon studied in various cultural groups or historical periods | Many interrelated phenomena studied in a single group |
| "Decontextualizes" behaviour research is seen as (quasi) experimentation | "Contextualizes" behaviour research is seen as hermeneutic interpretation process |
| Culture as a set of *behaviour-inducing conditions* | Culture as a *system* |
| Universalism | Relativism |
| Often implicit emphasis on cultural similarities | Often implicit emphasis on cultural differences |

*Source:* After Price-Williams (1989, p. 77).

a Hindu joint family. Each of these branches or derivatives claim chunks of common territory and frequently—often in a very vociferous manner—deny the legitimate claims of others. Each branch claims a common ancestry, but none could be said to be sitting at the main root. All of them operate in spheres that have common boundaries and a lot of territories overlap and are jealously claimed and guarded by one or the other branches. The situation results in intense "familial" dispute of legitimate rights of one of the other branches. The polemics and controversies that one often comes across between different proponents who have emphasized culture-behaviour relationship, appear to me to be unnecessary, futile and unproductive. These existing approaches to culturally rooted psychology do not appear contradictory but complementary. There is no question of exclusion and denial. On the other hand, there is a lot of benefit to be derived from mutual learning and communication, rather than disputes.

# Part II

# Human Development

# 5

# The Family Scenario in a Developing Country and Its Implications for Mental Health: The Case of India*

The main thrust in this chapter is on significant changes in the Indian family and their implications for healthy human development in the context of ongoing rapid socioeconomic transformations. Socio-cultural and economic development inevitably affect institutions and individuals. More specifically, the focus of this chapter is on the individual-level changes affected by the modifications that are taking place in the family. Though the emphasis is on social and cultural change, the chapter does not deal with the acculturation of social groups that involves mutual influence of two autonomous cultural systems. Taking the family in India as a case, an effort has been made to identify the changes that have occurred due to various kinds of development programs and the process of "modernization" in the country as a whole. It confines itself to socialization practices and experiences of the individual in the family, which itself is in a state of transition. It isolates factors in the changing family that are likely to have implications for healthy human development.

No large-scale and definitive study of the impact of these changes on human development has been conducted. There are, however, many

* Reproduced, with permission, from Sinha, D. (1988). The Family Scenario in a Developing Country and Its Implications for Mental Health: The Case of India. In P.R. Dasan, J.W. Berry and N. Sartorius (eds), *Health and Cross-cultural Psychology: Toward Applications* (pp. 48–70). Newbury Park, CA: SAGE Publications.

This text has been edited for typographical errors, stylistic consistency and sequential organization in order to make it suitable for inclusion in the book.

scattered studies that throw light on the socio-psychological antecedents of psychopathology and mental health. This chapter brings together these studies dealing with the Indian family and points to possible psychological consequences. It is felt that what is happening in the Indian family typifies the situation prevailing in most developing countries that are experiencing the whirlpool of rapid socioeconomic development.

No cross-cultural comparative analysis of families has been attempted. Rather, this chapter highlights contemporary change in the traditional Indian family structure, which is moving toward nucleation to meet the demands of industrialization, urbanization, and modernization generally. Yet comparisons have been made of the traditional family with the family in a state of transition. Second, throughout the chapter there are frequent references to family in the West to emphasize the nature and direction of changes. Therefore, though not in the strictest sense, this chapter is cross-cultural in orientation.

# General Framework of Development

In order to have a proper insight into the role of the family in human development, it is essential to understand the general framework as represented by the situation in which the individual functions at the national level. The key characteristic of the situation is the rapidity of changes at all levels that have brought many benefits to the individual and the communities at large. Though not very spectacular, there has been a steady rise in per capita income and a growth in national income per annum. In earlier years, India had been a victim of chronic famines resulting in millions of deaths. With the green revolution, famine became a thing of the past, and, in many respects, a food surplus has been generated. On the social plane, changes have been more far reaching. A rapid rise in education, and legislation covering economic, social, and political spheres pertaining to land, property rights, inheritance, the rights of women, marriage and divorce, and minimum wages, have radically altered the land ownership pattern, power, and relational norms in villages, family interactions, and in the politicization of the castes. Conferring rights on women and making divorce laws easier have dealt a fatal blow to the traditional pattern of joint family and have even generated familial tensions. We are not here to examine the benefits, or otherwise, of these changes, but are concerned with the social processes that they have unleashed and their socio-psychological repercussions. The total effect, on the social, economic, and political fronts, of all these changes coming more or less simultaneously has been to alter entire lifestyles, interpersonal relationships, power structures, and familial patterns. It is in this radically transformed social context that human development in other developing countries may have to be viewed.

# The Main Characteristics of Change

The three main features of these changes are (a) their all-embracing character, (b) their rapidity, and (c) their unfolding in a nonorderly sequence. These changes tend to encompass the entire society and relate to all levels of the functioning of the individual. It has often been observed that the nations of the Third World are impatient and set about to achieve within the span of a generation what the developed countries in the West took centuries to bring about. The sentiment is well expressed in the words of the late Prime Minister Pandit Jawaharlal Nehru, who, when opening the Economic Commission for Asia and Far-East in 1956, said, "We are not going to spend the next 100 years in arriving *gradually, step by step*, at the stage of development which the developed countries have reached today. Our pace and tempo of progress have to be much faster" (emphasis added). The process inevitably involves *telescoping* or "temporal compression" of change within a very short span of time. It involves a large-scale program of social change calculated to transform the entire society—modernization of the social structure, institutions, families, attitudes, and value systems. What is psychologically more significant is that these transformations are not coming about step by step or in an orderly sequence but, as Myrdal (1968) describes it, in *cacophonic* fashion.

Jahoda (1975) contrasts the core characteristics of the sociocultural milieu of the developed and developing countries. As against the relative stability and predictability of the former, the problems of the latter emanate from uncertainties and instabilities that constitute the core characteristics of the rapid socioeconomic changes. The two factors of temporal compression and the discordant sequence of changes in conjunction have produced a condition that is highly unsettling and stressful both for the individual and for the society (Sinha, 1984). The merging of diverse cultural practices produces cultural incongruities and disparities that are stress-inducing. An increase in social violence, riots, terrorism, suicide, crime, and delinquency, and other forms of social disorganization—alcoholism, anonymity, and the impersonality of modern life (Triandis, 1971), to mention only a few, are some of the negative manifestations of the condition of instability. The ambiguity of values and role models (Sinha, 1979), alienation, changing levels of aspiration, and increasing disparity between aspiration and achievement leading to dissatisfaction in work, higher incidence of psychosomatic ailments, "marginality," and "identity diffusion" are some of the other kinds of psychological fallout that have been observed (Sinha, 1984). The full implications to mental health of these societal transformations are not yet fully understood.

Viewed against this broad perspective, the psychological problems faced in the developing countries boil down to the possible impacts of the fast-changing environment on human development and mental health. In the sociopsychological context, the salient aspects of this environment are (a) a weakening and breakdown of age-old traditions that had regulated the lives of individuals and various institutions for centuries; (b) transformations in the family, religion, caste, and other social institutions; (c) the migration and uprooting of the population from its natural habitat in rural areas to cities and remote places in search of employment; (d) a new life-style that is "discontinuous" to what the individual had been used to for generations; (e) changes in attitudes and in basic value and belief systems; (f) changes in the individual's loyalties, group identifications, and patterns of intergroup relationships; and (g) general conditions of uncertainty and instability. Most of these conditions are psychologically stressful for the individual, and have obvious implications for mental health. Doob (1960), in his study of some African countries, formulated a set of hypotheses on the psychological effects of development. They were predictions about psychological differences between people who remain "unchanged," those who had "changed," and those who were "changing." Empirical evidence of definitive character was lacking, but there was support for his predictions that development increased initiative, independence, self-confidence, and the abstracting facility. Further, emotional states of discontent, aggression, ambivalence, and sensitivity tended to be associated with the process of transition. During transition, the stress level was also likely to be high.

It is to be noted that though the negative fallout has been emphasized, the consequences of rapid socioeconomic change are not always negative, and may have many positive effects. As Berry (1980), reviewing the impact of social and culture change, concludes, "Overall, it is clear that earlier assumptions that social change and acculturation tended to be psychologically devastating are no longer maintained" (pp. 264–265).

It is against this general backdrop that certain changes that have come about in recent years in the family in India have to be viewed.

# Family and Human Development

The relationship of familial experience and the development of the individual, especially from the point of view of his or her mental health, has been extensively investigated. In India, many investigators (Gomez, 1975; Radhamani, 1975; Shetty, 1975; Sood, 1971) have studied the family interactional patterns of psychotics and neurotics and have reported significant differences. They contend that there are recurrent interactive patterns occurring in families and that such processes support psychopathological behavior in one or more members. There is consensus that "a patient is only a symptom of a troubled family" (Channabasavanna & Bhatti, 1982, p. 149). Sanua (1980), in his chapter "Familial and Sociocultural Antecedents of Psychopathology" in the *Handbook of Cross-Cultural Psychology*, has reviewed the relevant studies. There he reiterates his earlier conclusion regarding the importance of familial factors especially with respect to schizophrenics: "Although the evidence of the importance of family factors ... is quite compelling, the pattern of the home environment needs to be more clearly defined and isolated from home patterns which lead to other types of psychoses, neuroses and anti-social behaviour" (Sanua, 1961, p. 265).

The literature on familial antecedents of mental health in the West is extensive. It mainly deals with the effects of socialization and processes of intrafamily communication and interaction. Factors in the family that may affect frequency of different mental disorders are (a) family composition (nuclear or joint), (b) kind of child rearing, (c) sex, (d) birth order, (e) social class, and (f) male dominance in the culture. Exclusive attachment to mother, extreme overprotectiveness, and babying have been found to be associated with schizophrenia (Sanua, 1961). In the context of social disorganization resulting from rapid change, Leighton (1974) contends that the relationship between psychiatric disorders and sociocultural factors is made possible by the breakdown of child nurturing and child-rearing patterns because of radical change in the social system, and from stress derived from experiencing the world as a series of frustrations and

**Figure 5.1**

*Schematic Model of the Relationship Among Social Change, Family and Psychological Consequences*

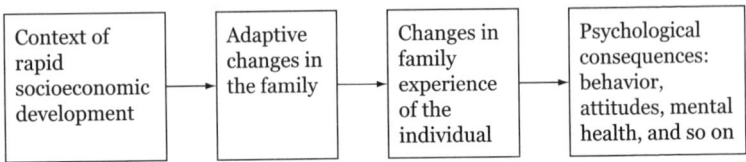

disappointments. In fact, in the relationship between sociocultural factors and mental illness, the family acts as an intervening variable. The family is important principally because of its strategic role in transmitting to its offspring conceptions of social reality that parents have learned from their own experience, and strategies for dealing with the problems of life (Kohn, 1972). A schematic model of the relationship among social change, family, and behavioral consequences is given in Figure 5.1.

Rapid socioeconomic changes that are occurring in the country induce certain adaptive changes in the family that in turn lead to modifications in socialization and child-rearing practices. The change in family experience that results is an antecedent factor to certain psychological and behavioral consequences in the individual.

# Salient Changes in the Indian Family

During the last three to four decades, the family in India has undergone phenomenal transformations. They involve both structural and attitudinal dimensions that have resulted in altered interrelationships among the members who constitute the family and changes in family obligations and decision making as well as modifications in the child-rearing and socialization processes (Sinha, 1982). The salient changes in the Indian family that constitute antecedent factors to the development of the individual and his mental health are:

(1) nucleation, or the transition from an extended-kin to a primary-kin system;
(2) the segregation of children from adults, and individuation;
(3) a change from indulgent to strict child rearing;
(4) inconsistencies in child rearing;
(5) the absence of clear-cut role models;

(6) changes in the status, role, and employment of women; and
(7) the impact of migration.

## Nucleation

Contemporaneously there is a distinct shift in family structure from an extended-kin to a primary-kin system. A number of sociocultural and economic factors have been responsible for the onslaught on the traditional type of joint family that has characterized the Indian society. In the traditional family, many scores of people related somehow with one another resided under one roof with a single authority, usually the oldest male, with a common family deity, and sharing in family income. With the growth of industrialization and the development of new cities, the employment structure has become altered, and the individual has before him or her the possibility of going beyond his or her caste and family occupations. Industrialization and consequent urbanization have been the strongest influence in the transformations that have come about in the traditional family structure. As has been observed, there is a conspicuous weakening of joint families in cities (Kapadia, 1966) as well as a rapid decline in the orientation toward kin and an increase in the orientation toward self-interest (Dube, 1958).

But the traditional family has not yet been completely replaced by primary-kin nuclear families. The Indian family is still in a "transitional" state. While it is fast assuming a nuclear character, it retains many of the features of the traditional family. Structurally, the extended family is tending to become nuclear, but functionally it is maintaining jointness (Gore, 1968). In short, the joint family is still capable of meeting certain needs of its members (Kapadia, 1966). Many people are not yet prepared psychologically to break away completely from the joint family. Many studies have emphasized the "limited changes" that have taken place in the Indian family. In terms of expressed closeness or psychological proximity, even the younger generation, though possessing a comparatively narrower view of what constitutes a family, still has a positive disposition toward "close relations" and "other relations" who were often regarded as elements of the family (Sinha, 1972). Gupta (1978, p. 73) observes that the new nuclear family type does not really exist as a separate entity but as a sector of the continuous extended family arrangement. It is apparent that most families fall somewhere in the middle and using the term *extended family* to refer to them seems most appropriate (Ramanujam, 1972). Attitudinally at least, the individual seeks to have a nuclear family without losing the advantages of the extended family life-style. In short, the pattern of family that seems to exist today is somewhat ambiguous and transitional. The ambiguity that the child faces in roles and expectancies is likely to have far reaching consequences on his or her development.

Further, with the increasing trend toward nucleation and the nonavailability of mother surrogates, the child's psychological surround has become drastically restricted, and the child's emotional access is limited to his or her parents. A highly restricted familial surround cannot provide enough emotional support and security, which has several implications for the development and mental health of the child. A number of studies (Sanua, 1980, p. 218) illustrate how the presence of strong family ties served to buffer the stresses of social isolation and deprivation, and the support of the family and the social system could be mobilized to reduce the effect of disorders and even eliminate them. Earlier, in times of crisis, the individual could always fall back upon his or her family. In this transitional phase, with family cohesion becoming weak, such support is not always forthcoming, which puts the individual in a situation of stress. The family support system had a special significance. It not only rendered emotional support, but even provided essential economic help in times of crisis, and took over the role of child care and child rearing whenever required. With nucleation, this role of the family is fast diminishing. As has rightly been observed (Sharma, Sethi & Bhiman, 1985, p. 73), "What we may be facing is the integration of an effective, spontaneous and a rich support system [represented by a joint family] and its replacement by a weaker substitute [represented by nuclear family]."

The family's role in care and support during illness has eroded and has been replaced by modern forms of institutional medical care, which are in most cases inadequate. This brings us to a significant aspect of the Indian norm in dealing with health and illness that is quite the reverse of what obtains in the West. Unlike in the West where illness is largely a matter of personal concern, in the Indian scene there is an *openness* with which it is discussed and shared with others. As Kakar (1982) points out, the most intimate details of an individual's distress are revealed, and its outcome and the curative procedure discussed and debated. In fact, the illness is fully *shared* by the family if not also by the community. It is not a rare sight to find that when a person is seriously ill and is admitted to a hospital, his entire family throngs, often camping on the hospital compound and even in the corridors. There is involvement and integration of the family, the relatives, and even the community in the healing process, whereas today, as is prevalent in the West, illness is fast becoming entirely an individual affair. The practice of relatives crowding the hospital has created innumerable problems for the hospital administration and is in no way commended. What is important, however, is to note that the family or public sharing of the illness helps to make it lose much of its private terror. But with the kind of changes that the Indian family is undergoing, family sharing and support of illness are diminishing.

The evidence regarding the relationship between nucleation and mental illness is somewhat ambiguous. In some studies (Dube, 1970; Thacore, 1973), the joint family system has been found to produce a greater amount of stress on the individual. It has also been observed that though the joint family provided a greater sense of security and a support system in times of crisis, it also had a greater incidence of mental illness (Sethi, Gupta, Mahendur & Kuman, 1974). But in bulk of the studies conducted in India, there is a clear indication that the traditional family is a better source of psychosocial support than a nuclear family (Agarwal, Mehta & Gupta, 1978; Sethi & Manchanda, 1978; Sethi & Sharma, 1982; Sharma, Sethi & Bhiman, 1984; Verghese, Beig, Senseman, Rao & Benjamin, 1973). It has also been observed that children from larger-sized families have significantly fewer problem behaviors such as sleeping and eating difficulties, unsocial behavior, aggressiveness, and delinquency than those from one- or two-child families (Murlidharan, 1969). There is evidence that as families are becoming more nuclear, support systems are getting weaker, thereby exposing individuals to greater stress.

# Segregation from the Adult and Individuation

Traditional and transitional families differ radically with regard to the development of autonomy and individuation. Earlier there was minimal demand on the child to function independently of the mother, and there was little encouragement toward individuation and autonomy. Ramanujam (1978) observes that separation and individuation of self simply do not take place in the Indian child and later adult personality as it does in the West. According to Roland (1980), traditional Indian child rearing and social relationships not only clearly emphasize more symbiotic modes of relation but also tend to inhibit separation and individuation. Separation, autonomy, and individuation, which are the ideals of Western society, are inhibited and have a pejorative connotation of selfishness and rejection.

Malhotra and Malhotra (1985), however, on the basis of their analysis of six- to ten-year-old children undergoing family therapy and psychotherapy, observed that the struggle for autonomy and identity, which is the cardinal conflict of adolescence in the West, is found at a much younger age in

India. A successful resolution of the conflict leads to mature and autonomous ego development while nonresolution or more prolonged resolution leads to impaired ego development fraught with high dependency leanings and the failure of the individuation and separation process in the early development of the self. Mahler and Jacobson (1964) stated that too much maternal symbiotic gratification resulted in severe borderline or psychotic psychopathology, whereas a strong symbiotic relationship existed between the Indian mother and child without such adverse effects.

Symbiosis as a mode of relationship involving emotional closeness and dependency is fostered in traditional Indian child rearing. In the early years, it leads to enormous narcissistic gratification both in the mother and in the child. After four to five years, the child is expected to conform to family expectations and be obedient, which not only destroys the heightened narcissistic well-being but increases anxiety to meet the new demands. Bassa (1978) terms it the "cardinal crisis of Indian childhood," and Ramanujam (1978) views it as "the main and only developmental conflict of Indian children." Along with these, Malhotra and Malhotra (1985) observed the simultaneous process of infantilization within the family environment leading to contradictory communication between what is fostered at home and what is expected outside. As a result, children are often found to be better behaved outside the family.

The use of physical punishment and authoritarian parenting as means of social control are said to develop poorly internalized controls: "The child learns to avoid displeasing the parent and eventual punishment rather than imbibe the norms" (Malhotra & Malhotra, 1985, p. 52). The child exhibits more approval-seeking rather than autonomous behavior. Fear of disapproval and loss of love are anxiety-generating.

In this context, the point made by Neki (1976) is worth noting. He gives signal importance to the relationship of dependency between the *guru–chela* (preceptor and pupil), regarding it as a model of interrelationship rooted in Indian culture and suggesting it as a paradigm for psychotherapy. Thus dependency that is fostered in the traditional family setup is not frowned upon and considered undesirable as in the West. On the other hand, it is viewed developmentally and considered functionally useful for interrelationships with parents, teachers, and superiors (Neki, 1976). Its utility is even perceived in the field of work and management (J.B.P. Sinha, 1980).

There is yet another aspect to the problem of nonsegregation of the child from the parents. In the joint family, no conscious effort is made to segregate children from adults. The child is free to witness adults interacting with one another in varying moods and tempers, thereby learning a great deal about the elders and their own roles just by observing and listening. The remark made by an Indian observer, as quoted by Murphy (1953), brings out the point very clearly: "You bring up your children; we live with ours." This is true not only in the physical sense. Psychologically also the child shares the emotions of the elders and develops a lifelong bond with his or her relatives. The child never becomes psychologically separated from the family. Verma and Poffenberger (1970) observed that when a family had guests, children were usually included in this socializing event. This is no longer the case. As the family is creeping more toward a nuclear structure, such sharing of life occurs much less frequently, and the inculcation of norms and values through collective living is no longer possible. In the context of recent changes, the psychological separation of the child from his or her family is not only earlier but more effective. The situation is more acute if the mother is employed. Not only is her availability to the child limited, she becomes "distant," and much of the socialization takes place through *institutional* child rearing in creches, nurseries, and day-care centers. As a result, the problem of conscious socialization has come to the fore. It should be noted that, in Indian vocabulary, there is no special word to denote "socialization." It was considered more a kind of *automatic* process that took place through living in the family. The expression nearest to it is *lalan-palan*, that is, loving and protecting. In the present context, as in families in the West, proper socialization of the child has become a matter of *conscious* concern, and there is also a greater dependence on external and institutional agencies for it.

All of these issues have important implications for development. The advantage of a symbiotic relationship with parents is lost in the transitional phase. Because the family has not become fully nuclear, full development of autonomy does not take place. Moreover, the child no longer has the advantage of *automatic* processes of socialization that happened to be a characteristic of the large extended family. It has not been adequately replaced either by institutional agencies or by the parents in nuclear families who have relinquished most of their socialization functions.

# From Indulgent to Strict Child Rearing

In a traditional type of family, there was a great amount of nurturance and indulgence by the mother and other caretakers in the first two to three years of the child's life. The child was constantly cuddled, held, crooned, and talked to and there was a lot of body contact with the mother, something very distinct from what prevails in the West. Kakar (1979,

p. 33) points out that an Indian mother is inclined toward total indulgence of her infant's wishes and demands, whether these be related to feeding, cleaning, sleeping, or companionship. Moreover, she tends to extend this kind of mothering well beyond the time when the "infant" is ready for independent functioning in many areas. Thus feeding is done on demand, and breast-feeding is continued as long as possible, often up to two or three years. In addition, body contact with the mother or her surrogate provide a source of security for the child.

In traditional families, there was no undue pressure for toilet training, and the child was allowed to proceed at his or her own pace to master skills such as eating, walking, and dressing. From almost unchecked indulgence and benevolence that characterized the early years of the child in a traditional family, there has been in the nuclear family a sudden switch to new inflexible standards for feeding, toilet, and sleeping practices. Analyzing the perception of changes in childrearing practices in a suburban village, Verma and Poffenberger (1970) noted that there was general agreement that children were breast-fed for a shorter period of time today than in the past and that villagers had become more strict regarding elimination habits and cleanliness. Dos and don'ts are strictly inculcated, and the child is supposed to discriminate clearly between the things to be done and not to be done. This shift from indulgent to disciplinary roles of the parents, and from permissiveness to strict control and the consequent decrease in affection, have become sources of insecurity (Asthana, 1956) and anxiety (Sinha, 1962) in the child. A few studies have clearly demonstrated the significance of this change to the development of the individual. Bhaskaran (1959), for example, found among upper-class Indian female psychotics a preponderance of dullness and apathy, which he attributed to the extremely strict upbringing to which these women were subjected. In another study (Bhaskaran, 1963), it was observed that 54% of schizophrenics had been indulged by their parents or surrogates and 18% had been rejected. Contradictions that were found in the family backgrounds of schizophrenics in the United States were also encountered in India.

It should also be noted that even in modern nuclear families, parents have not fully adopted the new norms, and many of the traditional practices have lingered, often generating not only conflict between parents as to what practices to follow, but also subjecting the child to contrary practices. Such interparental conflicts with regard to childrearing problems have been found to affect the child's adjustment and scholastic achievement adversely (Kakkar, 1970).

# Inconsistencies in Child Rearing

One of the outcomes of the transitional phase through which the family in India is passing is that the child is often exposed to unstable and even contradictory patterns of behavior from his or her parents. With traditional values of child indulgence and care being given up and some of the old values lingering at the same time, the new norms for child rearing have yet to emerge. As a result, parental roles vis-à-vis the child regarding affection and love, and reward and punishment, remain unclear. Sometimes the father and mother follow practices that they had themselves experienced during their childhood in their extended families, and at times they also tend to adopt the practices typical of modern nuclear families in the West. For the child, such ambiguity as to the parental roles generates conflict and anxiety. Such inconsistencies in parental roles have been considered to be one of the factors in the emergence of anxiety in children (Sinha, 1962).

This is also evidenced in the way punishment has been used for socializing the child. "Up to the age of five, the child should have affection and care; for ten years thereafter [physical] punishment is to be used. When he attains the age of sixteen, he is to be treated as a friend"—has been the traditional adage in this respect. Under the Western influence, the use of punishment in disciplining the child has been decried, though the old adage of "spare the rod and spoil the child" has not been given up. A study has revealed (Saraswati, Takkar & Kaur, 1979) that beating and physical punishment were frequently resorted to as forms of power assertion in working-class families, while scolding and threatening were more prevalent among middle- and upper-middle-class families. Here again, there is ambiguity with consequent repercussions on the psychological growth of the child.

There is yet another aspect of this question. In the traditional family, the mother usually did not exercise the role of a primary disciplinarian, which was often the father's role, that of elderly uncles or aunts, and sometimes even of grandparents. She was mainly the source of love and affection, and the child was clear about what to expect from her. The position has become complicated in the nuclear family. New roles now revolve around the parents, especially for the mother when the child is young, and for the father later on. This is of single importance in socialization. The mother, who is primarily concerned with affection, also takes an authoritarian role. Thus the child begins to perceive her not only as the chief source of affection but also of authority, from which punishment emanates. It is obvious that when the same figure becomes the source of antagonistic affects—love and fear, affection and avoidance—conflict in the mind of the child is inevitable, predisposing him or her to anxiety (Sinha, 1962). It is to be noted that in India such a figure is mythologically symbolized by the goddess Kali who is normally portrayed as fierce, powerful, and violent but at the same time is perceived also as a benign and protecting mother.

This factor has become accentuated when the mother is employed. With both of the parents working, they not only devote less time to child care, but sex-role diversity, which has been so characteristic of the traditional family, is being erased. Both of the parents share in household, child care, and other domestic duties. This results in sporadic alterations in mother and father roles, and the child finds it difficult to build clear-cut expectancies for his or her respective parents. Earlier, when asked, "Whom you love more-mother or father?" it was almost automatic and normal for the child to reply that it was the mother. Today when the same question is put to the children, they hesitate, feel confused, and often reply that they love both of them equally.

# Absence of Clear-cut Role Models

The gradual transformation of the family from the joint extended to the nuclear family has restricted the child's choice of the model that he or she can emulate. In a joint family, during early childhood, the main model for identification was the mother. As the boy grew up, he had the father, the grandfather, and other male members before him whom he could emulate. As the girl grew up, she had the mother, the grandmother, and other female members whom she could emulate. The multiplicity of role models resulted in identification being diffused. In an environment of multiple mothering and fathering, as Mead (1921/1951) observes, not only are the identifications multiplied, but there is diffused dependence with some flattening of affect. With nucleation, identification is less likely to be diffused. There are findings (Sinha, 1979), however, that indicate that the children and youth of today do not possess clear-cut role models and very seldom identify either with parents or with outstanding figures from mythology, history, or the world of science and learning. The traditional family of today is not fulfilling its socializing role in providing stable role models for the child. In the first place, parents in the changed environment have ceased to play a significant part in presenting models for conduct and life goals. Older relatives and grandparents are no longer there to transmit folk-tales and mythological stories about great characters who were models of conduct. Second, parents themselves often present an ambiguous facet. It is suggested (Sinha, 1979, pp. 63–64) that "elders of today when they were themselves young could easily identify and find role-models among the older generation of that time because the latter belonged to a more stable society and presented figures which were not torn by contradictions. But this is no longer the case." Due to contradictions and conflicts that have beset the fast-changing world, the older generation of today, which should have provided the guidelines for conduct that it had in its own time, has failed to provide stable models free from ambiguity and contradictions. In analyzing values and role models among Indian youth, Sinha (1977) found this reflected in the value ambiguities and diffused, unstable, and heterogeneous role models adopted by the youth. It is regarded as a kind of "role-refusal" on the part of the young, reflecting identity confusion.

## Change in the Status, Role, and Employment of Women

The spread of education among women, and a number of legislative measures like the Hindu Succession Act (1956), Special Marriage Act (1954), Hindu Marriage Act (1955), and many others—collectively forming what has often been called the Hindu Code Bill—have sought to give equal status to women in matters of inheritance, politics, and employment and to prevent discrimination on the grounds of sex. Though there is a distinct gap between legal rights and the social attitudes that stand in the way of the actual emancipation of women, these measures have unleashed social forces that have radically altered the position of women in the Indian family system. From a position of subservience as envisaged by the ancient Hindu lawgiver Manu—wherein a woman was to depend on her father in childhood, on her husband in young adulthood, and on her son in old age-she could now take on an independent role.

Here again there is a gap between what is legally possible and the actual situation. As Kapur (1970) observes, while women's roles and relationships have changed and are changing, there is still a wide gap between their legal, political, and economic rights and privileges and the *actual* rights and privileges that they enjoy and utilize. Society's attitude in general has not changed significantly toward the woman's role and status.

The situation is particularly evidenced with regard to women and employment. Taking menial, household, and agricultural jobs has been prevalent among the lower classes and has been accepted socially. But women of middle and upper-middle classes entering professions is a comparatively recent phenomenon. The spread of higher education among women and economic pressure to maintain a certain style of living have forced many women belonging to these strata of society to join various professions. It has resulted in a change in the status of women and their role in the family. From a purely subservient and dependent role in the traditional family system, women have begun to contribute to family earning. Because of their changed economic status, women have inevitably begun to have a say in decision making, and enjoy, at least partially, the income that they have earned. But with women taking to various kinds of professions, a corresponding attitudinal change in males has yet to come about: "They like their wives to take up jobs but dislike them to change at all as far as their attitudes toward their role and status at home is concerned and dislike their traditional responsibilities being neglected which results from their preoccupation with out-of-home vocation. Their attitude toward their wives is found to be ambivalent" (Kapur, 1970). Because consequential changes in men's attitudes have not occurred, women's employment has become a frequent source of familial conflict and marital maladjustment. Women have found it difficult to reconcile the demands of familial and professional roles. Due to conflicting demands, role conflict, tensions, and anxiety among women who are employed, especially among the middle and higher classes, have been observed (Kaul, 1974; P. Sinha, 1981).

The employment of women has repercussions on socialization and child-rearing practices as well. With the mother being employed, the child, at a very early age, has to be put in a creche, day-care center, or other institutional arrangement for care while the parents are away at work. Due to pressures of time and work, parental involvement in child rearing diminishes. As a result, parents have a limited socializing role. The child is consequently left to the care of maid servants or is put in day-care schools and nurseries from a very early age. Such services on an organized basis are essential when the mother is employed, but are not readily available or adequate except in large metropolitan areas. Putting the child into day care or nurseries may help in the early separation of the child, in greater individuation, and in the development of autonomous functioning and independence. The child does not develop the kind of conformist attitude to the traditional family norm. Because of the limited role of parents, the child goes out of the family early and gets into peer groups. With the weakening of the joint family and the trend toward a nuclear structure, there is a distinct relinquishing by the family of the socialization role. Peer groups have come to fill this gap.

An increasing number of studies have explored the effects of maternal employment on children. It has been observed that male children of working mothers are socially more participative than those of nonworking mothers, but they tend to be higher in "nervousness" (Prasad & Prasad, 1975). Adverse effects of maternal employment on socialization, child care, and behavior of the child have often been emphasized. But it is generally concluded that though many studies have pointed to its detrimental influence on the growing child, maternal employment per se had limited effect and such factors as family circumstances may be more critical than actual employment status (Eiduson, Cohen & Alexander, 1973). In a study where the pattern of maternal work, lifestyle, the age of the child, and the mother's general ability level were taken into account, there was no evidence of negative effects on cognitive, social, and emotional development of the child traceable to maternal absence due to employment alone (Zimmerman & Bernstein, 1983, p. 424). It is acknowledged that before making generalizations, more information is needed on the impact of maternal employment on the development of the child. On the other hand, maternal employment may also have a positive influence by offering the child a chance to explore a wider world, relate to other adult figures, socialize with peers at early age, and do more things for him- or herself with less supervision, interference, or restriction. It may also present different role models to the child with both parents working and sharing roles, thereby making sex-role stereotypes fade gradually (Zimmerman & Bernstein, 1983).

# Impact of Migration

Poverty, the rapid growth in population, industrialization, and urbanization have led to migration. Children are often part of rural families moving to urban areas in search of employment. They constitute around 50% of all migrants. Migration often means separation from the extended family and the experiencing of a new life-style in a changed environment. They usually live in slums or as footpath dwellers devoid of basic civic amenities and education.

Migration has taken different forms: the migration of the rural population to cities and industrial belts in search of employment, migration from poorer and less developed states in the eastern India to more prosperous areas like the Punjab where labor is scarce and expensive, and migration to Gulf countries, with migrants coming from Kerala especially and from the mostly Muslim populations of other states as well. In the case of the latter two groups, it is mostly the males who move for temporary periods—varying from a few months to two to three years—leaving their families in rural areas. The remittances that they send periodically and the savings that they bring back do lead to economic amelioration, but not without many sociopsychological consequences. Apart from the factor of "separation," the migrants are exposed to new lifestyles, some of which they adopt, coming back with newer ideas about the man–woman relationship and family interaction. Rejection of many of the traditional attitudes and values, and the generation of new norms, become sources of friction and stress in the families of migrants, with unfortunate effects, especially on children.

The prevalence of psychiatric and psychosomatic ailments has been found to be higher among migrants (Dube, 1970; Thacore, 1973). The rate of incidence has varied in different surveys—370 per 1000 (Bhaskaran, Seth & Yadav, 1970) to 96 per 1000 (Sethi, Gupta, Raj Kumar & Promilla, 1972)—but they are much higher than among local residents.

Migration, especially to remote places, has been a strong factor in family disorganization. The problem has not been investigated in any systematic manner as to its impact on child rearing and mental health. It has, however, been reported that there is a significant and disturbing rise in mental health problems and disruptions in the families of the Keralite migrants who have returned with considerable savings after their stints in the Gulf countries. Their economic status had risen remarkably but at enormous cost to their families and to their own adjustment.

# Summing Up

Changes in the Indian family in recent years have altered the pattern of socialization in a radical manner. As Khatri (1970) points out, these changes have in many ways increased the general vulnerability of the child to mental health disturbances. Findings from the studies discussed above indicate a nexus between familial antecedents and the healthy development of the individual. There is, however, the need to define and identify more precisely the specific aspects of the family situation in the context of the comprehensive changes taking place in the country, and to interrelate these aspects with the psychological development of the individual. It is likely that many sociocultural and economic factors enveloping the family are likely to confound the effect, and that familial factors per se have only a limited influence. Therefore, the conclusions regarding the relationship of changes in the family and psychological development discussed earlier are to be considered tentative, more in the nature of predictions to be verified through carefully designed investigations. One would tend to agree with Sanua's (1961, p. 265) assertion, made with respect to the familial factors in schizophrenia, that although the evidence of the importance of family factors is quite compelling, the patterns of the home environment need to be isolated and more clearly defined.

I will advance a few observations on the role of cross-cultural psychology in this context. As has been remarked earlier, the full psychological implications of the changes in Indian families that have occurred in recent years have not been fully understood. These changes and their full repercussions could be adequately recognized if comparative data from different cultures were available. It would be unjustified to regard them as psychologically desirable or even inevitable simply because the changes outlined seem to move in the direction of the family situation in the contemporary West, or to understand and interpret them entirely in terms of similar data and theories that have been generated in the West. Changes in the families in India have their own special characteristics. They are conditioned by the cumulative experiences in the sociocultural and historical contexts in which they have unfolded. Many of the changes that have occurred are peculiar to the Indian setting, and some old-fashioned traditional practices have persisted because they seem to have their own functional utility. Many of them would appear strange and even dysfunctional from the Western point of view. A case in point is dependency, which is almost a bugbear in the West, but it has been found to have its functional significance not only in psychotherapy (Neki, 1976) but also in the organizational setting and as a style of interrelationship with authority (J.B.P. Sinha, 1980).

As Jahoda (1975) has observed, data and theories of modern psychology are the products of a very special type of sociocultural milieu whose characteristics are not to be found in most developing countries. As a result, current psychological data and theories that are mostly Western in origin have only a limited utility and application to the sociocultural changes that are occurring in the developing countries. Therefore, cross-cultural methodology is useful. This new branch has done a yeoman service in successfully challenging panhumanism and the universality of mainstream psychology, which for decades were almost taken for granted. It has rightly emphasized the need for taking due cognizance of cultural variations. By providing comparative data from diverse cultures and often pointing to specific cultural bases of various patterns of behavior, it has given a new insight to the psychologist that he or she did not have before.

# 6

# Socialization, Family and Psychological Differentiation* (*with Shalini Bisht*)

Socialization may be described as a process which focuses upon the development of the individual as a social being and as the member of a society. It teaches the child the ways and norms of his society and moulds him in his early stages of, development, thus determining to a large extent his later personality structure and style of functioning.

As the structure of society varies, socialization patterns also vary resulting in differences in the consequent personality structure. Kardiner (cited in Whiting and Child, 1953) has spoken of the effect of a society's maintenance system (which he defines as its economic, political and social customs), on the child-rearing practices which in turn influence the personality of the individuals. Variations in the composition of social structure, for example, the type of village, the housing pattern, the type of neighbourhood, family size and structure will all influence and contribute to variance in child-rearing practices and the resultant personality. Thus, the type of family, joint or nuclear in which a child is reared, will have significant impact on his style of functioning. Whether a child's interaction is limited to his parents and siblings alone in his family or whether it extends to parent surrogates and his coevals like cousins and other relations will determine his psychological differentiation. Thus, the number of adult figures in the family and the consequent psychological distance of the child from his parents are important factors influencing

* Reproduced, with permission, from Sinha, D. Socialization, Family and Psychological Differentiation (with Shalini Bisht). In D. Sinha (ed.), *Socialization of the Indian Child* (1980). New Delhi: Concept.

This text has been edited for typographical errors, stylistic consistency and sequential organization in order to make it suitable for inclusion in the book.

differentiation of the child. Some three decades ago the family structure in India was what we call the joint family characterized by sharing of residence, property, income, etc. and comprising forty to fifty or even more members. Now this family structure is transforming itself into a nuclear family structure which comprises parents and their children, i.e., a limited number of members only. The change in the international relations and interactions within the family due to this transformation has great significance for the child's psychological differentiation since the two family types give entirely two different kinds of social environment to the child—one in which the child has less freedom to develop his self-identity and individuality by virtue of its authoritarian set-up (the joint family) and the other which encourages independence and development of a distinctive self on account of its more permissive atmosphere (the nuclear family). Studies have shown that family experiences and socialization are important determinants of psychological differentiation. We, therefore, have reasons to believe that children in these two types of families will differ in the extent of psychological differentiation achieved.

The present chapter deals with the pattern of family and its impact on psychological differentiation. More specifically, it analyses how differences in socialization practices as prevailing in a joint or a nuclear family are likely to influence a child's psychological differentiation.

# Concept of Psychological Differentiation

The concept of psychological differentiation was first introduced by Witkin et al. (1962/74) in the course of studies of individual differences in cognitive style. Briefly stated, "differentiation refers to the complexity of structure of a psychological system" (Witkin, 1978). A more differentiated system manifests itself in an articulated way of experiencing the world, an articulated body concept, greater self-nonself segregation and structured, specialized defences. The field independent cognitive style is related to greater differentiation while the field dependent style is related to lesser differentiation.

Several studies in the area of socialization have given considerable evidence that individual differences in the extent of differentiation are to a large extent the end products of differences in socialization experiences (Dyk, 1969; Dyk and Witkin, 1965; Witkin, 1965; and Witkin et al., 1962/74).

Working on studies of child-rearing practices and attitudes of mothers of relatively field-dependent and independent boys Dyk and Witkin (1965) and Witkin et al. (1962/74) found that mothers of field-dependent boys encouraged continued connection with her, emphasized conformity, discouraged aggressive behaviour and used severe training methods. Thus they hypothesized that child-rearing practices which encourage separate autonomous functioning foster the development of greater differentiation and a field independent cognitive style, while child-rearing practices which encourage continued reliance on parental authority are likely to make for less differentiation and a more field-dependent cognitive style.

The results of this early exploratory study were confirmed in independent investigations done by Seder (1957), Berry (1966) and Dawson (1967a, 1967b). Seder (1957) studied a suburban Boston group and found that "field-dependent boys were not allowed to set their own standards and were pressed towards standards and goals set by their parents, were severely punished for aggressive and assertive behaviour, were punished according to their parents whims and moods and were generally disciplined in an authoritarian manner." Dawson (1967a, 1967b) studied the Temne and Mende groups of Sierra Leone (Africa) and found that the Temne parents as compared to the Mende parents stressed authority, used physical punishment and were less consistent in their child rearing methods. As predicted the Temne were found to be more field dependent than the Mende. In another study of a similar kind Berry (1966) compared the Temne and the Eskimo groups and found that the Temne children who were severely disciplined and physically punished were more field dependent than the Eskimo children who were given much freedom, were rarely punished and were encouraged to assume responsibility early in life. A number of other studies have given similar results. Thus, it was found that parental strictness was associated with field dependence (Abelew, 1974; Baran, 1971; Vernon, 1965); parents of field dependent children discouraged separation (Claeys and DeBoeck, 1976; Edgerton, 1975; Irving, 1970; Jones, 1975; Ramirez and Price Williams, 1974a) and strongly dominated family interactions as compared to parents of field independent children who shared power (Dreyer, 1975); mothers of field-dependent children used relatively non-specific modes of comforting their children (Dyk, 1969); families with greater paternal involvement were likely to have field-independent boys (Busse, 1969; Dawsor, 1967b; Meizlik, 1973; Dreyer, 1975) while a mother salient surround was likely to have field dependent children (Dawson, 1967a, 1967b), and extended family structure was associated with field dependence while a nuclear family structure was associated with field independence (Witkin et al., 1974; Holtzman, Guerrero & Swartz, 1975).

Several other studies using a cross cultural approach to identifying socialization variables associated with psychological differentiation have implicated an important dimension called "social traditionalism" designated "social conformity" by Witkin et al. (1974). In this term they included "social settings characterized by insistence upon adherence to family and social authority and the use of severe or even harsh socialization practices to enforce this conformance" (Witkin et al., 1974). Studies subsumed under this title "traditionalism" or "social conformity" have been mostly done on Jewish subjects: Preale et al. (1970) compared young Israelis of Middle Eastern and Western origin. The Middle Eastern family was described as tradition oriented having an "authoritarian, patriarchal structure which tends to foster subordination to authority and restriction of emotional autonomy." Together with this "child-rearing functions of socializing agents in the families of Middle Eastern origin are more stereotyped and less differentiated than in the urban family of western ethnic origin" (Preale et al., 1970). The Middle Eastern group was found to be more field dependent than the Western group. In yet another study, Zadik (1968) found that Jewish socialization practices characterized by subordination to authority and reduced emotional autonomy were related to less differentiation. Similar results were found by Amir (1975), Arnir et al. (1970) and Weller and Sharan (1971).

Dershowitz (1971) also showed "traditionalism" to be an important variable in the development of cognitive styles. He compared boys from strictly orthodox Jewish families of East European origin with boys from assimilated Jewish and white Protestant families. The orthodox Jewish boys were found to be more field dependent than the latter group. Dershowitz described the orthodox Jewish groups as traditional in the sense that these families adhered strongly to the many particulars of Jewish religion, stressed religious training and followed values and patterns of traditional living. In such a family the father was more concerned with scholarly pursuits so that the mother alone looked after the children, which resulted in strong maternal domination over boys, inhibiting their development of autonomous functioning. Rand (1971) got similar findings on comparing the Jewish Moroccan families with Jewish families of European origin. The Moroccan family was authoritative, and patriarchal, stressed conformity, sheltered the child and used corporal punishments. Witkin et al. (1974) compared villages of Holland, Italy and Mexico differing in extent of emphasis on conformity and found that children of villages showing less conformity were more differentiated than children from villages emphasizing conformity. A review by Witkin and Berry (1975) and Berry (1976) of studies of subsistence level societies indicates that the nomadic hunting groups tend to be relatively more field independent than the sedentary agricultural groups on account of differential emphasis upon "social conformity". The nomadic groups described as "loose" societies are relatively less structured, stress autonomy training and put less pressure on social conformity, while the sedentary societies described as "tight" societies are stratified, use strict child rearing methods and press for conformity. Sinha (1978) found the nomadic Birhors to be significantly more field-independent than the sedentary Oraons. But the difference in extent of differentiation between the nomadic Birhors and the transitional agricultural Birhors (i.e., those nomads who have taken to sedentary life some twenty years back only), though in the expected direction was not found to be statistically significant.

According to Sinha this non-significant difference between the two tribes is probably because of the fact that the sedentary agricultural Birhors have changed from the nomadic life style to this new life style only recently, and this short time period has not been enough to change significantly their nature of perceptual style.

The studies reviewed above clearly imply that early family experiences contribute significantly to individual differences in development of psychological differentiation and suggest that families which emphasize autonomy, assertiveness, separation and are less authoritarian and autocratic foster field independence and greater differentiation while families which de-emphasize these and stress conformity and subordination to authority foster field-dependence and lesser differentiation.

The main features of socialization practices as related to field independence/dependence are summarized in a tabular form (Table 6.1).

**Table 6.1**

*Socialization Practices and Psychological Differentiation*

| *Field Dependence* | *Field Independence* |
| --- | --- |
| Strict disciplinary methods | Liberal disciplinary methods |
| Inconsistent and non-specific modes of child-rearing | Consistent and specific modes of child-rearing |
| Separation discouraged | Separation encouraged |
| Conformity is emphasized, and independence is discouraged | Independence and autonomy are encouraged |
| Parents dominate family interactions and authority lies with one parent | Parents share power and contribute equally to family interactions |
| Less paternal involvement and greater maternal surround | Greater paternal involvement and lesser maternal surround |

# Role of Joint and Nuclear Families in Socialization and Development of Psychological Differentiation

For every individual his family is the first social group that he encounters after birth and for the early part of his life he relates himself only to this limited "world". It is in the family alone that a child makes his first important relationships like relations with mother, father, siblings and so on, and through interactions with them begins his first attempt at discriminating the "self" from the "non-self" and working for "selfhood", thus taking his first step towards differentiation.

Every family socializes its child according to its own norms. Thus, socialization patterns vary according to variations in family structures. In India two dominant family patterns have been in existence regulating our way of life, viz., the nuclear and the joint family. Put in broad terms, a nuclear family consists of parents with married sons without children and other unmarried children, while a joint family is characterized by the presence of three or more generations of lineal descent who share property, residence, etc. The dominant interactions and influences in these two contrasting family types are very different, since the joint family is a large group of members belonging to three or more generations with shared interests, whereas the nuclear family is a small group of members belonging to only two generations.

## Dominant Interaction Patterns in a Joint Family

The Indian joint family is hierarchical in nature and the eldest male member, usually the grandfather, is the head of the family. Within him lies the locus of power and authority. He has command over the rest of the family and holds decision making power which he exercises in an authoritarian manner. The child who is at the lowest order in this hierarchy does not have any active participation in the family interactions. He is supposed to be obedient, respectful and rarely rebellious. This prevents him from carrying out his wishes and asserting his selfhood. He is not allowed to make his own decisions and set his goals so that he is unable to recognize his abilities and uniqueness. This strong emphasis on subordination to authority encourages stereotypes in behaviour and restricts autonomous functioning of the child, thereby interfering with the development of self-identity an attribute of differentiation.

Children in large families are severely disciplined (Whiting, 1961) and parental behaviour is autocratic and authoritarian (Elder & Bowerman, 1963). Generally an atmosphere of restraint exists between the older and the younger generation and liberty on the part of youngsters is not tolerated. Thus interpersonal relations between the different generation members in an extended family are authoritarian in nature allowing for limited interactions. Such strict and restrictive atmosphere gives less freedom to the child to explore his surroundings and function in an independent manner, and works against the identification of one's impulses and development of specialized coping strategies which are important features of a more differentiated system.

A joint family set-up demands for its stability and integrity, co-operation and conformity from its members at the expense of individual independence. Thus, a great premium is placed on conformity to family ideals and norms, and children are expected to conform to these ideals strictly. This fosters continued inter-dependence among members and inhibits autonomous development. Further, emphasis on conformity to a predetermined set of external standards makes it difficult to identify and develop one's unique abilities, interests and modes of coping again, with the result that specialization of psychological functions, a significant determinant of differentiation, is inhibited.

In joint family members do not have the freedom to take any initiative nor can they assert their independence. They have to work in the interest of the family and any attempts at gaining personal freedom are resented by the other members. A child thus cannot detach himself from the family and act independently. This prevents him from forming a sharply differentiated impression of himself and from separating himself from his family. Because of the large number of people in a joint family, a child is lost in the vast set-up and is recognized as just one of the group (Gore, 1978). In short then, a large family set-up discourages individuality and breeds in the child a dominating feeling of being "just one of the group". This works against the achievement of a "self" distinct from others and makes the child unaware of his own attributes as distinct from those of the others. In consequence again, the development of self-nonself segregation, a salient feature of differentiation, is hampered.

Because of the presence of a large number of relatives, the child has many adult figures for identification who act as parent surrogates. In a way, group child rearing is usually the mode of socializing a child in large families. It is not the mother alone who looks after the child; any female figure like grandmother, aunts or elder sisters may do so. Thus the child passes through many hands and encounters faces of many adults acting in *loco parentis*, thereby having multiple models before him. This leads a child to have a more diffused and less individuated conception of his self (Clausen, 1966). He "has to relate himself to many adults who represent sources of authority and gratification to varying degrees" (Gore, 1978), thus preventing him from forming a well-developed, articulated and clear-cut image of himself. In other words he lacks an articulated body-concept as an indicator of greater differentiation.

Moreover, since there are many people to look after a child, he is never without company even in the absence of his parents. Thus, infant indulgence is likely to be high in joint families (Whiting, 1961; Barry, Bacon & Child, 1957). Children are over-protected and sheltered which favours dependence on mothers and discourages separation. As a result, self-nonself segregation is again hampered.

A very prominent feature of Indian joint family is that father–child relationship is very restraining. According to Gore, "father's affective role is considerably circumscribed by social and cultural norms. He is to assume an authoritative rather than an affective role towards his children" (Gore, 1978). Because of father's psychological absence, the mother surround which makes the children more dependent on their mother and this as studies have shown fosters field dependence. In such family structures, with a female salient surround the developmental task of separating from mother is a difficult one, especially for boys, which thus hampers achievement of a sense of separate identity, a prominent characteristic of differentiation.

# Dominant Interaction Patterns in a Nuclear Family

A nuclear family is "an example of structural differentiation from the more composite structure of an extended family" (Singh, 1977). A nuclear family may be broadly defined as one which comprises two-generation members—parents and their children.

In a nuclear family the child encounters only the immediate members of his family. As compared to a joint family he has a much smaller social universe in which to grow up and there are not many adults and relatives with whom he may attach himself. There is a significant decrease in the number of adult models. The child, thus, forms very strong and intense personal bonds with his parents. There is active participation on the part of parents resulting in greater concentration and intensity of interaction between parents and children. This type of relationship gives the child ample scope for developing a clear-cut and distinct self-identity and for functioning in an individualized way, both of which are important features of differentiation.

In the nuclear family, the father is the head of the family who is usually readily approachable. As compared to a joint family the child in nuclear families is less severely disciplined and has a lot of scope for asserting his selfhood and independence. He has more freedom to take initiative and act independently. This helps the child in forming a distinctive and differentiated conception of his self, capable of separating from others, thus facilitating self-nonself segregation and working towards more differentiation. A distinctive conception of his self also helps the child in recognizing his abilities and coping methods thereby forming a well-developed and specialized defence system.

Further, since there are not many members in a nuclear family the child is on his own quite often which leads to autonomous and independent functioning. The playmates and friends of the child are often from outside the family which necessitates his going out of the family boundary and establishing relations elsewhere also. This encourages his separation from the family and makes him see his relations with others in a broader perspective, thereby facilitating self-nonself segregation which is a salient feature of differentiation.

The atmosphere in a nuclear family is more permissive, and the child is less severely disciplined and less harshly treated. He is under the supervision of his parents alone and elder siblings and is not hampered by excessive shelter and care available from others. This gives him opportunity for developing his self-identity and acquiring an articulated body concept.

While in the joint families the father is psychologically absent, in nuclear families he plays an important role in interactions thereby providing a suitable model to boys. Studies indicate that father's presence fosters field independence and greater differentiation (Busse, 1969; Dawson, 1967b; Meizlik, 1973; Dreyer, 1975). With an increase in the father's role, the mother's role is limited only to child care which helps the child in separating from the mother. This leads to individualized development and autonomous functioning and contributes to greater differentiation.

In summary, the child in a joint family is guided in his behaviour and attitudes by "external sources" such as the grandparents, parents, other relatives and behaviour and actions originating from within him are rejected so that the child is not able to recognize his unique capabilities and resources. The final outcome is a less differentiated self with no variety. In contrast, the child in a nuclear family is less guided by and oriented towards external sources and is encouraged to develop his inner capabilities and interests thereby resulting in a variegated and more differentiated self.

The dominant interaction patterns in two types of families are summarized in Table 6.2.

A close scrutiny of Tables 6.1 and 6.2 shows that some of the socialization practices associated with lesser or greater differentiation (Table 6.1) are the dominant features of joint/nuclear families (Table 6.2) respectively. Thus, such socialization practices as harsh child-rearing methods, stress upon conformity, discouragement of autonomy and separation and father's limited role as compared to mother's dominant role in child-rearing, which are associated with field dependence and less differentiation are in fact some of the characteristic features of a joint family. Conversely, socialization practices such as liberal child-rearing methods, emphasis upon autonomy and separation, and father's involvement in child-rearing with mother's role somewhat

**Table 6.2**

*Dominant Interaction Patterns in the Joint and Nuclear Families*

| Joint Family | Nuclear Family |
|---|---|
| 1. Hierarchical in nature | 1. Less structured |
| 2. Multiple adult models | 2. Fewer adult models |
| 3. Greater infant indulgence | 3. Lesser infant indulgence |
| 4. Authoritarian structure, use of severe child-training methods | 4. More permissive and use of less harsh methods |
| 5. Stress conformity | 5. Gives more freedom |
| 6. De-emphasize autonomy and separation | 6. Stress autonomy and separation |
| 7. Father's role is limited in childrearing and mother has a dominating role. | 7. Both parents share power and have nearly equal roles. |

limited, which are associated with field-independence and greater differentiation, are the notable features of a nuclear family. Our analysis of the dominant features of parent child relationship and socialization practices in two types of families and viewing the same in juxtaposition with the socio-cultural determinants of field dependence/independence cognitive styles suggest a close association between the two. It is only through a careful empirical investigation that it will be clear how far a child's experiences in the joint and nuclear families foster or inhibit psychological differentiation.

# 7

# The Young and the Old: Ambiguity of Role Models and Values among Indian Youth*

Youth is a distinct and important period in the life cycle of the individual. Sometimes youth has been stereotyped as being rash, indiscreet, impulsive and foolish, and the expression '*gadah pachisi*' ('donkey's twenty-five') is current in some regional languages, characterizing the tendency of youth to resort to unwise and impetuous behaviour which is expected of an individual up to the age of twenty five and which should be ignored by understanding elders. But in spite of certain derogatory and undesirable features sometimes ascribed to it, in certain respects youth marks the peak in the physical and mental growth of the individual. There are legends and stories in which great kings of yore resorted to penance and worship to maintain the vigour and grandeur of youth eternally, or to regain it after it had been lost with the onset of old age. The period after youth may be characterized by greater wisdom and maturity, but there is a widespread belief that a general decline, however imperceptible and gradual it may be, sets in soon after. Therefore, it is not surprising that youth is not only cherished, but that there is often a yearning in the later years to return to this phase of one's life cycle.

Youth is characterized by a biological 'coming of age'. It ends the period of one's childhood and adolescence, and marks an entry into adulthood.

* Reproduced, with permission, from Sinha, D. The Young and the Old: Ambiguity of the Role Models and Values among Indian Youth. In S. Kakar (ed.), *Identity and Adulthood* (1978, pp. 56–64). New Delhi: Oxford University Press.

This text has been edited for typographical errors, stylistic consistency and sequential organization in order to make it suitable for inclusion in the book.

However, psychologically speaking, this period has often been viewed as one of crisis which every individual has to face in varying degrees. It is only by resolving this crisis in some fashion that he can develop emotionally and socially into an adult. This period of crisis, whether it be in the life of an individual or that of a whole generation of young people, is often reflected in certain kinds of strains and stresses and has been variously described as a generation gap, vocational and social disorientation, alienation, ambivalence and 'identity confusion'. The concept of identity confusion, as defined by Erikson (1968), denotes 'a person's uncertainty about his future role in society, as well as a sense of discontinuity between his personal past and his future' (p. 87). As experienced subjectively, it means a feeling of fragmentation, of indecision, and of isolation from social and interpersonal contacts. It is not the purpose of this chapter to elaborate on the concept of identity confusion or its allied concept of identity crisis. It would be quite sufficient to say that an intensified form of such confusion is reflected in a variety of psycho-social disorders such as anxiety, anomie, despair, depersonalization, meaninglessness, isolation, loneliness, a feeling of anonymity, and pessimism, all of which seem to characterize contemporary youth.

At certain periods in history, the resolving of identity confusion on the part of individuals becomes particularly difficult. Certain cultural and historical factors influence this intensity, and an important one is the rapidity of change through which a particular society is passing. One of the features of modern Indian society is the rapid breakdown of traditional values, and the transitional character of its social, political and economic structures. This phenomenon of transition has been taken to underlie the general incidence of high anxiety which has been observed among the Indian student population (Sinha, 1962). There have been revolutionary changes in the entire pattern of life within the last three decades. Old values have tumbled and the new are still in a state of flux. The phenomenon characterizes most Asian countries. According to Leon Guerrero, once the Filipino Ambassador in London, the elements in all the movements in western history—the break-up of the Roman Empire, the overthrow of the feudal system, the Renaissance, the Reformation, the French and American revolutions, the disruption of the social system in the industrial revolution, the class-war of the Russian revolution—are all simultaneously bubbling in the Asian revolution. Gunnar Myrdal has also commented on this confusing rapidity and disorderly sequence of all-round changes that are taking place in India and other Asian countries: 'It is, then not only a telescoping in the sense that the changes are concentrated in a shorter time span, but there is also a break in the order in which the changes occur. What could in Europe unfold gradually and proceed as a grand symphony with one movement following the other in thematic sequence is by destiny syncopated in South Asia into almost a cacophony' (Myrdal, 1968, pp. 119–120). In such a period of rapid change, the problem of identity confusion is intensified by the breakdown of traditional values and traditional roles, where adult support for youth's search for identity is lacking and where the guidelines for accepted behavior get blurred and contradictory. On the plane of individual personality, it is often reflected in the experience of contradictions and inner conflicts, and a mode of life which has been characterized as 'compartmentalization' (Dawson, 1963). While analyzing the cultural factors in the emergence of anxiety, I have also remarked on the dichotomies inherent in the Indian situation and personality, and have characterized this as 'tolerance of dissonance' (Sinha, 1974). Nirad Chaudhuri designates it as 'Janus Multifrons', and talks of the 'terrible dichotomy' of Hindu personality with a large number of antithetical though connected traits shaping behavior. These 'opposites almost neutralize one another, and the indecisive tug-of-war stultifies all his actions' (Chaudhuri, 1966, p. 106).

Man inherits a limited repertory of responses. Most of the responses are learned, and a majority of them are learned from others, i.e., culturally acquired. In this respect, among other cultural influences, the perception of role-models which the individual tries to emulate and regards as providing guidelines for his conduct, and the perception of what is right and wrong, proper and improper, have a vital part to play in the psychological growth of the individual. The present chapter reports the results of a few studies conducted in 1969 and constituting parts of a larger project on intergenerational differences which reflect the ambiguities and confusion of Indian youth today (see for details Sinha, 1972). Directly, this essay is concerned with an analysis of choice of hero-image and role-models, and perception and evaluation of certain 'ambiguous' socio-moral traits as well as of some events and incidents representing transgression of certain accepted codes of behavior. The strategy of the study was to contrast the reactions of youth against those of persons belonging to the older generation. The sample studied consisted of 300 university and college students from the city of Allahabad, 150 younger teachers below 25, and 150 university and college teachers who were 40 years or above. The overall mean age of the older teachers was 48.18 years, that of younger teachers 23.03, and a little over 19 and 16 years respectively for university and college students.

The sample was subjected to three tests. The first consisted of perception of people and determination of role-models and hero-images. The subject was asked to name five persons from whose life he may have gathered inspiration and who, he considered, had influenced him in his life and behavior. Later, he was asked to name two of these persons in order, and to indicate the one he regarded as the greatest. Third, he was requested to name the qualities possessed by those two persons which made them notable. An analysis of responses indicated the role-models accepted by the subject as well as the qualities he considered significant.

On the second test, namely, the perception of events, the subject was required to evaluate a number of situations with socio-moral connotations. Each one depicted a transgression of some common social or moral code like misappropriation of public funds because the individual was in urgent need of money; burning of a shop by a crowd because it had not put down its shutters when a general strike was declared; having a secret love-affair with a married woman; travelling without a ticket; and similar other situations. The incidents were chosen to represent some typical, commonplace occurrences. The incidents were presented one by one to the subject, and he was required to indicate whether he considered each 'proper' or 'improper', or whether he was unable to decide about it ('neutral response'). The frequencies of each of the three types of responses were then analyzed.

The third study consisted of the presentation of a list of ambiguous behavior traits as well as other qualities like honesty, cheating, etc. which could be considered desirable or undesirable. A long list containing some desirable, undesirable, and ambiguous behavior traits, randomly mixed, was presented to the subject and he was asked to indicate whether each quality, when found in a person, would be considered good or bad, positive or negative, desirable or undesirable.

# The First Study

The analysis of choice of role-models and heroes revealed interesting age differences. The older generation of teachers displayed a higher degree of agreement among themselves regarding the choice of persons and personalities from whom they received inspiration. They belonged both to the past and the present and constituted figures from the political as well as religious world while some were social reformers. Among the young, both students and teachers, the choice of models was more widely dispersed. It was observed that the hero image and models for the younger generation were more varied and unstable. Barring outstanding personalities like Mahatma Gandhi, Nehru and Lal Bahadur Shastri, they did not seem to have any clear-cut role-models from whom they derived inspiration and after whom they would like to shape their conduct. The young displayed relatively greater variety in their choice. Apart from the three personalities mentioned earlier, they referred to a large number of figures from the political world, some being quite obscure local personalities, and even film stars and sports champions. It was also observed that all their models belonged to the contemporary world, and that in their choice, there was little general agreement among themselves. Unlike the young, the older sample mentioned even mythological and legendary personalities frequently, and confined their choice generally to well-known mythological, historical, or contemporary people famous for their contributions to the fields of science, literature, politics, religion, and social reform. Lack of agreement and a high degree of diversity in the choice of models reflect uncertainty and instability of role-models for the young. However, it is to be observed that when the subject was asked to indicate the qualities which he thought made those persons great, there was considerable agreement not only among the two groups representing the young, but also between the younger and older generations. The most frequently mentioned qualities were patriotism, statesmanship, humanitarianism, social reform and so on. It may be noted that though these were frequently mentioned by the young as qualities that made their heroes great, many of the heroes chosen (for example, film stars, cricket players, etc.) were such that these qualities could hardly be said to reside in them. This emphasizes further the ambiguity of role-models among the young.

## The Second Study

Similar uncertainty and instability was noticed in the analysis of evaluation of incidents representing socio-moral transgressions. It may be mentioned that compared with the older generation, the young displayed a more permissive and less condemnatory stance. This was true for six out of twelve events which were evaluated. However, what was more intriguing was that there was a sizable proportion of uncertain 'neutral' responses to most of these situations. This was particularly high among the two samples representing the young. In other words, when confronted with a socio-moral dilemma, the younger generation displayed considerable hesitation in judging it either as proper or improper, and preferred to suspend judgment. In at least half the incidents presented to them, one-fifth to one-third of the evaluative responses were 'neutral'. The corresponding figures among the older generation of teachers were some ten to fifteen per cent lower. In other words, faced with situations involving socio-moral issues, the younger generation tended to vacillate and suspend judgement more than the older. Thus, youth reflected a comparatively weak super-ego development and a failure to reconcile with the changing moral codes. The net result was a relative lack of certainty about their opinions and judgments. Or, to put it in the words of Nirad Chaudhuri, they were 'torn by their internal psychological tussles'.

# The Third Study

On the qualities considered desirable or undesirable in a person it was observed that there was no difference between the young and the old on the so-called 'cardinal virtues' like honesty, duty, non-violence and so on. However, it was observed that there was greater agreement regarding the importance of these among the two groups belonging to the same generation than between the groups representing different generations. Further, such a concurrence was small regarding qualities which were considered undesirable in a person. While the younger teachers and students agreed among themselves regarding qualities considered undesirable (correlation being 0.88), there was only moderate agreement between the young and the old (correlation being 0.49 between older teachers and students, and 0.48 between older teachers and young teachers).

On another measure, the difference between the young and the old was reflected in the perception and evaluation of some 'ambiguous' traits. During pre-testing, twelve behavior traits were found to yield 'ambiguous' responses, i.e., these traits were such that they had almost equal probability of being judged as either desirable or undesirable in a person. On these behavior traits differences were observed between the generations. Evaluation of some of these behavior traits among the young and the old was divergent. With regard to some, like cunning (*chalak*), opportunist (*avsarvadi*) and the like, the young tended to regard them more frequently as 'desirable', while the older generation viewed them as 'undesirable'. The case was similar with qualities like sentimental (*bhavuk*) and restless (*chanchal*) where the differences were in the reverse direction. In other words, such evaluative differences of a few so-called 'ambiguous' behavior traits were indicative of the divergence in values. Further, such differences in perception made it difficult for the young to adopt and accept the members of the older generation as their model.

# Conclusion

The above findings illustrate a number of points. There is a value ambiguity among the young, as a result of which they are not able to have clear-cut evaluative responses to certain socio-moral issues. This ambiguity reflects a socio-moral dilemma faced by them and a vacillation and uncertainty characterizing their handling of such situations.

The reason for this ambiguity in the young can only be guessed. One of the factors which is likely to be operating is the relative lack of exposure in the older generation to mass media while the younger generation is almost completely immersed in various mass media like radio, films, television, the press, and magazines so that the world of arts, sports, entertainment and contemporary events are constantly brought within their psychological field, leading to a proliferation of role-models available to them while the choice of the older generation was largely limited to the figures and personalities about whom they had heard from their elders in the form of stories and legends or read in books which projected more or less unambiguous roles for them, the young are confronted with a large array of 'not-so-important' figures that have been made familiar to them by the mass media. As a result, the young have available to them a wide range of models for making their choice. The proliferation of roles with which they are confronted, make it difficult for them to identify completely with any set of clear-cut roles or personalities, which is important in the formation of ego-identity. This is reflected in the fact that, barring a few exceptions, the frequencies of choice in selecting a particular figure as a hero was relatively low in the younger group. Since heroes for the contemporary generation were diverse, mostly consisting of minor personalities; it can be asserted that by and large there was an absence of what may be called normative models for the youth as a group. While the outstanding heroes could provide definite roles, the roles tended to get largely obscured in the person of minor heroes.

The young very rarely found their identification models among the great personalities of the past. This is indicative of the absence of a link with the past and with traditional values. A mature psychological identity presupposes a subjective sense of continuous existence, and a coherent memory. It is anchored in the past and at the same time links itself to the future. This continuity did not seem to exist in the case of the young.

It is often suggested that in the process of identity formation the individual looks to some persons, usually parents, teachers, elders or someone from his peer group, whom he tries to emulate and whose qualities he tries to introject into himself. They provide him with guidelines for conduct and help him in resolving identity confusion. But the sample of youth studied seldom found inspiration from personalities from the past, and also very rarely chose their parents or teachers as their role-models. The reason for this is not hard to find. It is quite likely that for the bulk of the rural youth who had 'migrated' from the villages to the university or the colleges with new aspirations and professional goals, the values and life-patterns represented by their parents, had very little worth emulating. Once they had shifted to the cities, they were completely overwhelmed by the pattern of life, the new norms prevalent on the campuses, and were dazzled by the new values. Parents in some cases may have been the focus of identification earlier, but at least at this stage they had ceased to play any significant role in providing models for conduct and life-goals to the younger generation.

A similar attitude is fostered by the students towards their teachers, which is indicative of the psychological distance between the two groups. A general attitude of hostility towards teachers has lately developed in many educational institutions. Whatever the reason for this rejection, the diversity and uncertainty of the response of youth indicate that they not only reject the past but also their parents and teachers. These have not been replaced by other stable models, so that as a group the young do not possess clear-cut role-models, which make the resolution of identity confusion more difficult.

It is further observed that the elders who could constitute the role-models for the young are themselves often perceived as presenting an ambiguous facade. It is suggested that the elders of today when they were themselves young could easily identify and find role-models among the older generation of that time because the latter belonged to a more stable society and presented figures which were not torn by contradictions (see also Sinha, 1962). But this is no longer the case with contemporary youth. Due to value contradictions and conflicts which have beset them in a fast changing world, the older generation of today, who could have provided guidelines of conduct, have in their own lives failed to provide stable models free from ambiguity and contradictions. It is felt that the consequent role-ambiguity and ambiguity of values which confront the youth have intensified the problem of resolution of identity confusion. It shows itself in a kind of 'role refusal' on the part of the young, and is reflected in unrest on the campuses, the development of a 'counter culture', end intergenerational differences which is creating tension in many spheres of India's social life. The absence of ideological commitment, which seems to characterize youth on many campuses, further complicates the problem of identity formation.

# 8

# Basic Indian Values and Behaviour Dispositions in the Context of National Development: An Appraisal*

In popular parlance as well as among serious-minded social scientists, there is a widespread view that people of a country or a nation possess some features that are distinct not only with regard to physique and skin pigmentation but also socio-psychological characteristics. They are not superficial behaviour descriptions or mere stereotypes but constitute 'high level abstractions that refer to stable, generalized dispositions or modes of functioning and may take great variety of concrete behavior forms' (Inkeles and Levinson, 1969, p. 426). In the present chapter an attempt has been made to identify certain values, systems of belief and behaviour dispositions that characterize the Indian people, and discuss their relevance in the context of national development. Without getting involved in the intricate controversies of defining basic values or of the existence or otherwise of what has been termed the 'national character', 'basic' or 'model personality', it is asserted that there exists in every society 'learned cultural behaviour' (Mead, 1951, p. 81), and that there is regularity with which certain values or patterned behavior sequences are manifested in any culture. It is suggested that the environment which

* Reproduced, with permission, from Sinha, D. Basic Indian Values and Behaviour Dispositions in the Context of National Development: An Appraisal. In D. Sinha and H.S.R. Kao (eds), *Social Values and Development: Asian Perspectives* (1988, pp. 31–55). New Delhi: SAGE Publications.

This text has been edited for typographical errors, stylistic consistency and sequential organization in order to make it suitable for inclusion in the book.

includes the socio-cultural system in which, the individual grows leaves an indelible mark on his outlook, attitudes and modes of behaviour. Individuals in a culture grow to adulthood with certain common capacities and incapacities for organizational behaviour and a shared approach to social interaction which is different from that found in other cultures. Without getting involved in controversies about the 'national character' or 'basic personality structure', it is observed that writers, novelists, historians, travelers and social scientists from time to time have given surprisingly similar impressions and characterization of the Indian people, their values, outlook to life and behaviour dispositions. An attempt has been made here to outline them and discuss their relevance in the context of the requirements of rapid economic growth and national development.

The discussion is organized under two broad heads: (a) basic values and attitudes that have been inculcated in the Indian as a part of his religio-philosophical and cultural heritage and historical experiences, and (b) basic dispositions, typical modes of behaviour and interactional patterns that have engendered through certain socialization practices, familial experiences and institutional demands. Both these dimensions are in close interaction. They have been discussed separately for the sake of clarity and convenience. Further, the treatment by no means is exhaustive. Some salient values and dispositions that have been emphasized by scholars of different callings and which appear to be significant to national development generally and to economic growth in particular have been selected.

It should be noted that due to enormous diversity it is risky to talk of Indian or even Hindu values and dispositions. Yet, in spite of much diversity there are common strands that run through its cultural, social, regional, linguistic and other divergences. There is a distinct Hindu view of life (Radhakrishnan, 1968). Nehru (1946/1981, pp. 61–62) in *The Discovery of India* while pointing to the diversities in physical appearances as well as in certain mental habits and traits of peoples hailing from different regions and divisions of Indian life based on castes, religions and degree of cultural development, asserted that 'all of them have their distinctive features, *all of them have still more the distinctive mark of India*' and in spite of all the differences 'yet have been throughout these ages distinctively Indian, with the same national heritage and the same set of moral and mental qualities. There was something living and dynamic about his heritage which showed itself in ways of living and a philosophical attitude to life and its problems' (emphasis added).

He frequently refers to 'the impress of India'. Irrespective of all the diversities, there has developed a unity of outlook and values that is peculiarly Indian.

# Basic Indian Values

Max Weber (1958a) in his essay *The Protestant Ethic and the Spirit of Capitalism* tried to isolate some aspects of culture and interrelate them to economic growth. The rise of capitalism was attributed to certain motivational and attitudinal changes which were an outcome of the reinterpretation of Christianity in the west which conferred sanctity on the pursuit of wealth but prescribed limitation, on its consumption. Though Weber (1958b) was aware of many pitfalls in his interpretation of Hinduism, he found the religion irrational and deeply rooted in the demoralizing and deadening pessimism of the law of *karma*. Hinduism was considered lacking the essence of Protestant ethic—something that was the crux of economic development in the west. As a result, failure of economic development in India was considered inevitable.

In spite of the criticisms leveled against 'Weber' his work has inspired many social scientists not only to identify the basic religio-cultural values of the Indian, but also to relate his religion and culture to economic development. Such efforts are controversial but represent an approach that all the same is useful in understanding the process of economic reconstruction in developing countries. In fact, the study of economic development can no longer ignore the analysis of the role of institutions, values and belief-systems and basic character and behaviour dispositions of people that develop in a particular socio-cultural environment.

Certain personality characteristics fostered by basic Indian values are considered dysfunctional to modern development. Narain's (1957) description based on the analysis of themes in films and proverbs, as 'mild, passive, dependent, other-worldly and non-materialistic, conditioned by the basic values of the Hindu religion such as renunciation and by social institutions, such as the family', or Spratt's (1966) characterizations passive, inner-directed and narcissistic are cases in point.

According to Segal (1966, p. 119), a famous writer of Indian origin from West India, it is due to the pervasive attitude of acceptance that 'such a society generates no mass revolution of rising expectations, and plans for any sustained economic advance must stumble constantly against popular indifference'. Emphasizing the non-economic aspects of economic development, Sovani (1963, p. 274) has asserted that the causes of the present malaise in India lie deeper in the Hindu culture and personality which have shown 'deadening efficiency' in maintaining the status quo. As such, 'one can hardly experience right type of social change to arise naturally from within the Hindu society'. Viewing the basic Indian values and character, Vikas Mishra (1962) has concluded that the attitudes and institutions associated with Hinduism, which encouraged economic development earlier, became hindrances after the advent of factories.

Kapp (1963) has made a distinct attempt to relate the Hindu culture and personality to economic planning and development in India. He has begun with the assumption that institutional arrangements often stand in the way of a more rational use of available resources and they may well offer the main explanation for the slow rate of development of many underdeveloped economies. Following Max Weber, he contends that the basic religious values of Hinduism, namely sanyas (renunciation), maya (illusion) and karma (action), and the social institutions of the joint family and the caste system are the main barriers to economic development. The deep-seated belief in *karma* and the endless cosmic causation inculcates in the individual an attitude of resignation and acceptance of the *status quo*, or whatever may befall the individual. The law of karma, in other words, lends a fatalistic coloring to the outlook of the individual, and the responsibility of action is regarded as belonging to the agency outside of him (i.e., external locus of control) and which has been in existence and operation over endless durations of time exceeding the life span of the individual. It is 'a perfect example of religious rationalization of existing incongruities of suffering' (Kapp, 1963, p. 15) and misfortune, and inculcates an attitude of fatalism. The causal relationship between the individual and his action assumes an almost mystical and supernatural character not subjected to rational comprehension and human control. It makes the acceptance of one's lot and that of others as the inevitable result of karma (action) which is not easily modified by human effort and action. It also leads to the attitude of acceptance of the imperfect world and the human condition without the desire to modify, master, or improve it. This attitude is very clearly reflected in a majority of the people who accept the status quo, however imperfect it may be by saying 'kya farak parta hai' (what difference does it make?) and is enshrined by the great epic poet Tulsidas in a verse in the Ramayana: *Kou nripa hohi hame kya hani*i (What harm does it come to me whoever may be the king?). Kapp (1963, p. 43) has observed cyclical time and cosmological causation belong to those basic categories of Hinduism which stand in the way of the emergence of one basic prerequisite of economic development, namely, the conviction that man does make his own history and that while the conditions under which he makes history are given, social and economic progress are not a matter of blind destiny but depend upon human choices and social action.

The conclusion was inevitable that Hindu culture and Hindu social organization are determining factors in India's slow rate of development. It is not only the lack of capital resources or skilled manpower which impedes the process of economic growth but non-secular pre-technological institutions and values such as the hierarchically organized caste system, the limited or static levels of aspirations, moral aloofness, casteism and factionalism—to name only a few of the major barriers (Kapp, 1963, p. 64). According to him the lasting solution of the problem of economic development could be found only in the gradual and systematic transformations of India's social system, her outlook to life and the levels of personal aspirations.

A foreigner invariably observes not only the rampant poverty and the fatalistic submission to it, but the indifference of the people towards human misery and squalor. Ronald Segal (1966, p. 14) pointedly remarked that Indian poverty is unique not because there are hundreds of millions of poor, but because of the indifference to poverty and the fatalistic submission to it. People in the degradation of slums live not with anger, hatred, violence and cruelty, but with death-like indifference. A recent observer of the squalid life and miseries of Calcutta slums, Dominique Lapierre (1986, p. 75) marvelled how 'people could actually remain good humoured in the middle of so much abjection'. 'They knew that if they were poor it was not their fault, but the fault of the cyclical or permanent maledictions that beset the places where they came from' (p. 45). The author was so impressed by the 'radiant expression' that people maintained in spite of all miseries that he called it 'The City of Joy'.

Roots of fatalism and the attitude of acceptance have been attributed not only to the religio-philosophical background but also to the nature of the physical environment and the climate that characterize the Indian subcontinent. Carl Jung once suggested that mountains restrict the horizons of the mind. In the same strain, the famous historian Professor A.L. Basham has hinted that the natural and geographical phenomena characterizing the Indian subcontinent have shaped the basic dispositions of the Indian people. To quote Basham (1971, p. 3),

It has often been said that the scale of natural phenomena in India, and her total dependence on the monsoon have helped to form the character of her peoples. Even today major disasters, such as flood, famine and plague, are hard to check, and in older times their control was almost impossible.

Many other ancient civilizations such as those of the Greeks, Romans and Chinese had to contend with hard winters, which encouraged sturdiness and resource. India, on the other hand, was blessed by a bounteous Nature, who demanded little of man in return for sustenance but in her terrible anger could not be appeased by human effort. Hence, it has been suggested that *Indian character has tended to fatalism and quietism, accepting fortune and misfortune alike without complaint.* (Emphasis added)

In view of the outstanding achievements of ancient times in the shape of splendid temples and immense irrigation works, Basham has doubted that the Indian attitude to life suggests a devitalized people.

He has added that:

If climate had any effect on the Indian character it was, we believe, to develop a love of ease and comfort, an addiction to simple pleasures and luxuries so freely given by Nature—a tendency to which the impulse of self-denial and asceticism on the one hand, and occasional strenuous effort on the other, were natural reactions. (1971, p. 4)

It is this aspect which is referred to as '*aram culture*' or a tendency to seek comfort and ease and the avoidance of sustained effort and hard work which is obviously inimical to a proper work culture.

There are some other basic values shared by the vast majority of Indians. The emphasis on *moksha* (salvation) is considered the ultimate goal in Hindu scheme of things. The fusion of the individual self (*atman*) with the infinite (*Brahman*) constitutes the terminal goal of life (*moksha*). Without getting into the details of how this ultimate goal is to be realized it is to be noted that 'release from worldly involvement' (Kakar, 1978) is regarded as its integral component and remains a vital goal of life even among the most modern Hindus. It has been suggested that the other-worldly attitude and the emphasis on non-involvement with the material world tend to detract the individual from the pursuit of economic objectives.

The pursuit of wealth (*artha*) and sexual satisfaction (*kama*) are, of course, components of the four cardinal values, and are considered legitimate in a phase of one's life. But in the Hindu view of life they are not given the same importance as the other two constituents, viz., *dharma* (duty) and *moksha* (salvation). They are subordinated to the overriding value orientation of Hindu religion which regards them as illusory, occupying a very inferior place of contemplation, renunciation and liberation. Thus, Kapp (1963, p. 18) observes that there remains 'an unresolved dualism within the present human situation which explains the paradoxical coexistence in one culture system of contradictory value orientations and actual behaviour patterns. This dualism must itself give rise to contradictory strivings and ambivalent feelings weakening human motivation'. Added to this is the general injunction of curbing one's aspirations and the attitude of 'desireless or detached action' as emphasized in the Bhagvadgita. Non-attachment to the fruit or consequences of action may be conductive to lessening of strain and stress (Pande and Naidu, 1986) but at the same time is likely to promote a lack of interest in the formulation of a proper plan of action and ultimately lead to an attitude of indifference to the results of one's action altogether. It is believed that such an attitude precludes proper operation of the reinforcement principle. With the attendant belief in *maya* or in the illusory and transitory character of the world, it operates as a factor weakening motivation. In any case, an attitude of non-attachment to fruits of action and renunciation along with the belief in the inevitable karma is generative of a limited or static level of aspiration and achievement which is not conducive to economic efforts. In fact, Taylor (1948) noted that the basic personality of the orthodox Hindu was characterized by low aspiration, passivity and conformity. Kusum Nair (1961), interviewing farmers and poor-peasantry, has reported a lack of desire and aspiration to raise living standards. She has observed that the levels of aspiration had a 'limited, static ceiling, but bottomless floor' (p. 193). Similar results have been obtained by Sinha (1969) who compared farmers from highly developed and extremely undeveloped villages on a number of measures of motivation. Irrespective of their level of economic development, villagers had a stagnant level of aspiration, low striving, absence of risk-taking. They were characterized by extreme caution and risk avoidance. Such a motivational syndrome was not calculated to provide the necessary and sustained urge towards socio-economic development among Indian farmers. Withdrawal of governmental support after a period of massive developmental activity has often been found to lead to a rapid decline in the areas concerned. The stagnant level of aspiration combined with the absence of striving and risk-taking account for the fact that Indian developmental programmes are not self-generating and self-sustaining. Kusum Nair (1961) has also pointed out that 'a community's attitude to work can be a more decisive determinant for raising productivity in Indian agriculture than material resources or for that matter even technology.'

McClelland (1961, p. 357), who regards need for achievement as the key psychological variable and an important factor in the entrepreneurial success of individuals and in the economic growth of nations, remarked that n-Ach is not encouraged by Hinduism. With Hinduism explicitly teaching 'that concern with earthy achievements is a snare and a delusion', it is hard to see how devout Hindu parents would set high standards of excellence for their son's performance. Thus, those who subscribe to his theory on the relationship of need for achievement with economic and entrepreneurial activities regard low n-Ach that Hinduism tends to generate as the most important block of development.

# Basic Dispositions, Typical Modes of Behaviour and Interactional Patterns

Apart from many basic values that are accepted widely and cherished some dispositions, modes of behaviour and interaction patterns that seem to characterize the Indian people have been commented upon in the context of the contemporary need for national development.

Once again, though historians, writers, psychiatrists, and psychologists have provided a very complex picture of the Indian psyche, it is indeed surprising that their portrayals are remarkably similar. It has been contended that the basic Hindu personality is characterized not only by low aspirations, but also by passivity and conformity (Taylor, 1948) and that the Indian child learns to conform at the cost of personal initiative and capacity to make decisions. Koestler (1960) has argued that the joint family and the caste system have been responsible for ingraining the reluctance to take decisions and evade responsibility. He has viewed the process of character formation in the family as kind of 'de-boning process inspired by the model of shapeless, spineless non-individuals, drifting through the world of illusions towards the ultimate deep sleep of "nirvan"' (p. 155). For him, 'out of the sacred womb of the Indian family only yes-men could emerge.' As result, he concluded that 'India is a democracy in name only; it would be more correct to call it Bapucracy' (p. 150).

In a controversial psychoanalytic portrayal of a group of individuals in a Rajput village, Carstairs (1957) has described the basic features of Hindu personality as being permeated with paranoid reactions of mutual distrust, emotional insecurity, ambivalence and indecision, which results from 'betrayal by the mother' of the child after initial indulgence. Such a sudden shift from total and almost unchecked indulgence by the mother to new inflexible standards of feeding, toilet and sleeping norms (Kakar, 1978, p. 33; Sinha, 1987) is said to produce insecurity and anxiety in the child (Sinha, 1962).

Another feature of the basic disposition that has been emphasized by many scholars is that of dependency and its attendant characteristics. Taylor (1948, p. 5) has remarked that the very nature of familial interactions develop an acute sense of dependence by the extreme, emphasis on subjugation to parental authority, minimizing of opportunities for personal initiative in socially significant fields of action, and the inculcation of a clear sense of subordination to social and religious sanctions which transcend even parental authority. As such, the Indian child learns to conform at the cost of personal initiative and the capacity to make decisions. Personal initiative is replaced by obedience and conformity, and security for the individual is associated with dependence upon superiors (Taylor, 1948; Asthana, 1956; Carstairs, 1957). On the basis of clinical experience, Ramanujam (1979) has reported that 'unarticulated bond between son and his father persists even after the son grows up. Even in (Indian) adults there are almost a nostalgic desire for approval and sanction of father at every step.' Analyzing the essential features of the socialization processes in Indian children, Minturn and Hitchcock (1966) have observed that there was sparing use of reinforcement, reliance almost solely on punishment to control the child and excessive use of 'don't' in guiding his behaviour. The content of the mother's scolding seldom contained a description of desired behavior. Training in self-reliance was almost as negligible as training in responsibility. The mother reinforced dependency, and seldom provided opportunities to the child to solve his own problems—a feature also noted by L.B. Murphy (1953). There is 'the crystallization of dependency complex' (Kapp, 1963, p. 59.) Dependence proneness is considered to be a common characteristic of Indians (J.B.P. Sinha, 1970). The roots of dependency do not lie simply in the familial reactions but in the religious tradition of bhakti (devotion) which demands from the devotee 'abandoning all commendable acts, seek shelter with me alone, I will liberate you from all sins; do not worry at all' (Bhagvadgita, Chapter 18, verse 66). In terms of the superior–subordinate relationship it implies complete dependence on the powerful, maintaining total dependency and affective intimacy and remaining faithful to him only. In other words, the strong demand of loyalty and compliance from the dependent seems to characterize interpersonal relationships in this country at all levels of functioning. As Pandey (1980) has observed, in this kind of relationship ingratiation is frequently employed which is 'a risk free strategy for manipulating each other.' Observers of the contemporary scene have often remarked on the sycophancy that is so rampant, and the modes of ingratiation that have been perfected in the superior–subordinate relationship. It has also been suggested that through ingratiation, the subordinate becomes part of the powerful entity and feels powerful. Dependency in such a relationship is a means to feel powerful (McClelland, 1975).

A related aspect of dependency in the Indian social system and relationship is the hierarchical structure (Dumont, 1970; Kakar, 1978; Roland, 1980) and cognitively arranging relationships in a hierarchical order (J.B.P. Sinha, 1982). Groups are socially isolated from others through elaborate regulations and restrictions imposed by the hierarchical position. Hierarchical structuring is so ingrained in India that it is easier to work in a superior–subordinate role than as equals (Kothari, 1970). Status differences and hierarchies were not only due to instrumental necessity but contained cultural and ideological, elements, and were a 'carry-over of preindustrial elements into modern work organizations' (p. 299).

As for the nature of interpersonal relationships, content analysis of stories from school text-books revealed that in all cases the image of the superior was that of an autocrat, either assertive or nurturant, who enforced his/her authority primarily by providing emotional rewards to, and arousing guilt in the subordinate individual (Kakar, 1971a). The acceptance of authority was so complete that it took the form of 'active submission of subordinates leading to the development of individuals with strong and enduring need for dependency as a part of their core personality' (p. 100). The image of the superior was nurturant or assertive, never impersonal or fraternal. In another study (Kakar, 1971b), the authority patterns in Indian organizations were found to be dominated by the parental ideology of authority relations.

There is ample evidence that in Indian organizations, be it governmental, officials, labor leaders and managers in both Indian and foreign-owned firms, assertive superiors dominate authority relations, and that top managements are authoritarian (Myers, 1960, p. 116). As Kakar (1971b) points out, 'Along with cases of paternalism, that is, nurturance, this element of assertiveness in superior behaviour is not only a characteristic of top management but also a feature of authority relations at all levels in organizations' (p. 299).

In the context of conditions for effective functioning of modern work organizations, it has been emphasized that autonomy, initiative, readiness to take responsibility and decision-making are considered to be highly functional qualities. The high degree of dependence, highly hierarchical relationship, excessive demands for compliance are often regarded as constraints, having a negative effect on subordinate performance and satisfaction. In fact, Pareek (1968) in his paradigm of development has not only emphasized the need for extension along with need for achievement but has also suggested that dependence motive contributes negatively to development.

A few other dispositions have been mentioned as characteristic of the behaviour of Indians, and are often considered not conducive to effective organizational functioning. In recent years, some scholars have contrasted individualistic and collectivistic orientations, viewing the latter as not being very conducive to rapid development (Triandis, 1984). It has also been contended that most eastern cultures foster collective orientation. It has been suggested that in the Indian psyche, there is constant affective reciprocity, strong mutual caring where emotional connectedness is always central, a constant flow of affect between persons, and any feelings disruptive to the relationship are contained and inhibited. Ego boundaries are more open to others and there is little psychological space around oneself (Roland, 1980). As J.B.P. Sinha (1982a, p. 153) has observed, 'Hindu experienced self is more structured around we, ours, and us than around I, mine or me. There is preference to belonging to a collectivity and to undermine autonomy, initiative, and individualism.' It has been observed that Indians tend to cluster together (McClelland, 1975). Even some novelists who have described the Indian setting have pointed to the 'network' of ties that bind the people in a collective whole. 'Every individual in India is always linked to the rest of the social body by a network of incredibly diversified ties, with the result that no one in this gigantic country of seven hundred and fifty million inhabitants could ever be completely abandoned' (Lapierre, 1986, p. 56).

With this ever present 'network' of ties, it is not surprising that personalized relationship is the common strategy in interpersonal functioning, and that 'contractual relationship of the West smells selfish and short-sighted' (J.B.P. Sinha, 1982b, p. 154). Interrelationships that characterize modern work organizations are contractual, rather than personalized. In the Indian setting, there develops a tendency to cultivate a relationship which, instead of requiring instant and exact exchange, is maintained by affect loaded reciprocity from both sides of the hierarchy with long time perspective (J.B.P. Sinha, 1982a, p. 154).

According to Kapp (1963, p. 581), both the collective orientation and the highly personalized kind of relational patterns that the Indian likes to develop are not very suited to the demands of modern organizations. He talked of group directed pattern of values and aspirations that emerges in the context of caste and joint family which are so integral to the developmental setting of the individual. The attitude of 'submergence of the individual in the group' is carried over into all performance and professional relationships which is not conducive to the development of an impersonal work discipline and commitment to an impersonal organization. Indeed, discipline, orderliness, precision and punctuality for the sake of such an impersonal organization, may be rejected as pedantic, tyrannical and intolerable (Kapp, 1963, p. 60). The individual prefers a more personal kind of relationship which a modern industrial complex is not likely to offer. There is lack of commitment to an impersonal work organization.

A few more behaviour orientations characterizing the Indian people have been discussed in the context of their relevance to effectiveness of developmental and organized activities. In spite of the collective orientation and a strong tendency to submerge the individual in a group, it is indeed paradoxical that in day-to-day functioning an average Indian is very selfish, displays extreme forms of egotism, and lack of consideration. He shows disregard for the 'others' who do not belong to the 'own' category (J.B.P. Sinha, 1982a, p. 157). Such blatant 'lack of concern for others' is encountered constantly whether in travel, civic behaviour or other places of daily activity. It has also been suggested that an Indian has no sense of neighoourhood and seldom thinks of himself as a member of a community. This coexistence of a high degree of individualism and a sharp 'self' and 'other' distinction with collectivism and the dictum of *vasudhaib kutumkam* ('the entire universe is your relation') makes the Indian psyche appear to be very paradoxical. In any case, this ego-centeredness, lack of consideration and concern for others make the emergence of shared and common goals of collective activity difficult.

Indians seem to possess an unusually strong disposition for social comparison. They 'tend to compare with incomparable ones for all conceivable things. Striving for material things along with a sense of insecurity that they may not have enough keep them extra concerned regarding where they stand on the scale of affluence' (J.B.P. Sinha, 1982a, p. 156). An intense social comparison makes even the most powerful person constantly insecure and he feels threatened about his own power base, and is always in the midst of imaginary threats. The phenomenon is well exemplified in the mythological story of Indra, the all-powerful king of the heavens. Whenever anyone undertook penance, austerity and meditation (tapasya) for his own spiritual uplift, he would feel a threat to his throne and to distract and disturb him Indra would dispatch the prettiest of heavenly damsels and dance girls. Such an insecure disposition affects the individual's interpersonal functioning and is inimical to collective effort towards common goals.

In the Indian psyche as well as in the modes of behaviour, juxtaposition of opposites has often been observed and commented upon. Down the ages, instead of assimilation or integration of diverse cultural influences into a unified system, what seems to have taken place is a kind of coexistence of disparate elements without any synthesis. An analysis of the situation over centuries provides the historical setting for such dichotomies that seem to characterize the Indian psyche. Down the ages, India was exposed to many cultural influences and most of these were by way of invasions from its north-western frontiers. In spite of the unique capacity of India and Hinduism to assimilate often hostile elements into some kind of a unique socio-cultural structure, there was nothing like a complete merger into one homogenous and cohesive system as seems to have been the case in European countries, where it was impossible for European tribes to coexist within the same territory, they invariably merged with one another. But in India, because an enormous number of dissimilar people had to find a way of living together, separate coexistence not merger became the pattern. As a Cambridge historian has observed, no single basic Indian culture has been developed and elaborated through the ages (Spear, 1968, p. 7). The wonder of India is that these layers which have not fused into one unified system have 'produced not an amorphous collection of hostile groups' but some kind of 'unity in diversity' reflected clearly in art, architecture and world view. It is clear that neither a 'melting pot' mechanism nor a 'local blending-machine' seems to have operated in the Indian context.

This historical phenomenon explains the lack of homogenization in Indian culture and religion into a unified system with one mainspring idea governing the entire life style. As the historian Schulberg (1968, p. 17), referring to the influx of diverse cultural groups into India through the ages, has remarked, 'Hinduism did not absorb those people; *it enfolded them*' (emphasis added). Any group with its special customs and life styles which came to India, lived apart and amicably side by side with those already there in a kind of cultural coexistence. Dumont (1970) has designated it as an encompassing system where seemingly contradictions of thoughts and actions, instead of leading to confrontation, are tolerated, balanced, accommodated and integrated (Marriot, 1976). It is this unique tolerance of contradictions which sometimes appears paradoxical in the Indian psyche, and has frequently been commented upon by travelers, social scientists and observers of the Indian scene.

The famous writer and a sharp critic of the Indian character, Nirad Chaudhuri (1966) has called Indians 'Janus Multifrons', 'torn by their internal psychological tussles', and has talked about 'the creation of a double consciousness, each complete and coherent but capable of shutting out the other when one is dominant'. He has also pointed out the 'terrible dichotomy' of the Hindu personality, a large number of antithetical though connected traits which shape his behaviour: 'a sense of solidarity with an uncontrollable tendency towards disunity; collective megalomania with self-abasement; extreme xenophobia with abject xenolaty; authoritarianism with anarchic individualism; violence with non-violence; militarism with pacifism; possessiveness with carelessness about property owned; courage with cowardice; cleverness with stupidity' (Chaudhuri, 1966). These 'opposites almost neutralize one another, and the indecisive tug-of-war stultifies all his actions'.

Arthur Koestler (1960) has also remarked about the Indian's basic predisposition to 'indifference to contradiction ... the peaceful coexistence of logical opposites in the emotional sphere.' Other writers have frequently talked about the same phenomenon. Ved Mehta (1959, p. 19) in *Walking the Indian Streets* has observed that India is a land of paradoxes, contradictions, and extremes on different planes. It 'has an uncanny way of bringing out extremes in people. . . . Our capacity for a single allegiance has been dulled. Instead we have developed an ability to be compassionate and cruel, sensitive and callous, deep and fickle' (p. 24). Again, in *Portrait of India*, Mehta (1962, p. 130) has pointed out that as in the past, to be a Hindu one does not have to practice any particular set of observances, adhere to any particular beliefs, accept any particular metaphysics. 'All gradations of beliefs, from the crudest to the most highly refined, have coexisted in Hinduism from the earliest times, making it the most syncretic religion in the world—what one of its students has called a tapestry of almost endless diversity of hues'.

In the slums of Calcutta, Lapierre (1986, p. 52) has observed similar contradictions, 'a land where the sublime often stood side by side with the worst this world can offer, but where both elements were always more vibrant, more human and ultimately more alluring than anywhere else', 'the best fortunately mixed with the worst' (p. 231).

Analyzing cultural factors in anxiety, Sinha (1962, p. 34) has remarked that an average Indian is 'caught in a chaos of conflicting patterns, none of them wholly condemned but no one of them dearly approved and free from confusion.' Such contradictions and queer juxtapositions are in evidence on the socio-political plane as well where khadi and handloom are combined with an expansion of textile mills, Gandhian sarvodaya with the building of a highly complex modern industrial society, cottage industry with mass production, private with public-sector, ahimsa (non-violence) with the worst kind of social violence (p. 35). Though some degree of 'cognitive compartmentalization' is observable in most societies in a state of transition (Dawson, 1963), 'tolerance of dissonance' appears to be specially characteristic of Indian social thinking.

Analyzing the evaluative responses to incidents of transgression of some socio-cultural norms, Sinha (1979, p. 61) has noted that young college students tend to be extremely vacillating, indecisive and prone to suspend their judgment. It was considered as indicative of value contradictions and inner conflicts that characterize the Indian psyche.

It has been suggested time and again that such unresolved conflicts and contradictions render the individual indecisive and stultify his action. This is reflected in vacillating and indecisive evaluative responses to incidents of socio-moral transgressions. The young manifested a strong propensity to suspend their judgment indicating thereby the value contradictions and inner conflicts that characterize the Indian psyche. It is, therefore, not surprising that India has been characterized as a 'soft state' (Myrdal, 1968) where there is a wide hiatus between what is resolved and what is put into action, between what is professed and what is practiced, and what is legislated and what is implemented. There are more 'rituals' and symbolic actions rather than actual action. A ritualistic start with a big fanfare often marks the fate of many of our large-scale developmental activities.

# Summing Up

It is generally agreed that despite an infinite variety and diversity in terms of ethnic characteristics, languages, religious and cultural backgrounds, there has been a sharing of some basic values, behaviour dispositions, and a common outlook to life that constitute the core of the Indian psyche. Some of the dominant values and dispositions have their roots in the religio-philosophical traditions in which the dominating influence has been that of Hinduism. These have been generative of the other-worldly outlook, attitude of renunciation, fatalism, passivity, static aspirations, dependence, hierarchical structure, preference for personalized relationships, emphasis on compliance and loyalty, collective orientation along with a lack of consideration, selfishness and distrust. Examined in the present day context of national development, they are considered as dysfunctional. To quote Singh (975, p. 94), 'disapproval of material and worldly things, lack of motivation for consumption, acceptance of the status quo, low aspirations, a pervasive sense of pessimism, fatalism, conformity, passivity, distrust, selfishness, and particularism' are all obviously great obstacles to economic development in India.

It is not the purpose of the present chapter to examine the concept of Indian national character or modal personality that is implied in most of the studies reviewed, or point to the drawbacks in their methodology and inadequate sampling. It would suffice here to say that the very heterogeneity of cultural influences that have operated and the diversities that constitute India make it highly risky to posit a modal Indian type in terms of values and behaviour modes. If one examines the literature closely, one comes across observations about values and dispositions of Indians that are often contradictory (Singh, 1975, p. 96). Carstairs (1957, p. 168), for example, says that there is less affection between Indian parents and children than what obtains in the west, and that in the presence of others they are indifferent to their children. On the other hand, Taylor (1948) and Minturn and Hitchcock (1966) have pointed out that there is more participation in adult life by Indian children. Carstairs (1957, p. 158) found weaning to be a very traumatic experience, while Minturn and Hitchcock (1966, p. 321) reported that weaning was not accompanied by any signs of emotional upset. Murphy (1953, p. 47) reported almost a complete absence of crying by children because they were put to the breast as soon as they became restless, whereas Minturn and Hitchcock (1966, p. 317) found that mothers took their own time to finish their jobs before attending to their children. Carstairs (1957) has observed deep feelings of emotional insecurity as a result of childhood experiences for some others it is just the opposite (Murphy, 1953; Taylor, 1948). What to speak of observations made by travellers and novelists, even those of psychologists and other social scientists appear to be impressionistic, crude and caricature-like and based on subjective observations. They constitute over-generalizations ignoring individual differences, often based on insufficient knowledge and prejudice rather than on systematic observations. Further, if one examines religious and philosophical literature, there are themes that are contradictory to what has been emphasized, especially by foreign observers and scholars. Though they may not be the most salient aspects of the Hindu way of life, wealth, worldly pleasures and themes supporting and encouraging economic and worldly pursuits have not been ignored or bypassed. There is no lack of practical values in Hindu society (Goheen,

Srinivas, Karve and Singer, 1958). Milton Singer (1956, p. 86) even goes to the extent of arguing that the theory of renunciation instead of being an obstacle has in fact been all along functionally linked to the material side of Indian life. Therefore, it is obvious, as Singh (1975, p. 100) has rightly observed,

> Any endeavour to examine the relationship between Hindu culture and economic development requires not merely a more comprehensive and more balanced consideration of Hinduism, that is, a consideration of both those aspects which may be detrimental to economic motivation and those which may be encouraging but empirical studies of attitudes and values induced by Hinduism and their exact relation with economic development.

There is need to know more about values and attitudes that *actually* form part of the Indian psyche, and the extent to which they operate in ordinary life rather than those inferred on the basis of Hindu metaphysical and ethical literature. The latter may be *expected* to mould Hindu attitudes and value system in a particular manner, but the same may not have actually occurred. There is always a gap between the expected or the ideal and the actual. From ancient texts and scriptures to contemporary attitudes and behaviour of Indians is a big leap fraught with dangers of erroneous over-generalizations.

In most of the studies reviewed it is implied, in some cases implicitly, that socio-cultural features of a traditional society interfere with the functioning of modern economic forces, and for proper growth they have to be changed and 'modernized' (Lewis, 1955; Rostow, 1952). Attitudinal modernity (Inkeles and Smith, 1974) and 'modernity syndrome' (Triandis, 1971), and certain psychological attributes are considered as essential requirements of modern industrial society. Value system and behaviour dispositions that characterize the traditional Hindu society have been regarded as incongruent to the demands of industrial and economic development. As Udy (1970, pp. 95–96) has observed:

> the main organizational transformation that must take place is a shift from socially determined to technologically determined forms of work. Crucial to this shift is the institution of contractual work, its successful competition with familial, reciprocal, and political work forms, and its development through employer specific and job specific arrangements to a firm position in a new occupational system grounded in industrial technology.

It is untenable to regard every aspect of a traditional culture, values, attitudes and modes of behaviour as dysfunctional per se, and thereby advocate wholesale adoption of western values and way of life or what goes by the name of 'modernity'. What is western or so-called modern is not the sine qua non of development. The negative consequences of economic growth and the expansion in the very concept of development to include social and human aspects besides that of economic progress has given way to that of human and endogenous development integrating economic, socio-cultural, psychological and other aspects of humans. Such a development corresponds to the internal characteristics of the society in question and its integrative qualities. As Alechina (1982, p. 19) has rightly pointed out, 'when a country develops endogenously, its way of life should be based on respect for its traditional values, for the authenticity of its culture, and for the creative aptitudes of its people'. Instead of blindly asserting that values and dispositions engendered by a traditional culture are invariably dysfunctional to development, it is necessary to examine the relationship more closely and identify those features which facilitate development in the particular socio-cultural context, and those that operate as obstacles.

The contention that Hindu culture and religious values weaken economic motivation and hinder development and modernization has not yet been conclusively supported by empirical studies. The few that have been conducted do not support a simple relationship and often yield conflicting findings. McClelland (1961) has demonstrated that need for achievement is an important factor in entrepreneurial success and in the economic growth of nations. Exposing individuals to a short programme of motivational boosting led to a significant heightening of entrepreneurial and business activities (McClelland and Winter, 1969). In Sinha's (1969) study, though the villagers generally manifested stagnant aspirations, risk avoidance and extreme caution, a comparison of farmers from highly developed and undeveloped villages did not reveal any motivational syndrome clearly associated with agro-economic development. Further, emotional aloofness combined with a high degree of control on the part of superiors, contrary to what is usually observed in American studies, seemed to have a positive effect on performance and satisfaction (Meade, 1967; Van den Ban and Thorat, 1968). Testing the functional utility of Indian authority patterns Kakar (1971b) found that affiliation had a significantly positive relationship and degree of task control had a significantly negative relationship both with performance and satisfaction. However, helping superior of the fraternal ideology was most positively related to work performance and satisfaction (Kakar, 1971b, p. 303). Cultural relativity of participative management has been emphasized and utility of establishing mutually supportive relationship has been pointed out (J.B.P. Sinha, 1974). Dependency is not regarded as an obstacle and a 'bugbear' as it has been done in the west. On the other hand, not only the applicability of the western model of participative and employee oriented leadership under Indian conditions has been questioned, but an alternative mood of nurturant task leader, more appropriate and effective under transitional socio-cultural conditions prevailing in India has been postulated (J.B.P. Sinha, 1980). It is task oriented having structured expectations from subordinate and draws upon familial and cultural values like affection, dependency, and need for personalized and mutually supportive relationship (De, 1974).

In this context, it should be noted that dependency as exhibited in Indian behaviour has not been properly understood and appreciated by western scholars. They have missed its developmental aspect—a progression from mere dependence to mutual dependence ultimately leading to 'dependability' (Sinha, 1986, p. 74). It represents the typical interpersonal transaction distinctive of a culture in which dependency is not only functional and developmental leading ultimately to a condition of mutual dependency and trust ('dependability'), but is also considered appropriate for therapeutic use (Neki, 1973). Dependency as exemplified by the guru chela (preceptor–pupil) relationship is not only regarded as a useful paradigm for psychotherapy, but can have its functional utility in the organized setting as well.

Another aspect which has not been properly appreciated by many Western scholars is the utility of collective orientation. It is doubtful whether untrammeled individualism practiced in some countries in the west can be functional in attaining the goal of economic development with social justice in the context of poverty and limited resources. There is experimental evidence to show that 'the usefulness of the n-Ach is burdened by the limitedness of resource.' Where resources were unlimited, higher n-Ach was found to yield maximum achievement in terms of quality and quantity of output. But when resources were limited, not only the total output suffered but the brunt was also borne by interpersonal and group liking as well as self-perception (J.B.P. Sinha, 1968). It also led to hoarding, use of resources for egoistic ends, monopolistic tendencies, and other undesirable practices (J.B.P. Sinha and Pandey, 1970) which are likely to be detrimental to rapid growth of the country. Rather than stretching the individualism–collectivism dichotomy too far, it is more useful to examine their relative utility and the extent of blend of the two that is functional to development under varying socio-cultural and resource conditions.

To throw light on the relationship between Hindu culture and need for achievement, Winter and McClelland (1975) made a comparative analysis of a few demographic and psychological characteristics of those who, as a result of n-Ach training programme, had changed in the desired direction and those who had not. The study had certain obvious limitations due to the small sample size and inadequacies in measuring significant aspects of Hindu culture. In any case, there was no evidence of a 'strong relationship between a participant's varna or caste grouping and whether he changes after the course' (p. 114). The conclusion was that 'one of the most significant differences between the changers and the inactives had nothing to do with religion or values' (p. 113). There is insufficient evidence to answer the question as to which aspects of Hindu culture encourage or inhibit need for achievement. As Winter and McClelland (1975, p. 123) have concluded, 'the connections between traditional values and modernization are neither so obviously true nor so simple as they might be thought to be'. Singer (1966) has rightly pointed out that change usually does not become consolidated by the disruption and destruction of the socalled 'traditional' values, but rather by reinterpretation or resynthesis along with new actions. A man can begin to act differently and yet hold traditional beliefs. Whatever resulting dissonance one would expect from this combination is handled by reinterpreting the old beliefs so that they do not conflict with new actions. Dissonance between the 'traditional' and the 'modern' may be reduced by presenting the new in a form that appears to be congruous with the old values. Usually dissonance is not handled by directly abandoning the old beliefs. In fact, abandonment of old beliefs may lead not to modernity but to confusion and cultural inertia (Shils, 1961). As Winter and McClelland (1975, p. 123) have remarked, 'Thus the notion that change can be, or must be, consistent with and harmonized with traditional values is not a naive sentimental hope', but to some extent a fact of life. Fatalistic religious beliefs by themselves do not necessarily inhibit commercial and economic growth. The manner and source of interpretation of these beliefs may be far more important. Given new interpretations, the so-called traditional beliefs may actually encourage economic activity, while abandoning these beliefs may lead to a situation where people are confused and interested only in the superficial prestige symbols of modern industrial culture (Winter and McClelland, 1975, p. 124).

The way in which old practices and rituals can be put to constructive use and be effectively utilized for mobilization of the people for nationalistic purposes has been well illustrated in the popularization of Ganesh Puja (worship of the elephant-headed god) in Maharashtra by Tilak and the prayer meetings and all the religious trappings that characterized Gandhi's various programmes of satyagraha against the British rule. There is not sufficient evidence to prescribe the necessity of wholesale modification of traditional values for national development even if such an enormous task was feasible. On the other hand, there are indications that many of the indigenous values and modes of behaviour can be effectively utilized for secular and developmental ends. In any case, the studies reviewed have emphasized the need for in depth analysis of the role of traditional social values and behaviour dispositions in national development. Merely asserting a relationship between the two, and that also a negative one, is not enough. What is more pertinent is the identification of those that are functional or otherwise, and unraveling the mechanism of their operation in various institutions and organizations that are the instruments of economic progress and development. Only through such an analysis their exact role can be understood and properly utilized for mobilization of human resources for national development.

# Part III
# Applied Concerns

# 9

# Towards an Ecological
# Framework of Deprivation*

Etymologically, the word "deprivation" is derived from the verb "to deprive" which means to dispossess or strip (a person or an object), and it implies a "felt loss". The reference obviously is to certain deficiencies in the environment, which are not only there but are also experienced as such by the individual. It relates to certain features or aspects of the environment that are absent or inadequate in certain degree which causes an impact on the functioning of the individual. Thus, when one talks of deprivation, the emphasis is on the relevant aspects of the environment which are deficient or wanted in some respects. Therefore, any conceptualization of deprivation should have due emphasis on the environment or the setting in which the individual operates. Unfortunately, despite behaviour being conceived in psychology as a result of interaction between the organism and the environment, one of the main weaknesses of this discipline for long has been the undue concern for individual variables and giving a short shrift to environment. If at all, only lip service is paid to environmental variables. Lewin's topological approach did try to set things on proper footing. But the individual and personalistic bias still persists. It is particularly the case with researches of psychologists in this country, as reflected in frequent papers and dissertations produced, that simply deal with the person and personality (and frequently using a vague omnibus expression like "psychological") variables, whether it be related to job

* Reproduced, with permission, from Sinha, D. (1982). Towards an Ecological Framework of Deprivation. In D. Sinha, R.C. Tripathi and G. Misra (eds), *Deprivation: Its Social Roots and Psychological Consequences.* New Delhi: Concept.

This text has been edited for typographical errors, stylistic consistency and sequential organization in order to make it suitable for inclusion in the book.

satisfaction, need for achievement, academic performance, adjustment and the like. Most of these ill-conceived researches implicitly at least imply that the individual functions as if in a vacuum. An individual's psychological processes can have meaning only if they are conceived in their proper setting or are viewed in terms of their interactions with the environment. Lewin's concept of "life space" does not seem to have made much impact on our thinking.

Further, in a lot of our studies, we find focus on a single variable at a time and attempt to "control out" all the others. This fear of "contamination" especially of the multifarious environmental variables underlies the fact that most of the psychological studies are of a nature which is removed from actual life situations. Concern for single variable has been largely responsible for generating artificiality in our studies so that the phenomenon studied remains removed from real life. 'More-than-one variable' experiments are certainly there. But even they have frequently not taken due cognizance of the environmental matrix. While the subject has gained in scientific rigour and taken it nearer to its goal of scientific precision and exactitude, it has been at a considerable cost. It has certainly made for scientific rigour, but often has in the process lost in relevance, so that it is frequently difficult to generalize to settings other than the one in which the experiment has been performed, and those concerned with practical applications of the results often find it useless when it comes to evolving an intervention programme. The emphasis on rigour has led to experiments that are elegantly designed but often limited in scope. Either the findings are too trite and commonplace, or of such a character that they are not generalizable to actual life situations. It is from this perspective probably that Bronfenbrenner in his invited address to the 1974 Convention of the American Psychological Association characterized much of contemporary developmental psychology as "the science of the strange behaviour of children in strange situations with strange adults for the briefest possible periods of time" (Bronfenbrenner, 1974a). If one substitutes the word "individual" or "organism" for "children", the statement is equally applicable to the bulk of contemporary psychology.

The main purpose of this discussion is to bring home some of the shortcomings of modern psychological researches, and to emphasize that behaviour is to be viewed not simply in terms of individual factors, nor the environmental factors as having isolated impact on the individual, but in the entire individual–environmental complex as a constant two-way interplay. Ecology, conceived as the study of biological forms in relations to their physical environment, or to put it in Lewinian terminology, as the study of these aspects of individual's environment which are important parts of his life space, provides a useful framework for conceptualizing most of the psychological processes. In its wider connotation, ecology is not confined to merely physical environment, but comprises the socio-cultural setting in which the individual operates. Two things are prominent in ecology: (a) a conceptualization of psychological adaptation in terms of person–environment congruence, and (b) a concern with effective coping (Holahan, 1977). Ecological perspective views psychological processes in true transactional terms. For example, in contrast to defining adjustment exclusively on the basis of internal personality dynamics, adjustment is construed in terms of transactional relationship between the individual and environmental setting in which he functions. Specifically, psychological adjustment may be defined as the state in which an individual's needs and proclivities for action are congruent with the demands and opportunities of the particular settings in which he operates. In addition, the ecological view emphasizes effective coping rather than adjustment or pathology.

Ecology provides a useful framework for understanding the psychological processes related to deprivation, and it has certain additional advantages in that it not only makes our research efforts more realistic, but also helps in suggesting some intervention strategies. In analyzing the impact of deprivation on certain perceptual skills, the author (Sinha, 1978) has followed closely a model suggested by Bronfenbrenner (1974a). The nature of environment provides the necessary sensory inputs, stimulation and experiential base for the development of perceptual skills of various kinds. The enduring environment of the child or his ecology may be conceived in terms of two concentric layers. The "upper" and the more visible layer contains his home, school, peer groups and so on, each providing three dimensions, namely, physical space and material, social roles and relationships of the child vis-a-vis other people, and his activities. The "supporting" or the "surrounding" layer embedding the former is provided by the geographic and physical environment and the institutional setting of the child in terms of his social class, caste and the general services and amenities available to him.

Home and its conditions in terms of over-crowding, space available to each member of the family, toys, pictorial and cultural materials in the home, technological devices used for general living and the like would constitute the most important visible "upper layer" influence on the individuals matched probably only by the nature and quality of schooling, and the facilities to which the individual child is exposed. In home as well as in the school, the nature of interpersonal relationships and activities that

**Figure 9.1**

*Ecological Model of Deprivation*

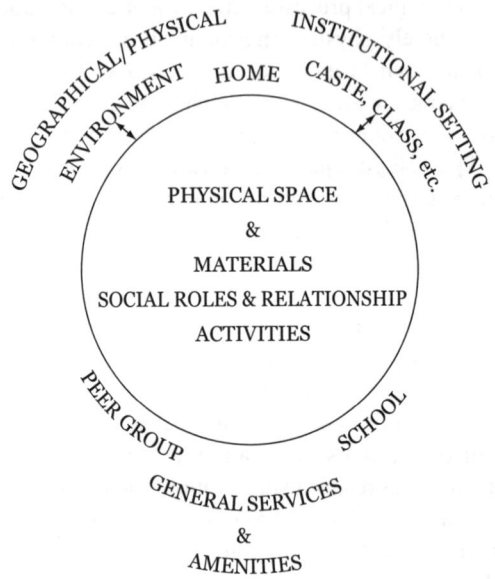

are encouraged or inhibited would constitute another kind of influence emanating from the family and the school. The third factor constituting the other visible layer is the nature of interactions and activities prevalent in his peer groups right from his childhood onwards. These three factors, namely the home, school and peer groups with physical facilities, nature of social interactions, and activities common in each, constitute the most important ecological influences on the psychological development of the child, and these influences are relatively easier to discern and examine. It may be borne in mind that there are other visible upper layer factors but are relatively minor in their import than the three outlined above.

These factors do not operate independently, but constantly interact not only with one another, but also are embedded in a larger and more pervasive setting constituting what have been designated as the "surrounding layers" of the child's ecology. They constantly influence the "upper layer" factors, but being pervasive and a little more diffused, their influences are not always clearly visible. The general geographical environment, nature of terrain which determine the mode of economic pursuits, space for play and other activities available to him outside the home including general congestion of the locality and density of population, space and facilities for play constitute the first element of the surrounding layer of ecology. To this may be added the topographical characteristics of the geographical environment (whether it is a flat, featureless, steppe-like grassland or undulating mountains) whose influence on our susceptibility to certain geometrical–optical illusions has been demonstrated, and which form the basis of the famous "carpentered world" hypothesis of Segall, Campbell and Herkovits (1963). Second element in the surrounding layer is the institutional setting provided by caste, class and other factors each providing certain role expectancies and strains, and imposing certain limitations on the individual, and prescribing certain kinds of preferred activities. The third factor is constituted by the general amenities available to the individuals residing in those places like drinking water, power, municipal and civic amenities, means of entertainment, and so on. These surrounding layers comprise the general environment, and being pervasive and common, their influences are taken for granted and not easily noticed. To all these may be added the factor of the level of poverty and general economic conditions which underlie all these, and which have repercussions on all the upper and surrounding layer factors in various degrees.

It may be observed that the visible and the surrounding layer factors often combine and interact with one another, and shape not only the economic pursuits, way of life, but also the socialization processes and interpersonal relationships and the general cognitive and perceptual functioning of the individual. Differentials in these, singly or in combination with others, are likely to have definite impact on the cognitive and perceptual competence of the individual as well as affect his motivations, style of coping with problems, and the general personality development.

Viewed in this perspective, the ecology of various socio-economic groups in India can be said to have a two-tiered concentric layer. For example, general poverty and the attendant congestions of the locality to which people belong, the limitations and roles enjoined by caste, and the facilities provided by the civic authorities to the areas where people reside can be viewed as the surrounding layer of ecology. Again, the conditions and facilities prevalent in home, the role relationships prevalent therein, and the activities encouraged or discouraged would constitute the outer and visible layer of ecology. Similarly, the conditions of the school and the nature and quality of schooling, as well as the nature of peer groups to which the child belongs would be regarded as other factors of outer layer ecology. The contrast in ecologies in both the layers is easily visible in comparing children from caste-Hindu families with those from the scheduled castes or the so-called "untouchables". For centuries, the scheduled castes have been living under conditions of intense social disadvantages, and prevented from sharing in the mainstream of socio-cultural and economic life of the Hindu society. The poor socio-cultural atmosphere in which they have lived for ages has resulted in their constituting the bulk of what is today called "the weaker sections of society" in India. Despite recent legislative and administrative measures to ensure their equality and eradicate discriminations against them, provide them with new roles and the provision of certain "privileges" to bring them rapidly up to the level of other social groups, they still suffer from many socio-cultural disadvantages which can collectively be regarded as "cultural deprivation". As Whiteman and Deutsch (1968) have observed, "social deprivation implies that the association between social grouping and specific environmental factors is not directly causal, but is mediated by more basic societal conditions such as unemployment, poverty, and inequality of opportunity in various areas". Apart from social disadvantages, poverty is another important factor constituting the environment of the scheduled caste children. But as Das and Singh (1975) have pointed out, the socio-cultural atmosphere in which a caste-Hindu lives would still be superior even between poor caste-Hindu and scheduled castes.

Thus, the socio-cultural disadvantages due to over-crowded neighbourhood, meagre civic amenities, and caste/class differentiation, may be regarded as the "surrounding or supporting layer" of the ecology of the child belonging to the scheduled castes. The upper or visible layer is provided by poor and deficient housing, the inferiority and discriminations which they still experience in various social relationships, and the inadequate schooling facilities available to them mainly because of poverty and indifference of their family towards getting them educated.

The above framework has been utilized by the author in a series of studies on the development of certain perceptual skills on urban, rural, and tribal children of various caste/religious statuses and exposed to differing qualities of schooling. One of these studies has been reported separately. In a recent paper (Bronfenbrenner, 1977) has suggested a more refined model. He argues that "the understanding of human development demands going beyond the direct observation of behaviours on the part of one or two persons in the same place; it requires examination of multiperson systems of interaction not limited to a single setting and must take into account aspects of the environment beyond the immediate situation containing the subject." He proposes scientific perspective of *ecology of human development* which can provide a useful framework for conceptualizing the psychological consequences of deprivation on human level. The author has followed closely his formulations regarding the same key concepts. Ecology of human development has been denned as "the scientific study of progressive mutual accommodation, throughout the life span, between growing human organism and the changing immediate environments in which it lives, as this process is affected by relations obtaining within and between these immediate settings, as well as the larger social contexts, formal and informal, in which the settings are embedded" (Bronfenbrenner, 1977). The conception of environment that is implicit here is considerably broader and more differentiated than that usually found in psychology. As Bronfenbrenner (1977) has stated "the ecological environment is conceived topologically as a nested arrangement of structures, each contained within the next." Following the terminology of Brim (1975), four successive levels have been proposed: *microsystem, mesosystem, exosystem*, and *macrosystem.* According to Bronfenbrenner (1977) a microsystem is "the complex relations between the developing person and environment in an immediate setting containing that person (e.g., home, school, workplace, etc.)". The factors of place, time, physical features, activity, participant and role, constitute the elements of the setting. In a psychological experiment, usually these elements are neglected, and roles other than those of the experimenter and the subject that may be operative upon the participants are disregarded, and "behaviour is examined primarily in terms of process (e.g., modes of interaction, reinforcement schedules, response rates) rather than content (e.g., the nature and purpose of the task)" (Bronfenbrenner, 1977, p. 514).

A mesosystem is conceived as comprising "the interrelations among major settings containing the developing person at a particular point in his or her life" (Bronfenbrenner, 1977, p. 514). It may encompass interactions among families, school, peer group, religious group and so on. It is a system of microsystems.

An exosystem as defined by Bronfenbrenner (1977) is "an extension of the mesosystem embracing other specific social structures, both formal and informal, that do not themselves contain the developing person but impinge upon or encompass the immediate settings in which that person is found, and thereby influence, delimit, or even determine, what goes on there. Major institutions of the society constitute the structure, and they encompass among others the world of work, neighbourhood, the mass media, agencies of the government, the distribution of goods and services, communication facilities, and informal social networks" (p. 515).

A macrosystem differs from these foregoing systems in that "it refers not to specific contexts affecting the life of a particular individual but to general prototypes, existing in the culture or subculture, that set the pattern for the structures and activities occurring at the concrete level".

A macrosystem refers to "the overarching institutional patterns of the culture or subculture such as the economic, social, educational, legal, and political systems, of which micro-meso, and exosystems are the concrete manifestations. A macrosystem is conceived not only as structures but also as carriers of information and ideology, explicit or implicit, that endow meaning and motivation to various social agencies" (Bronfenbrenner, 1977, p. 515).

It is not necessary to dilate upon the properties of each of these four systems. It would suffice to point to the characteristic of reciprocity and constant interaction within factors of each system and between the systems. In the present context, it is contended that deprivation can be conceived as certain deficiencies characterizing one or more of these systems with which the individual has to cope constantly. More the number of factors involved, greater would usually be the level of deprivation. Further, it is to be noted that deficiencies in the four systems or in factors within each one of them can best be conceived not in simple additive terms but as having an interactive relationship with each other. It is felt that with this four-level ecological perspective underlying any study of the effects of deprivation, the phenomenon is likely to be viewed in all its complexity and reality. Without sacrificing scientific rigour, relevance of the study would be assured.

The second framework of deprivation in your levels of ecosystems is not essentially different from the earlier formulation in terms of two concentric layers. It has, however, the advantage of being more differentiated, capable of conceptualizing various factors of deprivation in more specific, concrete, and realistic terms. Studies and experiments designed within this framework are not likely to suffer from the usual defect of artificiality and irrelevance.

Before concluding, it may be pointed out that the model that is conceptualized is not a rigid one. It represents essentially a perspective and a viewpoint which is relevant to a number of different content areas and problems. Ecological perspective, as Holahan (1977) has pointed out, is also applicable across different levels of problem analysis, including role relationships in an organized setting, the effects of physical environment upon behaviour, and the pervasive influences of culture and history on community processes.

The perspective has the utility in helping to evolve intervention programme which focuses on the individual's level of functioning. It draws our attention to the necessity of improving such skills that the individual needs to cope with particular institutional or environmental blocks for achieving the desired objectives rather than towards personality factors per se. If it is observed that a particular environmental setting has precipitated severe psychological handicaps in a large number of individuals, the intervention strategy would focus towards changing those characteristics of the environment that present serious obstacles to individual functioning. Moreover, effort will also be directed to identify and bolster those aspects of the physical and socio-cultural systems that can help the individual meet the demands of the situation more effectively. In this context, as Spielberger and Iscoe (1970) have observed, a psychologist can assume newer and innovative roles. Kelly's (1968) intervention project in Michigan on two high schools situated in areas which were environmentally highly discrepant supporting divergent types of effective coping behaviour provides a good example of the utility of this framework. This, the potential social policy relevance of the ecological perspective in contrast to the intra-psychic position augurs well in the context of increased emphasis on social relevance. As Holahan (1977) concludes, "facility in integrating a sound conceptual basis with social action enhances its viability".

# 10

# Interventions for Development
# out of Poverty*

Large tracts of the globe, often characterized as the Third World, suffer from acute poverty. Even in the most prosperous nations of the world, there are pockets of poverty in which a sizable proportion of people are underfed, underclothed, badly housed, and lacking in basic amenities of life. Studies on the psychological dimensions of poverty and their impact on individual functioning have been conducted not so much as academic exercises but with the specific purpose of devising measures for ameliorating their harmful effects. It is in no way implied that psychological dimensions exhaust the universe of poverty and constitute its main cause. It is generated and sustained by economic systems and social structures. Radical transformations are required for its eradication. But the condition of poverty does not restrict itself simply to the economic domain. Its spread is visible in social, psychological, health, and other areas affecting human existence and behavior patterns. Therefore, while recognizing the central role of economic and structural determinants, it is contended that outcomes of poverty include social and personal effects, including the coping processes of the individual. Understanding these processes is useful in devising strategies and programs for persons and groups to develop out of poverty and enjoy a life free from unnecessary and avoidable miseries and deprivations.

* Reproduced, with permission, from Sinha, D. (1990). Intervention for Development out of Poverty. In R.W. Brislin (ed.), *Applied Cross-cultural Psychology* (pp. 77–97). Newbury Park, CA: SAGE Publications.

This text has been edited for typographical errors, stylistic consistency and sequential organization in order to make it suitable for inclusion in the book.

# Conceptualization of Poverty

In the psychological literature, poverty has many conceptual nuances, and there is often confusion about the criteria used to classify groups as poor. Ignoring sophisticated measurement procedures, psychologists have preferred working with categorical-level variables, examining marginal groups like Blacks, Chicanos, Harjans, or those designated, as in India, as "weaker sections" of society.

Apart from purely economic factors, sociocultural indices have been frequently used for designating "poor" and "disadvantaged" groups. In addition to using a single criterion, investigators have used a whole catalogue of objects and possessions in the home (e.g., books, electrical appliances) or neighborhood (e.g., playgrounds), occupation, residence, educational facilities, and activities engaged in by the person. A standard procedure has been to develop a socioeconomic status (SES) scale or specific scales of poverty, like the "deprivation index" of Whiteman and Deutsch (1968) and the Prolonged Deprivation Scale of Misra and Tripathi (1980), taking into account the aspects of environment in relation to which individuals are impoverished.

Thus psychologists have conceptualized poverty as a situation with a number of attendant conditions that individually or collectively influence the development of people, rendering them less capable of overcoming poverty by personal efforts. The sequence of processes representing the relationship between poverty and its psychological and behavioral consequences is illustrated in a schematic model (Figure 10.1).

Poverty is associated with low income, low caste and class status, poor housing, overcrowding, lack of public amenities, various degrees of malnutrition, and high susceptibility to diseases. Further, the poor are exposed to a less stimulating environment, inadequate school facilities, lack of parental support, and the like. These attendant conditions individually or collectively affect people's psychological functioning. The common psychological effects are inappropriate perceptual and cognitive skills, attentional problems, learning disabilities, inadequate linguistic skills, stagnant aspirations, sense of helplessness, low self-esteem, and mental health problems. These, in turn, result in coping strategies that are dysfunctional for academic and other situations in life. The behavioral outcomes in the form of low competencies, low academic performance, high rates of dropout and wastage, low school attendance, stagnation, failure, and withdrawal imply that people are not able to successfully cope with their problems. All these, in turn, accentuate the condition of poverty.

**Figure 10.1**

*Schematic Model of the Relationship between Poverty, Its Psychological Consequences, and Their Outcomes*

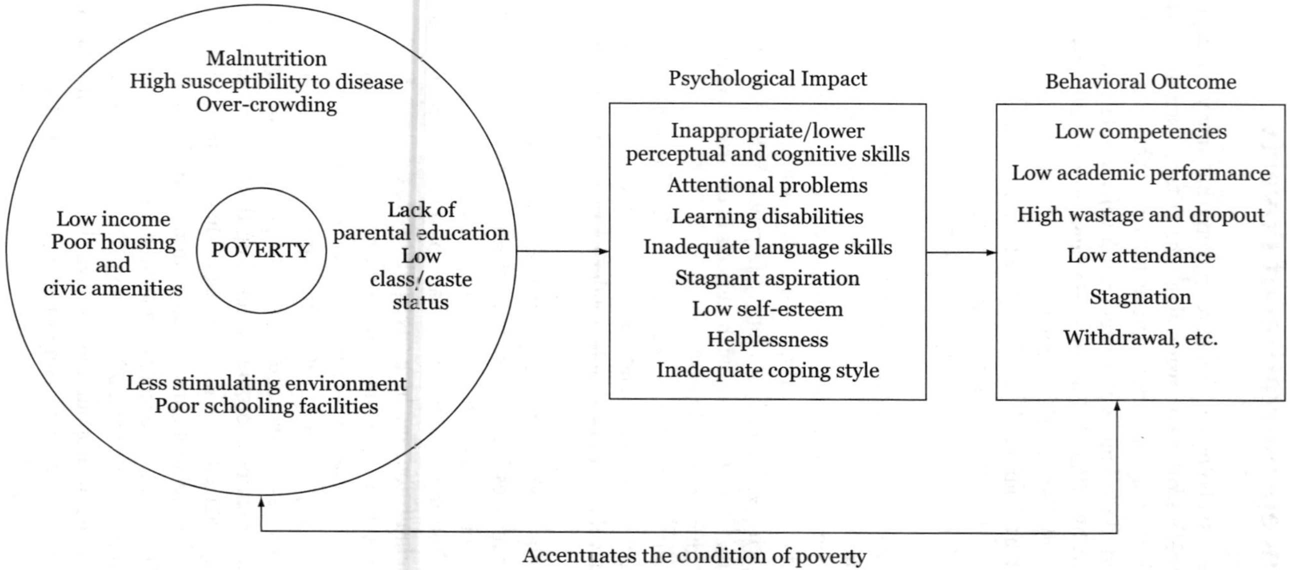

Behavioral Outcome

Low competencies
Low academic performance
High wastage and dropout
Low attendance
Stagnation
Withdrawal, etc.

Psychological Impact

Inappropriate/lower
perceptual and cognitive skills
Attentional problems
Learning disabilities
Inadequate language skills
Stagnant aspiration
Low self-esteem
Helplessness
Inadequate coping style

Malnutrition
High susceptibility to disease
Over-crowding

Lack of
parental education
Low
class/caste
status

POVERTY

Low income
Poor housing
and
civic amenities

Less stimulating environment
Poor schooling facilities

Accentuates the condition of poverty

In other words, psychological processes operate as mediators between the condition of poverty and its detrimental impact on behavior. It would be wrong to suggest that one is poor because of psychological limitations. But it is also true that a life of poverty produces many psychological ill effects rendering the individual less capable of coping with problems. A kind of vicious circle is created. What is emphasized is that, rather than being its cause psychological consequences accentuate the situation of poverty.

Psychology as a discipline is most competent to deal with behavioral dimensions, the understanding of which is likely to be helpful in devising action programs and policies for eradicating poverty. It is also emphasized that ignoring psychological variables may lead ameliorative programs to unexpected and at times undesirable consequences. Understanding the psychological characteristics of the poor is no less important than the analysis of the system that brought in the condition of poverty.

# Psychological Impact of Poverty

Psychological research on poverty can be classified under three broad headings: (a) malnutrition and its impact on development, (b) cognitive dimensions of poverty, and (c) personality and motivational dimensions. The areas of mental health and personal style including self-concept, success–failure orientation, time perspective, and coping behavior have been integrated with (c) in the present chapter. Moreover, (d) studies of self-fulfilling prophesies and (e) attribution processes have led to new insights. Each of these is discussed briefly, and policy and action implications of the major findings are spelled out.

## Malnutrition and Its Impact on Development

Malnutrition of various degrees is a condition most frequently prevalent in poor populations living under adverse socioeconomic and environmental circumstances. Although early and severe malnutrition occurs with considerable frequency in the poorer populations of developing countries (up to 20% in some instances), the most widespread type of malnutrition is that of mild-to-moderate, chronic under nutrition, which is most readily noted in some retardation of physical growth and development. Severe protein-calories malnutrition (PCM) includes the conditions of nutritional *marasmus* (starvation) and *kwashiorkor* (protein deficiency) typically occurring as a rather acute illness toward the end of the first or in the second year of life. Severe nutritional deficits alter the child's attentional competencies and responsiveness to the environment (Ricciuti, 1981) and lead to reduced activity and apathy. It has been observed that, although malnourished infants and toddlers seem less responsive to low or moderate levels of stimulation, they appear to be hyperactive at higher stimulus levels. It is highly probable that attentional deficiencies underlie the learning disabilities that are reflected in poor performance in school and various real-life settings. Although this aspect of malnutrition needs to be investigated more systematically, it is obvious that what gets affected adversely is attentional strategies and competence, or learnability, and not basic intellectual capacity. It should be kept in mind that attentional strategies affect IQ *scores*. This is one example of how IQ tests should not be taken as perfect measures of intellectual capacity. Therefore, if, in an intervention program, food supplementation is used along with measures to enhance responsiveness and learning competencies, the adverse effects of early malnutrition can be largely countered.

Mild-to-moderate malnutrition is more widespread. Studies conducted in India, Latin America, and other parts of the world have yielded considerable evidence that the physical development of children, particularly height and weight, go hand in hand with the development of other areas such as language and cognition. There were significant differences in head circumference and growth rate, in intelligence, and on measures of visual-motor development between adequately and inadequately fed lower-class nursery school children from New Delhi (Werner & Murlidharan, 1970). A comparison of 1,336 undernourished rural children at school entry (6–8 years) in Varanasi, India, with a sample of normal children demonstrated impairments of IQ, fine motor coordination, and immediate memory. The former were also slow in verbal reasoning, comprehension, and perceptual ability and displayed 10 adequacies, 10 social competence and communication. Even for those undernourished children with normal IQ, 16.3% had poor achievement indicating learning difficulties (Agarwal, Agarwal & Upadhyay, 1988).

Many studies have tried to assess the relative influences of malnutrition and social factors on mental development. Findings are not always consistent. Among Barbadian children of 5–11 years who had suffered moderate to severe degree of malnutrition during the first year of life, IQ was reduced, which was independent of socioeconomic factors. They also showed attention deficit, impaired memory, easy distractibility, poor school performance, and restlessness resembling the syndrome of attention deficit disorders (Galler, Ramsey, Solimano & Lowell, 1983). On the other hand, the importance of social influence was brought out by the fact that an acute episode of malnutrition in the first two years of life did not affect the intellectual development of children growing in favorable circumstances. In contrast, if the child was in an unfavorable environment for intellectual development, an early bout of malnutrition had marked effects on later mental attainment (Richardson, 1976). In fact, the role of long-term environmental stimulation on Korean orphans adopted in supportive American homes and social environment has indicated that observed behavioral effects of severe malnutrition disappear and children show higher IQ and better school performance as compared with those who returned to their existing environment (Lien, Meyer & Winick, 1977).

There is ample evidence that unfavorable early child-care practices and dysfunctional patterns of caregiver–infant interaction may contribute to an increased risk of malnutrition, growth retardation, and suboptimal behavioral development (Ricciuti, 1980). The importance of maternal intelligence, attitude, and socioeconomic status of the family for the nutritional well-being of preschool children has been emphasized. Early disturbances in mother–child interactions and inadequate mothering increase the risk not only of malnutrition but also of inadequate psychological development (Vazir, Bhogle & Naidu, 1988). When mothers were exposed to training in child care, food supplementation produced substantial acceleration in development in rural infants (Bhogle, 1979). A study of very poor tribal children from remote areas of Madhya Pradesh, India, indicated that a suitable educational intervention with mothers brought about marked improvement in language and cognitive development, no matter how poor the children were in their physical environment (Murlidharan & Kaur, 1987).

Many nutritionists and pediatricians concerned primarily with the effects of biological conditions like postnatal malnutrition upon the child's mental development often have tended to underestimate the degree to which mental development may be directly influenced by adverse social and learning experiences prevalent in environments characterized by endemic malnutrition (Ricciuti, 1977). There is a need to examine more precisely the manner in which unfavorable aspects of the child's early social and learning environment and various adverse biological influences interact in jointly shaping the course of the young child's psychological as well as physical growth and development.

Even though the exact mechanisms of influence are yet to be understood, the findings do provide a base for planning appropriate types of intervention concerned with facilitating the child's growth and development. There is strong evidence that the mother's role and the social environment have significant mediating influences. Adverse intellectual consequences of under nutrition and low birth weight are very much attenuated in favorable social environments. Therefore, provision of both nutritional supplementation and enhancement of the child's social, family, and learning environments is essential to promote both physical and psychological development (Ricciuti, 1977).

There are serious doubts about a direct causal and unidirectional relationship between malnutrition and cognitive development. By and large, the findings indicate that the effects of malnutrition are not irreversible if appropriate measures are taken early. This provides a note of optimism and has obvious implication for action programs in that if nutritional treatment, rehabilitation, and enrichment occur early, say, in the first year, the chances of recovery of normal or near-normal intellectual functioning appear quite good.

## Cognitive Dimensions of Poverty

There has been extensive research on the impact of poverty on various perceptual and cognitive processes. There is overwhelming evidence from cross-cultural studies and from those conducted on animals and children that environmental deficiencies adversely affect the acquisition of perceptual and cognitive processes. Adverse conditions associated with poverty operate as detrimental influences on intelligence, proficiency in pictorial perception, concept formation, learning, memory and mediational processes, linguistic skills, and academic performance.

Though the evidence is at times confusing, it has generally been observed that children growing in substandard environmental conditions are lower in intelligence than comparison children growing up under more favorable circumstances. Deprivation indices have been found significantly related to performance on both Lorge-Thorndike intelligence and vocabulary tests even within groups homogeneous in race and socioeconomic levels. More disadvantaged groups showed decreasing IQ with age (Whiteman & Deutsch, 1968). Further, socioeconomic status was positively correlated with scores on reading tests. These deficiencies, if left unchecked at early stages, caused irreparable damage to the cognitive and intellectual growth of children and resulted in the "cumulative deficit phenomenon," rendering them progressively more incapable of successful performance in classroom settings. As a result, the longer such children remained in school, despite equal facilities available to them, the further behind they fell in relation to the norms of their age and grade. Though some studies conducted in India (Rath, Dash & Dash, 1979) have failed to establish a clear-cut relationship between sociocultural disadvantage and performance on various kinds of intelligence tests, the trend of the findings is one of negative relationship between the two (Singh, 1976; Werner & Murlidharan, 1970).

The adverse effects of impoverished circumstances like (a) low economic class and caste status, (b) unsatisfactory school facilities and (c) residence in unstimulating environments and remote rural areas have been observed on a large variety of perceptual and cognitive tasks. It has also been observed that, although better school facilities do enhance the performance level of disadvantaged children, the differential between advantaged and disadvantaged groups tends to become accentuated with an increase in age and grade, causing a cumulative deficit phenomenon (Sinha, 1977).

Sociocultural disadvantage is associated with general impairment of learning, memory, and mediational abilities (Agarwal et al., 1988; Klein, Freeman, Kagan, Yarbrough & Habicht, 1972; Sahu & Mahanta, 1977). This occurs similarly with problem solving, concept formation and conservation skills (Dasen & Colomb, 1982; Misra & Tripathi, 1980). Although disadvantaged background interfered with the acquisition of these skills, provision of training (Rao, 1977) appeared to bring about considerable improvement, which remained stable (Mishra, 1987).

Bernstein (1973) has observed a close association between social class and linguistic skills. Though his contention is controversial, it has stimulated many studies related to sociocultural disadvantage and language development. The findings in general indicate the language skills ranging from basic structural aspects like speech articulation and grammatical usage to more complex functions such as descriptions and classifications were retarded in lower-class disadvantaged children (Chazen, Laing, Cox & Jackson, 1977). They also scored lower on word reading and verbal conditioning tests (Panda & Das, 1970). A study of scheduled caste (formerly called "untouchable") children in India revealed their "dialect" to be deficient and deviant from the standard language of upper-caste children (Suresh, 1984). Lower-caste 2- to 3-year-old children performed poorly on grammar comprehension, word meaning, and expression skills. The linguistic environment of the family associated with class status operated as a significant moderator variable. Verbal stimulation received in the family, especially from grandparents, exerted a positive influence and could counteract the adverse effect due to lower-class status (A. Singh, 1987).

Linguistic skills and the discontinuity between the language spoken by disadvantaged children and the one used in schools are of vital significance to scholastic performance. Because general language ability is the major differentiating characteristic between class groups, and is a central element in information processing, it is highly essential to give language training a central place in the intervention program framework (Ryckman, 1966).

With cognitive skills, learning and mediational processes, and linguistic abilities being highly relevant to the performance of the child in school, what adverse socioeconomic circumstances seem to do is to increase the discontinuity between skills possessed by the disadvantaged and attentional, cognitive, and linguistic skills requisite to school success: Children, therefore, encounter difficulties in the classroom generating progressive alienation between them and the teacher.

Studies lend ample support to the above contention. In India, at all levels of educational performance, difficulties encountered by the scheduled castes and scheduled tribes in comparison with the general population are reflected in their very low enrollment, irregularity in attendance, high dropout rates, and poor academic records. Specific studies designed for the purpose have demonstrated that the greater the degree of disadvantage, the more inferior the academic performance (Singh, 1980). Even when intelligence is matched, disadvantaged children displayed poorer academic performance. In the United States, it has recently been observed that, although Blacks and Mexican Americans have achieved the largest gain among all SAT takers, a corresponding improvement in their college performance has not taken place (Educational Testing Service [ETS], 1988, p. 2).

Family and social factors are significant in this regard. The family education index for scheduled castes and scheduled tribe groups with poor academic attainment was lowest, and their parents had the lowest aspiration for their children (Rath et al., 1979). Among the disadvantaged tribal and nontribal children, a combination of high intelligence and parental support favorably affected academic achievement. Parental support compensated for lower intelligence, offset adverse effects of low socioeconomic status, and encouraged academic achievement (Singh, 1983, p. 9).

Policy implications are obvious. The point of entry for improving the educational attainment of the disadvantaged is the family.... If, due to sheer poverty, correctives for disrupted homes, separation from parents, and lack of parental support may take long to be effective, the alternative strategy is to provide the child in the school what he or she lacks at home (Singh 1983). Because, even at a very early age and much before they enter schools, disadvantaged children lack many of the skills essential for success (ETS, 1988, p. 7), intervention has to occur early to constitute an effective "antidote" to deprived circumstances. School "enrichment" has to be supplemented by appropriate intervention at the level of the family to maximize the outcome.

# Personality and Motivational Dimensions

A number of studies have demonstrated, although not in unambiguous terms, the association between other indices of poverty and feelings of insecurity, anxiety, rigidity, conformity, emotional instability, mental health difficulties, lower self-image, extroversion, and some personality characteristics (see Sinha, 1976). The impact of sociocultural disadvantage on motivational variables is more marked. Pareek (1970) has elaborated the motivational syndrome induced by poverty. Apart from helplessness and powerlessness, he considers it as a structural component that produces a threefold motivational pattern characterized by low need for achievement, low need for extension (extending the ego to the society or concern for the common welfare of all), and high need for dependency. The latter is expressed in the form of lack of initiative, shifting responsibility to others, excessive fear of failure, seeking favors from superiors, overconformity, and aggressive rejection of authority.

The picture is ambiguous with regard to the need for achievement. But studies conducted in the West (Hess, 1970) and in India (Misra & Tripathi, 1980) have reported low aspirations on the part of the disadvantaged. It is traced to mother–child interaction, which has been described as a socialization of apathy and underachievement. Harsh authoritarianism of parents with emphasis on positive control, emotional and social distancing between themselves and their children, and early relaxation of close parental supervision generating feelings of unworthiness are factors responsible for it. Low aspirations of disadvantaged children seem like nothing else but the internalized projections of similar aspirations of their parents (Rath, 1973).

There is also evidence that typical adaptation techniques, such as time orientation, self-concept, success–failure orientation, reinforcement systems, sense of control over environment, and coping strategies generally, become adversely affected by the conditions of poverty. A negative relationship between deprivation and self-perception has been noted (Misra & Tripathi, 1980). As for time orientation, unlike the middle and upper classes, the poor hardly display a plan of future action and tend to live in the present or have fanciful ideas about the future (Sinha, 1969). An absence of clear-cut time perspective among the poor has been observed (Agarwal & Tripathi, 1980). They are oriented to the past and are vague about the future, displaying an indefinite, unstructured, and diffuse time orientation without consensual markers—a perspective that has little motivational value.

There are differences on incentive systems, reaction to success and failure, locus of control, and coping style generally. For disadvantaged lower-class children, immediate, material, and concrete reinforcers have been found more effective than verbal ones (Sharma, 1986). Analysis of control strategies used revealed that unskilled working-class mothers relied more on physical feedback, preferred control through implied threat, and seldom showed the child how to do various tasks (Hess, 1970). Lower-class black and white children displayed significant improvement in performance under praise and approval rather than disapproval (Rosenham, 1966).

Rotter's concept of locus of control has frequently been studied with respect to various castes in India. The disadvantaged tend to display a passive orientation and are more inclined to believe that external forces exclusively control the rewards that they receive. On the other hand, high-caste, advantaged children tend to be more internal (Das & Panda, 1971). In fact, analysis of reactions to success and failure of underprivileged university students has revealed that there is a strong tendency in them to refer success to external "uncontrollable" factors as God, luck, and teacher's kindness, and not to "controllable" factors like one's own effort, thereby failing to take adequate pride in accomplishments that would have a reinforcing effect. This appeal to externality produces a fatalistic outlook and superstitious ritualism, that is, performing some rites before undertaking a big task. Whereas success was externalized, failure was often attributed to oneself. With an unfavorable self-concept and a stringent standard for evaluating one's performance, students' self-image was lowered and their feelings of personal inadequacy were accentuated. They had, in fact, built a mechanism of self-discouragement that was entirely dysfunctional (Sinha, 1980).

The findings indicate that through parent–child interaction and socialization, the disadvantaged develop a pattern of motivation and coping style that is not functional to meet the demands of school settings and various life situations. Because a large part of this mechanism is learned in the family, intervention has to be focused on the family of the disadvantaged child. As many of the processes are learned early, the action program for development of effective coping strategies has to be forged in family situations before children enter schools.

## Rosenthal-Type Studies on Poverty

Rosenthal and Jacobson (1968) have suggested the possibility of the operation of a "Pygmalion effect" or "self-fulfilling prophesy" in the classroom so far as the poor and disadvantaged students are concerned. The teacher quite frequently regards those belonging to disadvantaged groups as possessing lower abilities. Students then perform poorly in examinations (Rath et al., 1979, pp. 93–96). Because teachers' expectations are to a large extent formed on the basis of social factors like class (Dusek & Joseph, 1983) and caste (Sharma & Tripathi, 1988), and because teachers mostly belong to the middle-class and upper castes, their expectations have serious implications for the academic performance of disadvantaged pupils. The essence of the position is that teachers get less from the disadvantaged because they expect less.

One can only guess about how the mechanism of expectation operates in influencing academic performance. It may affect the amount of attention and time that the pupil receives from the teacher; or, through nonverbal cues, the teacher may encourage or dampen the enthusiasm and motivation of the disadvantaged student. It is also possible that the phenomenon may influence the social–emotional climate of the institution, which has a very powerful impact on school performance.

These findings have definite policy implications. Because poor academic performance by disadvantaged students can be ascribed at least partly to the kind of expectations the teachers entertain about them (Panda & Behera, 1985; Rosenthal & Jacobson, 1968), the place of intervention is on the attitudinal plane. If teachers are, during the period of their training, made aware of how the poor performance of disadvantaged students is a demonstration of "self-fulfilling prophesies," and how one has to guard against this *unintentional* bias, it is likely to counteract the adverse influence and help improve academic behavior of pupils from disadvantaged groups.

## Attributional Studies

The search for causal explanations of social and natural events is an indispensable part of the human thinking process. Weiner's (1986) conceptualization of attribution behavior has influenced many studies on poverty. He suggests that causal attributions of success and failure significantly influence self-esteem and future expectations, and that success is generally attributed to internal, and failure to external, causes. The nature of causal attribution shows interesting cross-cultural as well as ethnic and social class variations. It has generally been observed that Whites judge internal causes to be more important than external in the case of success and take greater credit for success. They attributed failure to external causes like luck and chance. On the other hand, Asians and Blacks attributed success to external causes but assumed more personal responsibility for failure (Friend & Neale, 1972; Fry & Ghosh, 1980). Analysis of causal attribution of poverty in general revealed that low-income respondents attributed success more to fate and luck than high-income people. This tendency acts as an impediment in successfully meeting the challenges of various life situations.

Further, the success of students identified as "good" and "bright" was attributed by the teachers to family, ability, and effort, and failure to chance and nature of the task. But, for those considered as "not good," failure was ascribed to their family, ability, and effort. When a student's performance was not in congruence with teacher's expectations, more attribution was made to external categories (Sharma & Tripathi, 1988). It is highly probable that teachers' attributions (both with regard to the advantaged and disadvantaged) are somehow communicated to the students so that there is often a high congruence between teachers' attributions and those of the students. It is obvious that attributions help in improving the performance of higher-class, advantaged students but prove detrimental to the performance of the disadvantaged. Thus any intervention program aimed at improving the performance of students coming from disadvantaged circumstances should aim at developing strategies to modify attributions made by teachers and students.

Attributional analysis has its practical utility. There is evidence to suggest that attributional dimensions of locus of control, controllability, and stability are linked with important properties of behavior (Hewstone, 1983) in that they are systematically related to affective reactions and future expectations. Internal (ability) attributions are related to expectations, persistence, and other aspects of achievement behavior. Because attributions made by the disadvantaged involve cognitions, they are more flexible and manipulable; there is greater possibility of changing them as compared with personality traits (Misra & Jain, 1988).

Attributional analysis is relevant in yet another way. Experience with poverty eradication programs, especially in India, has revealed that they have underplayed or missed altogether the subjective reconstruction of poverty by people that helps them to maintain feelings of self-worth along with a sense of control over their lives (Y. Sinha, 1988). The meaning thus construed by the person has behavioral implications, which, in turn, influence the extent of participation in, and the efficacy of, antipoverty programs. The type of attributions of achievement usually made by the disadvantaged subjects, that is, failure is due to lack of ability and effort (internal factors) and success due to fate, chance, or God's will, generate an attitude of dependency on some external agency (government or private). This dependency must be eliminated or at least reduced, and achievement (in this case, development) must be regarded as a result of one's effort and ability (internal attribution). With this pattern of attributions, the process of poverty eradication has a greater chance of being self-generating and self-sustaining. A suitable strategy, therefore, has to be worked out to bring about the necessary cognitive transformation in attributions that reduces dependency and generates initiative and independence in people.

Attributional analysis can also be used to monitor and evaluate poverty alleviation programs. As it is implied that an individual or a group can successfully develop out of poverty if success is attributed to internal causes like personal endeavor, effort, and hard work, periodic analysis of attributions made by the beneficiary groups would be an index of whether the development programs are inducing the appropriate kind of psychological transformation in the people. If development continues to remain "externalized" in the minds of the people, sooner or later it is bound to run into difficulties.

# Some Intervention Programs

## The United States

Studies conducted in different parts of the world indicate that, as a result of being disadvantaged, children have acquired such cognitive and linguistic skills and patterns of motivation that, when they first arrive at school, they already have certain limitations for pursuing school programs successfully. Therefore, if education is to be an equalizer and a factor to help disadvantaged children to grow out of poverty, intervention has to be made before they enter school. Encouraged by the initial success of many small-scale compensatory educational projects in the early 1960s, an elaborate and ambitious intervention program called Operation Head Start was started by the federal government. It was an eight-week program at 2,500 child centers involving over half a million children. Its goal was to equip economically deprived children with skills that they would need when they entered public school. Although there were variations, most of the programs emphasized all aspects of the child's early development. In addition to educationally oriented activities, health and nutritional requirements and emotional and social concerns were considered. Some programs focused only on the schools, others were home based, and some were a combination of the two.

Evaluations of the program consistently showed that children made significant gains in IQ, vocabulary, and school readiness skills such as understanding letters, numbers, and concepts. The gains were large, especially among children with initially low IQ. A disturbing finding, however, was that the early benefits were deceptive in that short-term gains tended to fade out during elementary school years. Little long-term good could be evidenced unless a high-quality educational environment was maintained.

To reexamine the effectiveness of the programs of the 1960s, a consortium of 11 investigators from different parts of the country was formed in 1976. Follow-up data were gathered on those who had participated in programs and who were then 10 to 17 years old, more than 90% being Black from low-income families. Comparison with matched control groups revealed that they had fulfilled the achievement requirements of their schools. They less often repeated a grade or were assigned to a special class for slow learners. They performed better on reading, mathematics, and intelligence tests. They more often completed high school and were more likely to be employed thereafter. Preschool also had some desirable noncognitive outcomes. Mothers' aspirations for their children were raised relative to the children's own aspirations. They were more likely to give achievement-related reasons for being proud of themselves. They rated themselves as better students than their peers and tended to have more realistic vocational aspirations (Lazar & Darlington, 1979, p. 14). The general conclusion was that "children who participated in preschool intervention programs were more likely than control children to meet at least the minimal standards of their schools" (p. 8). Rather than entertaining early disillusionment with the project, the findings suggested that carefully designed early education programs can produce lasting benefits for economically disadvantaged children and can be a powerful factor in their development out of poverty (Lazar & Darlington, 1982).

## Latin America

A World Bank review of 15 projects mostly from Latin America, with emphasis on one of the three aspects of service delivery, caregiver education, and community development, revealed that the effect of the intervention on psychosocial development was positive. When compared with children outside the project, those who participated tended to become "more alert," sociable, and curious. There was evidence that those from lower-income and marginal families benefited more, cognitively and socially, than their more privileged peers, and that supplementary nutrition was effective in motivating school attendance (Myers & Hertenberg, 1987, p. 36). Though no attempt was made to look at long-term effects, the evaluations supported the contention of Halpern and Myers (1985, p. 28) that early childhood intervention yields a picture of modest positive effects on initial adjustment to the demands of primary school. Particular factors enhancing this adjustment appeared to be some combination of earlier age of enrollment, improved school readiness, and improved health and energy levels.

A program of intervention through infant stimulation conceived on a national scale for the systematic development of human intelligence was organized by the government in Venezuela from 1979 to 1983. Its main constituents were (a) the "Learning to Think" project, directed mainly at primary school students; (b) the "Instrumental Achievement" project, aimed at increasing the levels of cognitive development and hence the capacity for learning and school achievement among socioculturally underprivileged children; (c) "Project Chess," aimed at developing a problem-solving way of thinking among schoolchildren; and (d) the "Family Project," directed at children from 0 to 6 years and their families. The last project, which was the largest, consisted of a program of integral stimulation for the development of the child in which audiovisual and printed materials were used on 150,000 mothers conveying information on how to attain optimal development of the newborn and how to stimulate speech and different sensory processes.

The program has been received with different degrees of enthusiasm, approval, humor, skepticism, and downright rejection. The main objection to it has been that it did not give sufficient importance to structural variables like living conditions and health (Salazar, 1989). The program operated in a political context and was discontinued with a change in the government. Due to its political overtones, no objective evaluation of its effectiveness has come forth. However, it constitutes an important step in the development of intelligence and cognitive skills by providing enrichment to millions of underprivileged children and bringing them to the level of the rest of the children. It is an important and unique attempt to use psychological technology for accomplishing national goals of human development in a developing country (Salazar, 1984, p. 121).

## India

Facing widespread poverty, it is not surprising that the main thrust, especially of the recent five-year national plans, has been the eradication of poverty. Because the main concern has been with disadvantaged children, some details of the Integrated Child Development Services (ICDS) in India will be discussed as another intervention program of enrichment and infant stimulation conceived on a national scale

ICDS is a massive intervention program concerned with urgent nutritional, health, and other developmental problems faced by the Indian child. It has been conceived to provide adequate services both before and after birth and through the period of growth to ensure children's full physical, mental, and social development. Apart from Improving health and nutritional status of children in the age group 0 to 6 years, it aims to lay the foundation for proper psychological, physical, and social development; to reduce the incidence of mortality, morbidity, malnutrition, and school dropout; and to enhance the capability of the mother to look after normal health and nutritional needs through proper nutrition and health education. This package of early childhood services is delivered through *anganwadi* (a grass-roots institution organized in the village or the city), which acts as a focal point for delivery of child development services such as immunization, health checkup, referral, supplementary nutrition, nutrition, and health education for expectant mothers, nonformal preschool education, and water and sanitation services. Because women have a key role in the development and welfare of the child, expectant and nursing mothers as well as other women have been brought into the scheme.

Independent evaluations sponsored by UNICEF (Krishnamurthy & Nadkarni, 1983) have shown that it has been making a dramatic impact on malnutrition, infant mortality and morbidity, immunization coverage, school enrollment, and reduction in school dropout rate. From a small beginning, the ICDS now involves more than 200,000 people in 1,738 centrally sponsored and 136 state-sponsored projects, each covering about 18,000 children and 2,000 pregnant and nursing mothers. The focus is mainly on nutrition and health aspects. Psychological facets have so far been neglected mainly due to resource constraints. But it is a colossal intervention program calculated to encourage the development of disadvantaged and underprivileged children so that they are able to combat the situation of poverty.

# Epilogue

Research on the psychological impact of poverty and its associated variables has considerably enhanced our general understanding of the concomitants of poverty. A general point that emerges is that the detrimental effects of poverty on academic achievement are mediated by a number of intervening processes that are generated on the cognitive, motivational, social, and family planes. These adverse effects are accentuated in the unfavorable proximal environment of the child in which the place of the family is vital. Therefore, intervention strategies have to be targeted not only on specific cognitive, linguistic, or motivational drawbacks but also on the family setting of the disadvantaged if maximal outcome is desired. To ensure that the gains of the intervention are lasting, improvements in the family setting and the educational environment of the child have to be enduring.

What poverty seems to do is not to adversely affect the basic abilities and intelligence but rather to arrest greatly the acquisition of certain skills that are relevant to proper functioning in school. Therefore, interventions have to be directed at the removal of these learning disabilities and incompetencies. What the disadvantaged child lacks in his or her learning environment has to be provided either by the enrichment of the environment or the school setting.

In general, findings indicate that the deficiencies generated due to the circumstances of poverty are not irreversible. It should, however, be noted that no less than 33% of the scholastic attainment profile of children is already decided when they start the first year of primary school (Bloom, 1964): Therefore, appropriate action has to be taken early in order to attenuate most of the effects of disadvantage.

In conclusion, the findings indicate that the psychological damage caused by acute malnutrition and disadvantaged circumstances can be largely counteracted provided that remedial action is taken early and provided that the improved environment is an enduring one. If proper intervention is made at the appropriate time, the disadvantaged child need not remain in the condition of poverty but can acquire appropriate cognitive, linguistic, and other skills to develop out of it.

# 11

# Motivational Syndrome of Farmers, Education and Rural Development*

The present review chapter is an attempt to demonstrate the role of education in the rural development. Indian farmers regard education important and vital for their children in getting government job but not with reference to the rural needs. Regarding motivational aspect, reluctance to take risk, stagnant aspiration and strong fear of failure have been characterized as being typical of Indian farmers. Various rural development programmes have failed in inculcating a new urge and aspiration of better living. A comparison of farmers between highly developed and underdeveloped villages has set out that farmers from highly developed villages have higher level of aspiration, high positive goal discrepancy index, greater flexibility in adjusting their level of aspiration to their performance. The chapter recommends that some amount of education closely integrated with rural needs and inculcating certain skills that are useful in development is likely to have the right-kind of impact.

Education as an important instrument in development has been recognized by everyone. It enhances human potential and as such is an important ingredient of development in different spheres. Though education is supposed to foster rural development, it has been in

* Reproduced, with permission, from Sinha, D. (1986). Motivational Syndrome of Farmers, Education and Rural Development. *Indian Journal of Current Psychological Research*, 1, 65–72. S.N. Rai Publisher.

This text has been edited for typographical errors, stylistic consistency and sequential organization in order to make it suitable for inclusion in the book.

a way counterproductive. When we were conducting field survey on motivational dimensions of rural development in some villages around Allahabad and were looking for subjects with different levels of education, we found it difficult to get "resident" villagers with educational qualification higher than high school. Most of those who had crossed the high school level tended to migrate to cities or to different industrial areas in search of jobs. As a result, whatever skill or useful attitudes and orientation had been generated by education were not available for the development of rural areas. Further, in course of the study, it was also observed that the kind of education that was provided in village schools was considered remote and irrelevant to the natives of the villages. Low enrolment and high dropout rates among poorer sections of the rural and tribal children are largely because of the irrelevance of what is taught in schools for the needs of the villages. Therefore, it is not surprising that villagers have not often displayed very strong need for education. In our study (Sinha, 1969) when villagers were asked to conceptualize what constituted a happy life, it was found that education was not an important constituent in the rank order of various categories of needs expressed by the villagers, it was way dawn and occupied eleventh and twelfth ranks out of the possible 30 and odd ranks among villagers from highly developed and very poorly developed areas respectively. Moreover, in another study where hopes and aspirations of villagers were analyzed, though education came within the ten most frequently mentioned items of hope, it was hardly referred to by a little over one fourth of the subjects. In a study conducted in Maharashtra in which the existing interrelationship between programme of adult education and rural development was examined and methods of improving its functioning as a functional component of rural development were explored, it was observed that though the programme had certain level of acceptance, it was not being associated with immediate economic benefits or skill development or employment, and did not seem to have the demand from the people (Muthayya and Prasad, 1982).

Thus, for the farmers as such, need for education has not been very salient though when projections are made for children, education is often considered vital. Probing the reasons for the same, it has been observed that farmers regard education for their children as one of the principal means by which they can get into the government service and obtain jobs in cities. Therefore, even when need for education of children was strong, it was not with reference to the needs of the rural areas as such, but for enhancing potential for getting into various services.

# Motivational Syndrome of Successful Farmers

As far as motivation is concerned, a number of studies have thrown light on the motivational syndrome of farmers who have displayed high level of agricultural development. Before spelling them out, some of the general findings of studies conducted by us in rural areas around Allahabad between the period 1964 to 1970 would be outlined. Analyzing the motivation of farmers, it has been observed that it was generally characterized by apathy and disinterestedness. On various measures of motivation and level of aspiration, Indian farmers have been found to display extreme amount of caution and stagnant level of aspiration. Fear of failure and reluctance to take risk were common features. If high aspiration was there, it was usually unrealistic, fantasy-oriented and vague. In fact, when required to spell out their hopes, fears and the elements of what constituted happy life for them, they were unable to do so in very clear and definite terms. Protocols were generally characterized by paucity of content and the range of needs expressed therein was highly restricted, being generally confined to items of immediate necessities and subsistence. In their concept of what constituted happy life, they were overwhelmingly concerned with immediate economic values. Community needs and general psychological needs like prestige, status, recreation, and values occupied only a secondary place in their need-value structure. On a conventional measure of level of aspiration, villagers were found to be overcautious. They tended to keep their goals tied down to the last performance and showed great reluctance to raise them very much. As a result goal-discrepancy score was generally small. There was little urge to take chances and constant desire to avoid risk. They displayed strong fear of meeting with failure. As such, they seldom set their goals very much higher than what they had done in the past. In short, their behaviour was characterized by high degree of caution and lack of enterprises. Furthermore, on some other measures, they did not seem to view the future with a degree of hope and there was absence of optimism.

The above presents the general picture of the kind of motivation which one tends to find among Indian farmers. Through different development programmes and schemes, effort has been made to alter the situation. It has been hoped that bringing about overall development in the villages would generate the right kind of motivations and urges which would keep the process of development sustained and make it self-generating. Moreover, when community development and other rural development projects were conceived, the important role played by motivation as a component of development was well recognized. Various rural development programmes have aimed at inculcating among villagers a new urge and aspiration for better living and a strong desire to improve their material condition and to have a more constructive outlook towards future development. As early as 1958, Mr. V.T. Krishnamachari who had a large part to play in initial stages in drawing up various programmes to bring about improvement in rural areas, remarked that "No measure for improvement will achieve successful result unless governments can make agriculturists change their old time outlook and arouse enthusiasm in them for new knowledge and new ways of life. There should be created in them burning desire for higher standard of living ... a will to live better".

This being the case, we tried to analyze the differences between farmers hailing from villages which had shown excellent agro-economic developments over the years and those who came from villages which had not displayed much by way of agro-economic development, but were comparable in terms of size, accessibility, distance from the city, topography and so on. Comparisons on a number of measures of motivation and level of aspiration did not yield a very clear-cut picture though some interesting differences were visible which did indicate a kind of motivational syndrome associated with successful farming. In comparative terms, farmers from highly developed villages who tended to have higher overall level of aspiration, higher positive goal-discrepancy index, were more flexible in adjusting their level of aspiration to their performance and estimated their past performance more accurately. They tended to set their goals higher as trials progressed. On the other hand, villagers from undeveloped areas consistently showed lower aspiration, lower positive goal-discrepancy index stronger tendency to under estimate their performance and an attitude of indifference. More progressive farmers from developed villages had a significantly stronger tendency to set higher goals and had larger positive goal discrepancy score. They also displayed greater proneness to face risk of failure in their performance. Further, in spite of the general similarity in the pattern of hopes and aspirations, villagers from developed areas did exhibit some awareness of community and national needs which were almost absent among those from very backward villages where personal needs tended to get projected on to the level of community and national spheres. In fact, among farmers from undeveloped areas, hopes and aspirations were largely circumscribed within the spheres of personal and family life and seldom transcended beyond to encompass community and national aspiration. Same was the case with fears and worries where personal, community and national levels were not clearly differentiated on a striving scale, past and present were rated low. There was little sense of accomplishment over the past five to seven years, though some ray of hopeful expectancy was displayed while viewing the future. It was also noted that sense of accomplishment was more pronounced amongst villagers from developed areas. Further, when conceptualizing happy life, villagers from developed areas were clearer about their goals, could verbalize their needs better and were more reality-oriented rather than fantasy-oriented.

A number of studies by other investigators have also pointed to the significant role of certain patterns of motivation in rural development. Using a unidimensional measure of agricultural innovativeness based on whether a farmer had ever used ten recommended practices, Roy, Fliegel, Kivlin and Sen (1968) observed that economic betterment had brought about an increase in aspiration of farmers. Sachchidananda (1970) in his study observed that adoption of improved farm practices was associated closely with need for achievement planning orientation and optimism. Comparing farmers around Delhi, who were classified as traditional and progressive, Narayan Singh (1970) noted the progressive farmers took moderate risk while the traditional agricultural entrepreneur; whether successful or unsuccessful. Sinha and Chaubey (1974) comparing farmers from highly developed and undeveloped villages, found relatively strong motive to avoid failure rather than motivation to achieve success among the older age group. It was contended that the important role played by old and aged farmers in making decisions regarding cultivation had hindered economic growth in the undeveloped villages. Chaubey (1974) observed significant effect of age on expectancy as well as risk-taking behavior. Boys and adults displayed high expectancy and higher preference for intermediate risk. In fact, the entire finding of Chaubey's study using different types of measures for need for achievement and risk-taking revealed a close association between moderate risk-taking and rapid economic development. Those from developed villages had a stronger preference for moderate risk in comparison to their counter-parts from undeveloped villages. The latter were also found to be more conservative and displayed a very strong tendency of risk avoidance (Chaubey and Sinha, 1974). Satvir Singh (1976, 1978) who compared two brothers who were both engaged in farming but one of them had shown significant advancement while the farms of the other were in a bad shape, concluded that certain psychological variables differentiated successfully the fast and slow progressing farmers. The progressive farmers' behaviour was associated with decision making, activity preference, upward striving, positive attitudes towards earning, pride in work job involvement, and risk-orientation. The slow moving farmers were significantly higher on interaction orientation. It was concluded (Singh, 1978, p. 68) that comparison of data for the extreme groups on the basis of farm output suggested that attitude towards money making on the farm, cautious decision making, pride in work, personal standing in his own eyes and in the eyes of others, striving for better standard of living, preference for work rather than being idle were the strongest and most consistent sources of growth in agricultural productivity. The identified—retarder of farm output was more interested in maintaining interpersonal relationships. In another study (Singh, 1976), the high growth rate group of farmers were found to have significantly higher level of need for achievement. Singh and Gupta (1977) have observed the significant effect of need for achievement on the exponential growth rate scores of their subjects. On the other hand, need for power and need for affiliation were not significant effects. However, the interaction between need for power and need for affiliation was a significant variable in agricultural growth.

## Education and Motivation

The results of some of the studies that have been reviewed earlier indicate the importance of a distinct pattern of motivation to successful farming. It has been frequently contended that modern agriculture necessitates certain amount of risk-taking and a distinct pattern of need structure among the farmers. Playing all the time safe and with no desire towards betterment have been found negatively associated with agricultural growth. Moreover, of the factors which seem to generate proper kind of motivation, education has generally been found to be significant. In our own studies (Sinha, 1974) we observed that educational background of the farmers did seem to affect the score on motivation on some of the measures used, especially the conventional type of test of level of aspiration. Those with some amount of formal education tended to set higher performance goal, had higher positive goal-discrepancy index and, generally speaking, displayed greater striving in comparison to illiterate farmers. Among farmers from highly developed villages there was a moderate relationship between education and some measures of level of aspiration. In their study (Roy, Fliegel, Kivlin and Sen, 1968) also education was found to have positive relationship with adoption of innovations in farming. Chaubey and Sinha (1972) while comparing farmers from highly developed and undeveloped villages observed that education unto the middle level is associated with intermediate risk-taking and higher level of aspiration. It was concluded that if education is a variable, then any programme calculated to raise the level of aspiration of farmers will have to take into account their level of education (Chaubey, 1971). Muthayya (1971) found most of his subjects in the lower aspiration group to be either illiterate (63%) or literate with no formal education (29.6%). Muthayya (1971, p. 47), on the basis of his findings, concluded that "Thus it may be said that level of education of respondents with high aspiration and middle aspiration is greater than with low aspiration suggesting a broad generalization that one's level of education influences one's level of aspiration as the former may provide the necessary confidence to forge ahead with regard to any endeavor" (p. 47).

# Role of Education

A number of points emerge from the above reviews of some studies on farmers relating to their motivation and education. Firstly, education at least up to middle level seems to be a factor associated with higher aspiration and greater urge towards improvement which in its turn seems to characterize successful farmers. Secondly, if a distinct motivational syndrome is associated with higher level of rural development, steps are needed to generate and inculcate the right kind of urges among farmers. Thirdly, while there is no direct evidence relating to higher levels of education, the studies reveal that education at least up to middle level is closely associated with the right kind of motivation. Therefore, some amount of education closely integrated with rural needs and inculcating certain skills that are useful in development is likely to have the right kind of impact.

Reluctance to take risk, stagnant aspiration and strong fear of failure have been characterized as being typical of Indian farmers. This kind of motivational syndrome has its roots in various socio-cultural and religious factors and it is not necessary here to delve into them. It would be sufficient to point to the need for generating what is usually called realistic or intermediate risk-taking attitude which is consistently considered as an effective motivational factor in development. Furthermore, reality-orientation and clarity of needs are other components of effective motivational syndrome. These have to be inculcated through various programmes of training. The author is not much enamored by the "instant coffee" type of programmes for boosting motivation that have become fashionable these days. What is required is judicious use of institutional and group influences to enhance motivation of individuals inculcation of realistic risk taking through children's games and provision of inputs contingent upon the desired change of behaviour among farmers. So far our development strategy, especially concerning the distribution of inputs, has generally produced among farmers dependency on government and other external agencies. It is contended that this dependency is detrimental to sustained and self-generating development. Easy money does not bring genuine motivation (Bogaert, 1984). It is suggested that instead of providing inputs in unilateral manner it should be modelled on instrumental learning paradigm, making availability of inputs contingent upon necessary motivation and change in behaviour. These are some general suggestions for inculcating the desired motivational syndrome through education and other processes. They require testing.

To conclude, we will summarize the main findings of a very interesting and significant paper presented to the regional workshop at ANS Institute of Social Studies, Patna, by Father Bogaert (1984) which indicated the nexus of relationship between education, motivation and development. Through the method of "participatary evaluation", an assessment was made as to what adult education programme had done to tribal development. It had "changed people rather than provide any material benefits". To put it more specifically, as a result of the adult education programme, the tribals felt that they were no longer considered *buddhus* (stupid), and had developed an understanding about how the block, banks and post-offices worked. Their eyes had opened to the problems of the village. Fear and confusion were removed, and they had developed self-confidence and a positive attitude to life which had made them ready to take risks involved in modern agricultural practices. They began to care for each other, had experience of power when they organized themselves into groups (like Gram Vikas Kendra) for group decisions and collective action towards village improvement. They started to participate in the process of development rather than allow things to happen to them. As they themselves put it, from being like "chicken without feathers"—naked and utterly vulnerable before lower block administrators, they could not approach them with confidence. As a result, the petty officers had to be careful, and corruption was reduced. In fact, while obtaining loans from the banks, they had to part with 25% or more in the form of bribe. Now, the rate had come down to roughly 15%.

The programme had also broadened the communication network and increased their contacts with the project personnel, visitors and so on. It was stated that because of the adult education programme, people began to send their children to schools and expected the teachers to teach.

It is difficult to say that all these changes were specifically brought about by the adult education programme. Definite causal nexus is difficult to establish. But what is important to note is that these reflect the causal relations as perceived by the people. That itself is of significance.

It is also to be noted that these changes were resented by the petty administrative functionaries as it meant a reduction of their power, loss of income and a compulsion to discharge their duties. Psychologically, it can be said that education had generated among the people a general state of arousal and awareness so that they had become sensitive to their environment, and developed an urge and a capacity to utilize it, and had opened channels of communication. All these helped to build a pressure for development from below so that the developmental effort from being a purely government-sponsored Sarkari programme became a people's programme. Father Bogaert's study gives an indication of the linkages between education, motivation and development.

# 12

# Applied Social Psychology in India*†

As a psychologist I always feel somewhat jealous of economics, which compared to other branches of social science is a little "unsocial". Of all the social sciences, it puts the least emphasis on socio-cultural factors. But if you look at your life, economics seems to have made the largest contribution whether for good or bad. Many of us seem to feel that an ordinary man would have been better off, and life much simpler and more comfortable if the economists had not meddled with it so much. But whether we like it or not, the economists are here to stay, and have the largest say in matters of planning and policy making. Their developmental theories and models manufactured in the London School of Economics, Cambridge, or Harvard are taken cognizance of by everyone concerned. The question of whether they are applicable or not to our setting is irrelevant. As far as the formulation of national plans, policies, and strategies for their implementation are concerned, it is the economists who matter. It is only recently, probably due to the experience of failure

* Note: Inaugural speech at the first seminar on applied social psychology organized by the Department of Psychology, Bhopal University, Bhopal. The seminar was held from the 9th to 12th February, 1987. Normally I don't like delivering inaugural speeches or keynote addresses, for I prefer sitting on the other side. But it was the insistence of Girishwar, as well as the fact that this subject is of great importance and has been of concern to me and dear to my heart that made me accept the invitation. In any case, I am thankful to the authorities of Bhopal University, in particular to the Department of Psychology and to Girishwar, and to all those who thought of me and conferred this honour.

† Reproduced, with permission, from Sinha, D. (1990). Applied Social Psychology in India. In G. Misra (ed.), *Applied Social Psychology in India.* New Delhi: SAGE Publications.

This text has been edited for typographical errors, stylistic consistency and sequential organization in order to make it suitable for inclusion in the book.

of some of our plans in spite of their being so "rational", that other social scientists like the sociologists, anthropologists, and to some extent political scientists have tended to come into the picture, though only as second-class citizens. We psychologists are discontented at being left out. As it has been put half humorously, "economic development is much too serious a topic to be left to economists" (Meier & Baldwin, 1957). Therefore, if development is *too serious* a subject for the economists to deal with satisfactorily, other *serious* people like sociologists, anthropologists, and even psychologists have to come in. Within the next few minutes I shall try to give a bird's eye view of the situation, and what psychologists can do to justify their entrance into this new field.

In spite of the primary position occupied by economics as an applied social science, there is prevalent dissatisfaction with the application of economic principles even among the economists. I would start by quoting a Nobel Laureate economist, Wassily Leontief, whose input–output ratio is well-known, and who has had a great impact on the thinking in this country. Leontief in his presidential address to the 23rd American Economic Association in 1970 is reported to have expressed an "uneasy feeling about the present state of the discipline" though "it is riding the crest of respectability and popular acclaim so far as the social sciences are concerned". What was the cause of this uneasiness? He contended that it was not the *irrelevance* of the practical problems to which the economists addressed their efforts, but the palpable inadequacy of scientific means with which they tried to solve these problems. He regarded the consistently indifferent performance in practical applications as a symptom of the fundamental imbalance in the present state of the discipline. If Leontief had an "uneasy feeling" about economics, I wonder what degree of uneasiness a sensitive psychologist would experience about social psychology and its applications, particularly as far as India is concerned. Though social psychology is so intimately related to man and his many interactions, in its present form it is probably the least connected with human affairs and with problems that really matter. The only mitigating factor in this context is that social psychology in the field of its application is a comparatively new phenomenon. Before 1950, textbooks rarely, if at all, mentioned its applications. Even in the 750 odd pages of the two volumes of the *Handbook of Applied Psychology* by Fryer and Henry, published in 1950, the expression "applied social psychology" as such did not appear either in the index or as a chapter heading, although the collection contained quite a lot that could be called applied social psychology.

The textbook by Krech and Crutchfield (1948) was probably the first book on social psychology which had a subheading "applied social psychology" running into just about a page-and-a-half. Even the famous two-volume *Handbook of Social Psychology* (Lindzey, 1954) contained only one chapter on the applications of social psychology. There has, however, been an increasing interest in applications of social psychological knowledge especially since the mid-fifties, i.e., since the post-World War II years. The war experiences have made us wiser. The second edition of the *Handbook of Social Psychology* published in 1969 (Lindzey & Aronson, 1969) provides an example of this trend. The entire fifth volume of this edition is devoted to applications and includes discussions on a wide range of topics. There are nine chapters which give an idea of the scope of applications. These are: prejudice and ethnic relations, effects of mass media on communication, industrial social psychology, psychology and economics, political behavior, social psychology of education, social psychological aspects of international relations, psychology of religion, and social psychology of mental health. Except for social psychological aspects of international relations and psychology of religion, social psychologists in India have been making contributions to almost all of the above areas. Except for a couple of papers by Dr. A.K.P. Sinha and O.P. Upadhyay (1960a, 1960b), we have not contributed considerably to the area of international relations. The two surveys of researchers in psychology in India sponsored by the ICSSR—one up to 1970 and the other extending to 1976, edited by Mitra (1972) and Pareek (1980–1981) respectively, give a general idea of the nature and quality of work by Indian scholars in the applied social field.

Without going into the details of the studies or critically examining them in any specific manner, it is to be observed, as I have done elsewhere (Sinha, 1986a), that the general shortcoming of all our researches in all these spheres is that in a lot of them we have followed the dictum of endless repetitions and aimless replications. We have used instruments which are rarely appropriate to the sample under study, and have also used all kinds of questionnaires of very doubtful character in our surveys, so much so that sometimes social psychology in India has been very rightly characterized as *Questionnaire Psychology* (Sinha, 1981, p. 14). I would like to add the word 'bad' to the questionnaire psychology, because most of the questionnaires are really worth very little. This was the situation till some years ago though now it seems to have changed considerably.

Another shortcoming limiting our utility as an applied science is that most of our researches are of an *ad hoc* nature, lacking a sound theoretical base or conceptualization. These researches are mostly empirical studies for the sake of empiricism. It would be beneficial to remember what Kurt Lewin has said about the importance of theory in empirical research. Moreover, there has been a lot of imitation and borrowing from the west—we have used conceptualizations which are hardly ours and have forgotten, as I have always said, that the model of man which is implicit in our thinking is western. Take, for example, the concept of adjustment. The way we have been using it implies that control of external environment is essential. As far as our outlook is concerned, there is no question of controlling the environment, there is no question even of the dichotomy between man and nature, so that the idea of control does not become important. As far as our model of man is concerned, man and nature are in a kind of symbiotic relationship where there is complete identity between one and the other. Therefore, adjustment is not control: adjustment is *learning to live with your environment*. In any case, it is rightly said that when we transfer concepts and techniques, we are doing something which is not quite justified. It is very difficult to transfer concepts, and it is equally difficult to transfer tools to a cultural setting which is entirely different. Most of our tools and concepts have been developed in the west, and we just cannot afford to borrow and use them uncritically.

Jahoda (1973) has very rightly pointed out that psychological data and theories are products of a very specific social milieu of advanced industrial societies whose features are literacy, impersonality, universality, and a wide range of available beliefs, ideas, and attitudes. It is true that the theories, derived in such countries have found reasonably good applications in a very limited area of our life, for example, in industry, educational institutions, clinical settings, and so on. In these spheres, the applied theories have certainly made valuable contributions because these institutions share to a considerable extent some of the stable characteristics of the environment from which these theories have been derived (Jahoda, 1980). But such conditions of relative stability are in general almost totally absent not only in India but in most of the Third World countries. All the time people are facing uncertainties and instabilities that are the core characteristics of the rapid socioeconomic changes taking place in these countries. Therefore, when faced with issues that are mainly the accompaniments or consequences of rapid change, the generalizations and theories that we have borrowed appear to have very little relevance or utility on problems like violence, student unrest, intergroup tensions, divided identities, and loyalties-tenacities of the subnational entities based on linguistic, ethnic, and regional considerations and countering the ill-effects of such environmental factors as migration and overcrowding, to mention a few—the existing western theories and principles only permit post hoc explanations and interpretations hardly providing any scientific basis for policy decisions or action programs. One tends to agree with Jahoda (1980) when he says that "Social psychology is still very weak as regards theories relevant to the studies in developing countries." This is a very significant statement and should be remembered. In order to be useful for the proper understanding of issues confronted by these countries, theories and principles should articulate the relationship between the socio-psychological processes and particular kinds of social systems, preferably taking into account social change.

Thanks to Professor S.C. Dube, being an urban oriented, rural born person, I was once again taken to the rural areas. Whatever I have done in these areas I owe to Professor Dube because he forced me out of the comforts of working in the rarefied atmosphere of a laboratory to working in a much more complex but exciting field of agro-economic and rural development (Sinha, 1969). The rural areas have since become popular. When I look upon the kind of studies which are now quite voluminous in the country, it is strange that even while studying naive and illiterate people from remote villages or tribal areas, we uncritically use verbal techniques, western personality inventories and scales without bothering to find out whether their items are even comprehended, or if the concepts are present in the minds of the respondents. Items are taken out of their context and irrespective of the mental framework of the person, they are applied, data gathered, and with readily available computers, the most sophisticated analysis is generated resulting in a very neat junk that gets published.

I recently prepared a paper entitled "Psychology in Rural Areas: The Case of a Developing Country" (Sinha, 1985a), which has been published in a volume called Cross-Cultural and National Studies in Social Psychology edited by Diaz-Guerrero. I pointed out that the rural and urban constitute two largely independent subsystems which require separate tools for data collection, and separate parameters for analysis and understanding in their own right. One cannot understand the rural by applying the parameters and principles derived from urban samples. Psychology, as it has developed in the west and which we have borrowed so uncritically, is a discipline whose data have been largely derived from the study of the urban middle class educated samples. Data and models of this urban discipline provide inadequate basis for understanding rural culture and behavior. The core characteristics of rural environment make it qualitatively distinct from the urban and any analysis of rural life has to be done against its own backdrop: In spite of all the limitations, the contribution of Indian psychology in analyzing rural problems has been considerable. I would go to the length of saying that we have set our mark in this area, and have thereby extended the boundary of social psychology as it traditionally existed. As in sociology, we have helped to develop a new sub discipline of "rural psychology". In the book that I am preparing on this subject, I will show that whenever we have been innovative and conscious of the social reality, we have done our job well, and whenever we have been imitative, we have made a mess.

Change being the core characteristic of our social, cultural, economic, and even of our physical environment social psychology, has to take into cognizance, at all times, the phenomenon of social change. Almost all of our social problems have to be conceptualized and understood against this background. In a recent paper on family, I have used change as a kind of ever present phenomenon (Sinha, 1984a). Socialization or the mental health problems of a growing child cannot be understood without taking into account the general backdrop of rapid social change. In fact, in the developing countries, social change and development have almost become a value and a kind of slogan so much so that in the name of development you are allowed to denude forests and permanently damage the ecology. However, leaving aside the seamy side, it is through developmental efforts and effecting large-scale social transformations that quick eradication of poverty and establishment of an egalitarian society, which constitute our main goals, are possible. In this context some advice to psychologists who want to work in the field is timely. Before the talks of applied social psychology commence, it is essential to be fully familiar with the planning documents, because they provide the framework in which one has to operate. They lay down the main national goals, and outline the various areas of development and strategies. After getting to know these documents properly as a psychologist, you have to see if you have a role to play and in what way you can contribute to planning and development. Thus, to those who talk about national development and social change from a psychological angle, I suggest that they should first read the introductory chapter of the first Five Year Plan which Nehru is supposed to have written, and then the current plan.

To bring about quick economic growth with social justice and to bridge the gap between the rich and the poor, with overall improvement in the quality of life, involve certain processes that are unsettling and have obvious psychological repercussions. All developing countries are in a hurry, as it were, to improve their socio-economic condition. If you look at a typically Indian scenario, but which applies to other countries as well, you will find that they are eager to catch up with the level of economic development that has taken the west generations to attain. The processes that have brought about the present level of development in the west started with the downfall of the Roman empire and was followed by the Renaissance; the Reformation; the French, American, and Russian revolutions; the breakdown of feudalism; and was rapidly accelerated by the industrial and agricultural revolutions with their accompanying scientific innovations and change in lifestyle, and more recently the revolution in electronics. Now, think of the time span covering all these processes and then think of the time within which we are trying to enter the 21st century. What have these changes done? Two processes have occurred which we as social psychologists must take into account. The first is the telescopic nature of change, i.e., changes which took centuries to come about in the west we are trying to compress in a generation or two. The second, which is more important and about which Myrdal (1968) in his book *Asian Drama* has discussed, is the cacophonic nature of change. Similar to disharmony, in which notes do not follow the order in a symphonic or regular pattern so that there is melody and harmony, but are jumbled together. The cacophonic and temporal compression of changes in conjunction has produced a condition that is highly unsettling, both for the individual and the society. Such instability is accompanied by an increase in the incidence of riots, suicides, violence, crime, delinquency, alcoholism, alienation, and all types of social disorganizations. It is against this general setting of change and instability that problems have to be viewed. The problems arising out of change are the ones that require immediate attention of social psychologists. They are to be studied, though not in a routine and stereotyped manner by using western concepts, personality inventories or measures which are hardly applicable, but by looking afresh at the problems and understanding them in their proper socio-cultural context. Social psychology which had been absent from the arena of social change has begun to take into its purview problems arising from it.

In most books on social psychology, social change does not even find a place in the index, let alone merit a discussion on it. It has no place in Lindzey's first edition of the *Handbook*. It finds a place, though only peripherally, in the second edition of the *Handbook*, where topics like developing countries and change are mentioned in about half a dozen places in the course of thousands of pages of its five volumes. It is only recently that things have begun to change, and I think I deserve some credit for it. As far back as 1966, during the Chandigarh session of the Indian Science Congress, the theme of my presidential address to the Section of Psychology and Educational Sciences was "Psychology on the Arena of Social Change" (Sinha, 1966). Utilizing a study of agro-economic development that I had conducted, which was sponsored by the National Institute of Community Development (Sinha, 1969), I made a plea that it is time for the psychologists to enter the arena. I indicated the kind of studies that we should be undertaking. It is satisfying to know that the notion became popular. About a year later in 1967 a conference was held at Ibadan (Nigeria) where some very prominent social psychologists from all over the world, including one from India, were present. They laid down the agenda of work for social psychologists in the context of development and social change (DeLamater, Hefner & Clignet, 1968). Some of us have been active in various international organizations and forums. We have not only hosted many symposia on psychology and social change and development, but we have instituted, for almost a decade, a section called the Division of National Development under the International Association of Applied Psychology. Now we have a special project of the International Union of Psychological Science called the International Network of Institutions and Individuals which deals with problems of the Third World countries, of which I am the coordinator. In every international meet, the topic of applied social psychology occupies a reasonably prominent place. However, reflecting their ethnocentric bias, the scholars in the west have not even bothered to look at the work of Indian and Asian scholars many of whom have been published in western journals.

The topics that are coming into prominence in our country, so far as research in applied social psychology is concerned, are motivational dimensions of rural development; communication and diffusion of innovations related to agriculture; health and population control; leadership in rural and industrial settings; political behavior; political efficacy; power redistribution, especially in the context of the rise of trade unions; new style of management; factors in organization building; family in change; socialization; and health behavior research. The last topic has recently come into prominence. It is interesting to note that a comparison of the census figures for 1971 and 1981 reveals that we Indians have the dubious privilege of having the disease of poverty as well as the disease of affluence. Because of malnutrition and poverty in India, we are highly susceptible to all the communicable diseases and at the same time because of certain changes in lifestyle we are increasingly becoming the victims of cardio-vascular ailments.

Apart from socio-psychological factors in the health behavior, socio-demographic and cultural aspects of mental-health are also receiving attention. Further, psychological correlates of poverty, problems of identity, social prejudice including secularism, values, basic Indian character and development, social violence, ecocultural factors in human development, and many others represent the main areas of research interest of social psychologists in India. These studies contribute toward imparting a new look to the discipline. Their special features are not only that they are characterized by growing sophistication as far as method of analysis is concerned but that they yield data which are suggestive of newer principles, models and concepts, and are also "relevant" indicating strategies for intervention. To give an example or two, Neki (1973) developed a new model of psychotherapy, i.e., the *guru–chela* relationship paradigm. Dr J.B.P. Sinha (1980) has also worked out a new model of effective management in this transitory phase, called the "nurturant task-leader" which is task oriented with structural expectations from subordinates, and draws upon cultural values like affection, dependency, and need for personalized relationship.

We have also been innovative with regard to our tools. Father Bogaert (1984), while making an assessment of the adult education program came forward with a new technique of data collection called "participative evaluation". In a study analyzing the tensions, cooperation, competitions, and alignments among caste groups in some villages, not only have the conventional techniques like questionnaire and interview schedules popular in social sciences been used, but historical material, depth interview, and diary of events in the village over a period of time have also been utilized (J. Gopal & Tiwari, 1985). The methods used for data collection display innovativeness and are appropriate to the semi-literate rural setting of Bihar. I have been responsible for developing tests for measuring levels of aspiration (Sinha, 1969), and for psychological differentiation (Sinha, 1984) by utilizing their (the tests), original paradigms and by suiting the test materials and procedures to the life and culture of the people. Many others have been active in this direction. In the process a new look to the subject is being imparted, and it is becoming more "Indian". In a recent paper I have called this the process of indigenization of psychology (Sinha, 1996b). Whether this trend is good or bad, I leave to your judgement.

Let me now conclude. I have been giving you a somewhat rosy picture of social psychology in India so far as researches are concerned. As regards their utilization, the picture is very disappointing. In spite of the fact that many of us have tried to show how the reinforcement principle could be utilized for dealing with many of the problems like campus violence, inducing developmental activities, when it comes to implementation, the principle is forgotten and goes back to preconceived notions, ideas, and hunches, I need not go to any length into this question of utilization of scientific data in decision making. One good exercise would be to know how much of the scientific input, including that from economics, is actually used by administrators in planning and in the implementation of programs. Rarely are they based on sound scientific data concerned with planning. Professor Harish Ganguli (1971) rightly remarked that the association of psychologists with governmental efforts in planning and implementation of national programs is less than that of other social scientists. Pareek (1980) observed that "there are signs of growing crisis in psychology" in the sense that it has "failed to make a thrust in the national life." The situation is similar in Africa. Referring to the Zambian scene which is typical of the African situation, Alastair Heron (1975) comments that psychologists are likely to be seen somewhat as a luxury by developing nations even when they demonstrated their potential as contributors to national development. We Indians are not unique. The disease is much more widespread.

The question is why have we been neglected? Why do people rarely bother about psychology? It is not necessary to go into the general question of utilization of social sciences by planners and policy makers. I would confine myself to psychology. Looking at the discipline I always feel that though we deal intimately with human nature and interrelationships, as a science we still tend to remain esoteric, investigating segmented phenomenon often leading to trivialities, so that insight and understanding have been sacrificed for methodological sophistication. We break reality into bits and pieces, because it is difficult to use sophisticated techniques in total reality. Therefore, the dictum followed is that it is best to use sophisticated techniques rather than know and understand social reality. Such researches frequently lack external validity. The main concern seems to be methodological sophistication, neatness, and experimental design and control even at the cost of distorting, if not entirely falsifying social reality. The data obtained may be easily amenable to sophisticated statistical analysis, but as far as understanding of the reality is concerned, they are of little use. Shunning away from the complexities of social reality and playing about with micro-variables seems to be done more for the sake of convenience rather than for gaining insight. Following Baumrin's (1970) statement in an APA publication called *Psychology and the Problems of Society*, I would assert that "doing disinterested science or science for the sake of science is likely to be immoral." It is rather an extreme statement but it does strike a friendly and harmonious chord in my heart.

Two things are necessary for social psychologist for doing relevant research. First, it is essential to widen the horizon and become a little more multidisciplinary. You cannot understand social reality if you have a narrow vision. Second, you cannot afford to fight shy of the systemic and structural variables which you tend to do because of your preference and unique skill in dealing with microcosmic variables. I would make a plea for "macropsychology" (Sinha, 1985b) which by its orientation is likely to be more useful in understanding the many pressing problems of social change and development facing the country, and also help in evolving strategies for their solution. I hope that the social psychologists in this country would accept the challenge and make a significant contribution in the world of psychology and thereby widen the conventional frontiers of the discipline.

To conclude, I would quote an economist and once again a Nobel Laureate. This time it is Jan Tinbergen who said in the conference of the Third World economists that "the economists of rich countries can perhaps permit themselves the luxury: sometimes to engage in research of little use; just for fun, intellectual or otherwise." He asserted that "let us choose our subjects with intentions to be of some use to the masses forced to live below the poverty line. Let us not discuss theoretical details unless they are relevant to empirical testing of relationships we need to know for policy design. Let us not discuss models that rest on assumptions far from reality." I strongly feel that social psychologists in India should carefully bear in mind Tinbergen's advice and be of some use to people on whose resources they exist.

# References

Abelew, T. (1974). Sex role attitudes, perceptual style, mathematical ability and perceived parental child-rearing attitudes in the adolescents. Unpublished Doctoral Dissertation, Fordham University, USA, *Dissertation Abstracts International*, 35, 1439 B.

Adair, J.G. (1989). *Development of the discipline and its contribution to social development in developing countries.* Paper presented at the Inter American Congress of Psychology, Buenos Aires, Argentina.

Adair, J.G. (1992a). Empirical studies of indigenization and development of the discipline in developing countries. In S. Iwawaki, Y. Kashima, & K. Leung (eds), *Innovations in cross-cultural psychology* (pp. 62–74). Amsterdam/Liisse: Swets & Zeitlinger, B.V.

Adair, J.G. (1992b, January 3–7). *The indigenization psychology bandwagon: Cautions and considerations.* Paper presented at the Asian Regional Conference of the IACCP, Kathmandu.

Adair, J.G., Puhan, B.N., & Vohra, N. (1993). Indigenization of psychology: Empirical assessment of progress in Indian research. *International Journal of Psychology*, 28, 149 169.

Agarwal, A., & Tripathi, K.K (1980). Temporal orientation and deprivation. *Journal of Psychological Researches*, 24, 144–152.

Agarwal, A.K., Mehta, U.K., & Gupta, S.C. (1978). Joint family and neurosis: A study of the wives of male neurotics. *Indian Journal of Psychiatry*, 20, 232.

Agarwal, K.G. (1975). Psychology or adaptology? *Social Scientist*, 1–5.

Agarwal, K.N., Agarwal, D.K., & Upadhyay, S.K. (1988). Malnutrition and mental functions in school children. In K.N. Agarwal & B.D. Bhatia (eds), *Update growth*. Varanasi: Institute of Medical Sciences, Department of Pediatrics, BHU.

Agarwar, R., & Misra, G. (1986). A factor analytic study of achievement goals and means: An Indian view. *International Journal of Psychology*, 21, 717–731.

Akhilananda, S. (1946/1948). *Hindu psychology.* London: George Allen & Unwin.

Akhilananda, S. (1952). *Mental health and Hindu psychology.* London: George Alien & Unwin.

Al Faruqi, I.R. (1988). *Islamization of knowledge: General principles and work plan.* Washington D.C.: International Institute of Islamic Thought.

Alechina, I. (1982). The contribution of the United Nations system to formulating development concepts. In *Different theories and practices of development.* Paris: UNESCO.

Allport, G.W. (1955). *Becoming.* New Haven: Yale University Press.

Allport, G.W., & Pettigrew, P.P. (1957). Cultural influence on the perception of movement: The trapezoidal illusion among Zulus. *Journal of Abnormal and Social Psychology*, 55, 105–111.

Amir, Y. (1975). Perceptual articulation in three Middle Eastern cultures. *Journal of Cross Cultural Psychology, 6*, 406–416.

Amir, Y., Sharan, S., & Preale, I. (1970). Perceptual articulation, socialization patterns and task effectiveness. *Megamot, 17*, 262–268

Anand, B.K., Chhina, G.S., & Singh, B. (1969). Some aspects of electro-encephalograpnic studies in yogis. In C. Tart (ed.), *Altered states of consciousness* (pp. 503–516). New York: John Wiley.

Andrews, F.M., & Withy, S.B. (1976). *Social indicators of well-being: American's perceptions of life quality*. New York: Plenum Press.

Ardila, R. (1982). Psychology in Latin America today. *Annual Review of Psychology, 33*, 103–122.

Ardila, R. (1985). Psychology in Latin America. In R.J. Corsini (ed.), *Encyclopedia of psychology* (Vols. 1–4, pp. 141–142). New York: Wiley.

Asthana, H.S. (1956). Some aspects of personality structuring in Indian (Hindu) social organization. *Journal of Social Psychology, 44*, 155–163.

Atal, Y. (1981). The cult for indigenization. *International Social Science Journal, 33*, 189–197.

Averasturi, L.G. (1980). Psychology and health care in Cuba. *American Psychologist, 35*, 1090–1095.

Azuma, H. (1984). Psychology in a non-western country. *International Journal of Psychology, 19*, 45–56.

Baran, D. (1971). *Development of validation of a TAT-type projective test for use among Bantu-speaking people*. Johannesburg, South Africa: National Institute for Personnel Research Council for Scientific and Industrial Research.

Bartlett, F.C. (1923). *Psychology and primitive culture*. Cambridge: Cambridge University Press.

Bartlett, F.C. (1932). *Remembering*. Cambridge: Cambridge University Press.

Basham, A.L. (1971). *The wonder that was India*. Calcutta: Rupa & Co.

Bassa, D.M. (1978). From the traditional to the modern: Some observations in Indian child-rearing and parental attitudes with special reference to identity formation. In E.J. Anthony & C. Chiland (eds), *The child and his family in a changing world*. New York: John Wiley.

Baumrin, B. (1970). The immorality of irrelevance: the social role of science. In F.F. Korten, Cook, S., & Lacey, J.I. (eds), *Psychology and the problems of society*. Washington, D.C.: American Psychological Association.

Beena, C. (1990). *Personality typologies: A comparison of Western and ancient Indian approaches*. New Delhi: Commonwealth Publishers.

Berman, J.J., Murphy-Bebman, V., & Singh, P. (1985). Cross-cultural similarities in perception of fairness. *Journal of Cross-Cultural Psychology, 16*, 55–67.

Bernstein, B. (1973). *Class, code and control: Vol. 2. Applied studies towards sociology of language*. London: Routledge & Kegan Paul.

Berry, H., Bacon, M.K., & Child, I.L. (1957). A cross-cultural survey of some sex differences in socialization. *Journal of Abnormal and Social Psychology, 55*, 327–332.

Berry, J.W. (1966). Temne and Eskimo perceptual skills. *International Journal of Psychology, 1*, 207–229.

Berry, J.W. (1972). Radical cultural relativism and the concept of intelligence. In L.J. Cronbach & P.J.D. Drenth (eds), *Mental tests and cultural adaptations* (pp. 77–88). The Hague: Mouton.

References 187

Berry, J.W. (1974). Canadian psychology: Some social and applied emphases. *Canadian Psychologist, 15*, 132–139.

Berry, J.W. (1976). *Human ecology and cognitive style: Comparative studies in cultural and psychological adaptation.* New York: Wiley.

Berry, J.W. (1980). Social and cultural change. In H.C. Triandis & R.W. Brislin (eds), *Handbook of cross-cultural psychology* (Vol. 5, pp. 211–279). Boston: Allyn & Bacon.

Berry, J.W. (1986). Multiculturalism and psychology in plural societies. In L.H. Ekstrand (ed.), *Ethnic minorities and immigrants in cross-cultural perspective* (pp. 35–51). Lisse: Swets & Zeitlinger, B.V.

Berry, J.W., & Dasen, P.R. (eds). (1974). *Culture and cognition.* London: Methuen.

Berry, J.W., Mishra, R.C., & Tripathi, R.C. (2003). *Psychology in human and social development: Lessons from diverse cultures.* New Delhi: SAGE Publications.

Berry, J.W., Poortinga, Y.H., Segall, M.H., & Dasen, P.R. (1992). *Cross-cultural psychology: Research and applications.* Cambridge: Cambridge University Press.

Berry, J.W., & Wilde, G.J.S. (eds) (1972). *Social psychology: The Canadian context.* Toronto: McClelland & Stewart.

Bhanthumnavin, D. (1987). Social history of psychology in Thailand. In G.H. Blowers & A.M. Turtle (eds), *Psychology moving east* (pp. 71–88). Boulder: Westview Press.

Bhaskaran, K. (1959). A psychiatric study of schizophrenic patterns in an Indian mental hospital. *International Journal of Social Psychiatry, 5*, 41–46.

Bhaskaran, K. (1963). A psychiatric study of paranoid schizophrenics in a mental hospital in India. *Psychiatric Quarterly, 37*, 734–751.

Bhaskaran, K., Seth, R.C., & Yadav, S.N. (1970). Migration and mental ill-health in industry. *Indian Journal of Psychiatry, 12*, 102–116.

Bhogle, S. (1979). Effects of supplementary food on motor development of rural infants. *Social Change, 9*, 18–22.

Bloom, B. (1964). *Stability and change in human characteristics.* New York: John Wiley.

Boesch, E.E. (1991) *Symbolic action theory and cultural psychology.* Berlin: Springer.

Bogaert, M.V. (1984, March). *Adult education input for tribal development.* Paper presented to the Regional Workshop on educational components of rural development projects. ANS Institute of Social Studies; Patna.

Brim, O.G. (1975). Micro-structural influences on child development and the need for childhood social indicators. *American Journal of Orthopsychiatry, 45*, 516–524.

Brislin, R.W. (1983). Cross-cultural research in psychology. *Annual Review of Psychology, 34*, 363–400.

Bronfenbrenner, U. (1974a). *Experimental human ecology: A reorientation to theory and research on socialization.* Invited Address, American Psychological Association, New Orleans, August.

Bronfenbrenner, U. (1974b). Developmental research public policy and the ecology of childhood. *Child Development, 45*, 1–5.

Bronfenbrenner, U. (1977). Towards an experimental ecology of human development. *American Psychologist, 32*, 513–531.

Busse, T.V. (1969). Child-rearing antecedents of flexible thinking. *Developmental Psychology, 1*, 585–591.

Campbell, A., & Converse, P. (1970). *Monitoring the quality of Americanl life: A proposal to the Russell Sage Foundation.* Ann Arbor: Survey Research Centre, University of Michigan.

Campbell, D.T. (1968). A comparative multinational opinion sample exchange. *Journal of Social Issues, 24*, 245–256.

Campbell, D.T., & Naroll, R. (1972). The mutual methodological relevance of anthropology and psychology. In F.L.K. Hsu (ed.), *Psychological anthropology* (pp. 435–468). Cambridge: Schenkman.

Cannon, W.B. (1932). *The wisdom of the body.* New York: Norton & Co.

Carstairs, G.M. (1957). *The twice-born: A study of the community of high caste Hindu.* London: Hogarth Press.

Channabasavanna, S.M., & Bhatti, R.S. (1982). A study of interactional patterns and family typologies in families of mental patients. In A. Kiev & A. Venkoba Rao (eds), *Readings in transcultural psychiatry* (pp. 149–161). Madras: Higginbotham.

Chatterjee, S.C., & Datta, D.M. (1939). *An introduction to Indian philosophy.* Calcutta: Calcutta University Press.

Chaubey, N.P. (1974). *A study of motivational dimensions of rural development: A study of risk-taking, risk-avoidance and fear of failure in villages.* Allahabad: Chaitanya Publishing House.

Chaubey, N.P. (1974). Effect of age on expectancy of success and on risk-taking behaviour. *Journal of Personality and Social Psychology, 29*, 774–778.

Chaudhuri, N. (1966). *The continent of Circe.* Bombay: Jaico Publishing House.

Chazen, M., Laing, A., Cox, T., & Jackson, S. (1977). Development of children from deprived home background. In *Studies in infant school children: Vol. 2. Deprivation and development.* New York: Basil Blackwell.

Cherns, A.B. (1969). Social psychology and development. *Bulletin of the British Psychological Society, 22*, 93–97.

Ching, C.C. (1984). Psychology and the four modernizations in China. *International Journal of Psychology, 19*, 57–63.

Claeys, W., & De Boeck, P. (1976). The influence of some parental characteristics on children's primary abilities and field independence: A study of adopted children. *Child Development, 47*, 842–845.

Clausen, J.A. (1966). Family Structure, Socialization and Personality. In Lois W. Hoffman & M.L. Hoffman (eds), *Review of Child Development Research*, Vol. 2. New York: Russell Sage Foundation.

Cole, M. (1995). Culture and cognition development: From cross-cultural research to creating systems of cultural mediation. *Culture and Psychology, 1*, 25–54.

Cole, M., Gay, J., & Glick, J. (1968). A cross-cultural study of information processing. *International Journal of Psychology, 3*, 93–102.

Conant, J.B. (1953). *Modern science and modern man.* New York: Double-day.

Danziger, K. (1983). Origins and basic principles of Wundt's Volkerpsychologie. *British Journal of Social Psychology, 22*, 303–313.

Das, J.P., & Molloy, G.N. (1975). Varieties of simultaneous and successive information processing in children. *Journal of Educational Psychology, 67*, 213–220.

Das, J.P., & Singh, P.S. (1975). Caste, class, and cognitive competence. *Indian Educational Review, 10*, 1–18.

Dasen, P.R., & Colomb, E. (1982). The use of Piagetian original scales in the assessment of the impact of malnutrition on cognitive development. In R. Rajalakshmi (ed.), *Nutrition and development of the child.* Baroda, India: M.S. University, Biochemistry Development.

Dasen, P.R., Dembele, B., Ettien, K., Kabran, K., Kamagate, D., Koffi, D.A., & N'Guessan, A. (1985). N'glouele, l'intelligence chez les Baoule. *Archives de Psychologie, 53*, 293–324.

Dash, U.C., & Panda, K.C. (1971). *Effects of certain non-intellective variables on cognitive performance.* Unpublished manuscript, Regional College of Education, Bhubaneshwar.

Dawson, J.L.M. (1963). Traditional values and work efficiency in West African mine labour force. *Occupational Psychology, 37*, 209–218.

Dawson, J.L.M. (1967a). Cultural and physiological influences upon spatial Perceptual Processes in West Africa. Part I. *International Journal of Psychology, 2*, 115–128.

Dawson, J.L.M. (1967b). Cultural and physiological influences upon spatial perceptual processes in West Africa. Part II. *International Journal of Psychology, 2*, 171–185.

De, N.R. (1974). Conditions for work culture. *Indian Journal of Industrial Relations, 9*(4), 587–598.

Delamter, J., Hefner, R., & Clignet, R. (eds). (1968). Social psychological research in developing countries. *Journal of Social Issues, 24*(2).

Dershowitz, A. (1971). Jewish subcultural patterns and psychological differentiation. *International Journal of Psychology, 6*, 223–231.

Diaz-Guerrero, R. (1977). Editorial response. *LACCP Newsletter, 11*(3), 4–6.

Diaz-Guerrero, R. (1984). Contemporary psychology in Mexico. *Annual Review of Psychology, 35*, 83–112.

Doob, L. (1960). *Becoming more civilized.* New Haven, CT: Yale University Press.

Drever, J. (1952). *A dictionary of psychology.* Harmondsworth, Middlesex: Penguin Books.

Dreyer, A.S. (April 1975). Family interaction and cognitive style: Situation and cross-sex effects. In H.B. Biller (Chair). *Beyond father absence: Conceptualization of father effects.* Symposium presented at the meeting of the Society for Research in Child Development, Denver.

Dube, K.C. (1970). A study of prevalence and biosocial variables in mental illness in rural and urban community in Uttar Pradesh, India. *Acta Psychiatrica Scandinavica, 46*, 327–359.

Dube, S.C. (1958). *India's changing villages.* London: Routledge & Kegan Paul.

Dumont, L. (1970). *Homo hierarchicus: The caste system and its implications.* Chicago: Chicago University Press.

Durojaiye, M.O.A. (1985). Psychology in Africa. In R.J. Corsini (ed.), *Encyclopedia of psychology* (Vols. 1–4, pp. 105–111). New York: Wiley.

Dusek, J.B., & Joseph, G. (1983). The base of teacher expectancies: A meta analysis. *Journal of Educational Psychology, 75*, 327–346.

Dwivedi, C.B. (1982, September 21–23). *Towards operationalization of human motivation according to traditional Indian psychology.* Paper presented at the symposium on Human Motivation in the Indian Context, Department of Psychology, Allahabad University, Allahabad.

Dwivedi, C.B. (1986, November 15–17). *Indian concepts of anxiety: An overview.* Paper presented at the national seminar on Anxiety, Department of Psychology, Banaras Hindu University, Varanasi.

Dwivedi, C.B. (1987). On Yogadarsana's *asampramosa* doctrine of memory. *Journal of Indian Psychology, 61*, 1–6.

Dyk, R.B. (1969). An exploratory study of mother-child interaction in infancy as related to the development of differentiation. *Journal of the American Academy of Child Psychiatry, 8*, 657–691.

Dyk, R.B., & Witkin, H.A. (1965). Family experiences related to the development of differentiation in children. *Child Development, 30*, 21–55.

Edgerton, N.E. (1976). The relationship of cognitive style of young children to maternal child rearing practices. Doctoral Dissertation, Florida State University (1975) *Dissertation Abstracts International, 36*, 5135A.

Educational Testing Service. (1988). Minority students in higher education. *Focus* (Princeton, NJ: ETS), 22.

Eiduson, B., Cohen, J., & Alexander, J. (1973). Alternatives in child-rearing in 1970s. *American Journal of Orthopsychiatry, 43*, 721–731.

Elder, G.H. Jr., & Bowerman, C.E. (1963). Family structure and child rearing patterns: The effect of family size and sex composition. *American Social Official Review, 28*, 891–905.

Enriquez, V.G. (1977). Filipino psychology in the Third World. *Philippine Journal of Psychology, 10*, 3–18.

Enriquez, V.G. (1982). *Towards Filipino psychology: Essays and studies on language and culture.* Quezon City: Psychological Research and Training House.

Enriquez, V.G. (1987). Decolonizing the Filipino psyche: Impetus for the development of psychology in the Philippines. In G.H. Blowers & A.H. Turtle (eds), *Psychology moving east* (pp. 265–287). Boulder: Westview Press.

Enriquez, V.G. (1990). *Indigenous psychologies.* Quezon City: Psychology Research and Training House.

Erikson, E.H. (1968). *Identity: Youth and crisis.* New York: W.W. Norton and Co.

Freeman, G.L. (1948). *The energetics of human behavior.* Ithaca, N.Y.: Cornell University Press.

Friend, R.M , & Neale, J.M. (1972). Children's perceptions of success and failure: An attributional analysis of the effects of race and social class. *Developmental Psychology, 2*, 124–128.

Fry, P.S., & Ghosh, R. (1980). Attribution of success and failure: Comparison of cultural differences between Asian and Caucasian children. *Journal of Cross-Cultural Psychology, 11*, 343–346.

Fryer, D.H., & Henry, E.R. (eds), (1950). *Handbook 'of applied psychology.* New York: Rinehart.

Galler, J.R., Ramsey, F. Solimano, G., & Lowell, W.E. (1983). The influence of early malnutrition on subsequent behavioral development, I. Degree of impairment in intellectual performance. *Journal of American Academy of Child Psychology, 22*, 8–15.

Ganguli, H.C. (1971). Psychological research in India: 1920–1967. *International Journal of Psychology, 6*, 165–77.

Gellhorne, E., & Kiely, W.F. (1972). Mystical states of consciousness: Neurophysiological and clinical aspects. *Journal of Nervous and Mental Diseases, 154*, 399–406.

Goheen, J., Srinivas, M.N., Karve, D.G., & Singer, M. (1958). India's cultural values and economic development: A discussion. *Economic Development and Culture Change*, October 1958, 1–12.

Gomez, K.C.L. (1975). Interactional patterns of families of schizophrenics. Unpublished D.P.S.W. dissertation, National Institute of Mental Health and Neurosciences, Bangalore.

Gopal, S. (1989). *Radhakrishnan: A biography.* Delhi: Oxford University Press.

Gore, M.S. (1968). *Urbanization and family change.* Bombay: Popular Prakashan.

Gore, M.S. (1978). Changes in the family and the process of socialization in India. In Anthony E. James & C. Colette (eds), *The child in his family*, Vol. 5. New York: John Wiley & Sons.

Gupta, G.R. (1978). The joint family. In M.S. Das & P.D. Bardis (eds), *The family in Asia* (pp. 72–88). New Delhi: Vikas.

Halpern, R., & Myers, R. (1985). *Effects of early childhood intervention on primary school progress and performance in the developing countries* (mimeo). Ypsilanti, Michigan: High/Scope Educational Research Foundation.

Heelas, P., & Lock, A. (eds). (1981). *Indigenous psychologies: The anthropology of the self.* London: Academic Press.

Heron, A. (1975). Psychology and national development: The Zambian experience. In J.W. Berry & W.J. Lonner (eds), *Applied cross-cultural psychology* (pp. 13–17). Amsterdam: Swets & Zeitlinger B.V.

Hess, R.D. (1970). The transmission of cognitive strategies in the poor: The socialization of apathy and under-achievement. In V.L. Allen (ed.), *Psychological factors in poverty.* New York: Academic Press.

Hewstone, M.E. (1983). *Attribution theory: Social and functional extensions.* London: Basil Blackwell.

Hiriyanna, M. (1951). *Outlines of Indian philosophy.* London: George Allen & Unwin.

Ho, D.Y.F. (1988). Asian psychology: A dialogue in indigenization and beyond. In A.C. Paranjpe, D.Y.F. Ho, & R.W. Rieber (eds), *Asian contributions to psychology* (pp. 53–77). New York: Praeger.

Holahan, C.J. (1977). The role of ecology in community psychology: A tale of three cities. *Professional Psychology*, 8, 25–32.

Holtzman, W.H., Diaz-Guerrero, R., & Swartz, J.D. (1975). *Personality development in two cultures: A cross-cultural longitudinal study of school children in Mexico and the United States.* Austin, Texas: University of Texas Press.

Huxley, A. (1954). *The doors of perception.* London: Chatto & Windus.

Huxley, A. (1957). *Heaven and hell.* London: Chatto & Windus.

ICSSR. (1973). *A report on social science in India*: Vol. I. New Delhi: ICSSR.

ILO. (1969). *International standard classification of occupations.* Geneva: International Labour Office.

Inkeles, A., & Levinson, D.H. (1969). National character: The study of modal personality and socio-cultural systems. In G. Lindzey & E. Aronson (eds), *Handbook of social psychology*, Vol. IV (pp. 418–506). Reading, Mass.: Addison-Wesley.

Inkeles, A., & Smith, D.H. (1974). *On becoming modern.* London: Heinemann.

Irving, D.D. (1970). The field-dependence hypothesis in cross-cultural perspective. (Doctoral Dissertation, Rice University,) *Dissertation Abstracts International*, 1970, 31, 3691B.

Jahoda, G. (1973). Psychology and the developing country: Do they need each other? *International Social Science Journal*, 25, 461–75.

Jahoda, G. (1975). Applying cross-cultural psychology to the third world. In J.W. Berry & W.J. Lonner (eds), *Applied cross-cultural psychology.* Amsterdam: Swets & Zeitlinger.

Jahoda, G. (1980). Cross-cultural comparisons. In M.H. Bornstein (ed.), *Comparative methods in psychology* (pp. 105–148). Hillsdale, N.J.: Erlbaum.

Jahoda, G. (1980). Has social psychology a distinct contribution to make? In. F. Blackler (ed.), *Social psychology and developing countries* (pp. 21–31). Chichester: John Wiley.

Jahoda, G., & Krewer, B. (1997). History of cross-cultural and cultural psychology. In J.W. Berry, Y.H. Poortinga, & J. Pandey (eds), *Handbook of cross-cultural psychology, 1* (pp. 1–42). Boston: Allyn & Bacon.

Jha, H., Sinha, J.B.P., Gopal, S., & Tiwari, K.M. (1985). *Social structure and alignment: A study of rural Bihar*. New Delhi: Usha Publications.

Jones, P.A. (1975). Socialization practices and the development of spatial ability. In J.L.M. Dawson & W.J. Lonner (eds), *Readings in cross-cultural psychology*. Hong-Kong: Hong-Kong University Press.

Kakar, S. (1971b). Authority patterns and subordinate behavior in Indian organizations. *Administrative Science Quarterly*, 16, 298–307.

Kakar, S. (1971a). The theme of authority in social relations in India. *Journal of Social Psychology*, 84, 93–101.

Kakar, S. (1978). *The inner world*. Delhi: Oxford University Press.

Kakar, S. (1979). *Indian childhood: Cultural ideals and social reality*. Delhi: Oxford University Press.

Kakar, S. (1982). *Shamans, mystics and doctors: A psychological inquiry into India and its healing traditions*. Delhi: Oxford University Press.

Kakkar, S.B. (1970). Family conflict and scholastic achievement. *Indian Journal of Psychology*, 45, 159–164.

Kao, H.S.R. (1989). Insights towards a trans cultural psychology: Spotlighting the middle kingdom. *Supplement to the Gazette* (University of Hong Kong), 36, 85–92.

Kapadia, K.M. (1966). *Marriage and family in India*. Bombay: Oxford University Press.

Kapp, W.K. (1963). *Hindu culture, economic development and economic planning in India*. Bombay: Asia Publishing House.

Kapur, P. (1970). *Marriage and the working women in India*. New Delhi: Vikas.

Kardiner, A. (1939). *The individual and his society*. New York: Columbia University Press.

Kaul, B. (1974). *Study of adjustment of women in employment*. Unpublished D. Phil. thesis, Allahabad University, Allahabad.

Kelly, J.G. (1968). Towards an ecological conception of preventive interventions. In J.W. Carter (ed.), *Research contributions from psychology to community mental health*. New York: Behavioural Publication.

Kennedy, S., Scheirer, J., & Rogers, A. (1984). The price of success: Our monocultural science. *American Psychologist*, 39, 996–997.

Khatri, A.A. (1970). Personality and mental health in Indians (Hindus) in the context of their changing family organization. In E.J. Anthony & C. Koupernik (eds), *The child in his family* (Vol. I, pp. 389–412). New York: John Wiley.

Kim, U., Park, Y.S., & Park, D. (2000). The challenge of cross-cultural psychology: The Role of the indigenous psychologies. *Journal of Cross-Cultural Psychology*, 31(1), 63–75.

Klineberg, O. (1938). Emotional expression in Chinese literature. *Journal of Abnormal and Social Psychology*, 33, 517–520.

Koestler, A. (1960). *The lotus and the robot*. New York: Harper and Row.

Kohn, M.L. (1972). Class, family and schizophrenia: A reformulation. *Social Forces*, 50, 295–304.

Kothari, R. (1970). *Politics in India*. New Delhi: Orient Longman.

Krech, D., & Crutchfield, R.S. (1948). *Theory and problems of social psychology*. New York: McGraw-Hill.

Krishnamurthy, K.G., & Nadkarni, M.V. (1983). *Integrated child developments services: An assessment*. New Delhi: UNICEF Regional Office for South Central Asia.

Krishnan, L. (1992). Justice research: The Indian perspective. *Psychology & Developing Societies*, 4, 113–151.

Krutch, J.W. (1954). *The measure of man*. New York: Bobbs-Merill.

Kumar, K. (1979). Indigenization and transnational cooperation in social sciences. In K. Kumar (ed.), *Bonds without knowledge*. Honolulu: East-West Cultural Learning Institute.

Kuppuswamy, B. (1985). *Elements of ancient Indian psychology*. New Delhi: Vikas Publishing House.

Lagmay, A.V. (1984). Western psychology in the Philippines: Impact and response. *International Journal of Psychology, 19*, 31–44.

Lapierre, D. (1986). *The city of joy*. London: Arrow Books Ltd.

Lazar, I., & Darlington, R. (1979). *Lasting effects after preschool: Summary report* (A report of the Consortium for Longitudinal Studies). Washington, DC: U.S. Department of Health & Human Services.

Lazar, I., & Darlington, R. (1982). Lasting effects of early education: A report from the Consortium of Longitudinal Studies. *Monograph of the Society for Research in Child Development, 47* (2–3, Serial No. 195).

Lee, H.W., & Petzold, M. (1987). Psychology in the People's Republic of China. In G.H. Blowers & A.M. Turtle (eds), *Psychology moving east* (pp. 105–125). Boulder: Westview Press.

Leighton, A.H. (1974). Social disintegration and mental disorders. In S. Arieti & G. Kaplan (eds), *American handbook of psychiatry*. New York: Basic Books.

Lewis, W.A. (1955). *Theory of economic growth*. London: Allen & Unwin.

Lien, N.M., Meyer, K., & Winick, M. (1977). Early malnutrition and later adoption into American families. *American Journal of Clinical Nutrition, 30*, 1734–1739.

Lindzey, G. (ed.), (1954). *Handbook of social psychology: 2 Vols.* Cambridge: Addison-Wesley.

Lindzey, G., & Aronson, E. (eds), (1969). *Handbook of social psychology 5 Vols.* Reading, Mass: Addison-Wesley.

Lonner, W. (1989). The introductory psychology text and cross-cultural psychology: Beyond Ekman, Whorf, and Biased I.Q. tests. In D.M. Keats, D. Munro, & L. Mann (eds), *Heterogeneity in cross-cultural psychology* (pp. 4–22). Amsterdam/Libbe: Swets & Zeitlinger, B.V.

Loomba, R.M. (1953). Towards a universal psychology. *Proceedings of the Indian Philosophical Congress*.

Mahler, M., & Jacobson, B. (1964). *The self and the object world*. New York: International University Press.

Malhotra, S., & Malhotra, A. (1985). Culture-conflicts and psychopathology in Indian children. *Indian Journal of Social Psychiatry, 1*, 48–53.

Maller, J.B. (1933).Studies in character and personality in German psychological literature. *Psychological Bulletin, 30*, 209–232.

Malpass, R. (1977). Theory and method of cross-cultural psychology. *American Psychologist, 32*, 1069–1079.

Marriot, K. (1976). Interpreting Indian society: A monistic alternative to Dumont's dualism. *Journal of Asian Studies, 36*, 189–195.

Marriott, M. (ed.). (1990). *India through Hindu categories*. New Delhi: SAGE.

Maslow, A.H. (1954). *Motivation and personality*. New York: Harper.

Mataragnon, R.H. (1988). *Pakikiramdan* in Filipino social interaction: A study of subtlety and sensitivity. In A.C. Paranjpe, D.Y.F. Ho, & R.W. Rieber (eds), *Asian contributions to psychology* (pp. 251–262). New York: Praeger.

McCelland, D.C., Atkinson, J.W., Clark, R.A., & Lowell, E.L. (1953). *Achievement motive*. New York: Appleton-Century.

McClelland, D.C. (1961). *The achieving society.* Princeton: Van Nostrand.

McClelland, D.C. (1975). *Power: The inner experience.* New York: Free Press.

McClelland, D.C., & Winter, D.G. (1969). *Motivating economic development.* New York: Free Press.

Mead, M. (1951). *Coming of age in Samoa.* New York: New American Library (Original work published 1928).

Mead, M. (1951). The study of national character. In D. Lerner & H.D. Lasswell (eds), *The policy sciences.* Stanford: Stanford University Press.

Meade, R.D. (1967). An experimental study of leadership in India. *Journal of Social Psychology, 72,* 35–43.

Mehta, V. (1959). *Walking the Indian streets.* London: Faber and Faber.

Mehta, V. (1962). *Portrait of India.* New York: Penguin Books.

Meier, G.M., & Baldwin, R.E. (1957). *Economic development.* New York: John Wiley.

Meizlik, F. (1973). The effect of sex and cultural variables on field independence/ dependence in a Jewish subculture. Unpublished Master's thesis, City University of New York.

Miller, J.D., Bersoff, D.M., & Harwood, R.L. (1990). Perceptions of social or personal decisions? *Journal of Personality and Social Psychology, 58,* 33–47.

Minturn, L., & Hitchcock, J.T. (1966). *The Rajputs of Khalapur, India.* Six Cultures Series, Vol. III. New York: John Wiley.

Mishra, H., Mishra, S., & Mubthy, H.N. (1974). *TM: As a behavior therapist views it.* Proceedings of the Vth All India Convention of Clinical Psychologists, New Delhi.

Mishra, R.C. (1987, December 25–27). *Cognitive stimulation, training and perceptual-cognitive task performance by socially deprived children.* Paper presented to the U.G.C. National Seminar on Strategies for the Development of Deprived Sections of Indian Society, Department of Psychology, M.K.P. (P.G.) College, Dehradun.

Mishra, V. (1962). *Hinduism and economic growth.* Bombay: Oxford University Press.

Misra, G., & Gergen, K.J. (1993). On the place of culture in psychological science. *International Journal of Psychology, 28,* 225–243.

Misra, G., & Jain, U. (1988). Achievement cognitions in deprived groups: An attributional analysis. *Indian Journal of Current Psychological Research, 1,* 77–88.

Misra, G., & Tripathi, K.N. (2004). Psychological dimensions of poverty and deprivation. In J. Pandey (ed.), *Psychology in India revisited: Developments in the discipline. Vol. 3 Applied social and organizational psychology* (pp. 118–215). New Delhi: SAGE Publications.

Misra, G., & Tripathi, L.B. (1980). *Psychological consequences of prolonged deprivation.* Agra, India: National Psychological Corporation.

Misra, V.N. (1979). *Hindu dharma: Jivan me sanatan ki khoj* [Hindu dharma: The search for the eternal in life]. New Delhi: Radhakrishna Prakashan.

Mitra, S.K. (1972). *A survey of research in psychology.* Bombay: Popular Prakashan.

Mitra, S.K. (1973). Progress of psychology. In *A decade (1963–72) of science in India.* Calcutta: Indian Science Congress Association.

Moghaddam, F.M., & Taylor, D.M. (1986). What constitutes an 'appropriate psychology' for the developing world? *International Journal of Psychology, 21*(1–4), 253–267.

Moghaddam, P. (1987). Psychology in the three worlds: As reflected by the crisis in social psychology and the move towards indigenous third-world psychology. *American Psychologist, 42,* 912–920.

Moghni, S.M. (1987). Development of modern psychology in Pakistan. In G.H. Blowers & A.M. Turtle (eds), *Psychology moving east* (pp. 23–38). Boulder: Westview Press.

Mohan, V., & Sandhu, S. (1986). Development of scale to measure sattvik, rajasik and tamaski gunas. *Journal of Indian Academy of Applied Psychology, 12,* 46–52.

Mohanty, A. (1988). Beyond the horizon of Indian psychology: The Yankee doodler. In F.M. Sahoo (ed.), *Psychology in Indian context* (pp. 1–8). Agra: National Psychological Corporation.

Moscovici, S. (1972). Society and theory in social psychology. In J. Israel & H. Tajfel (eds), *The context of social psychology* (pp. 17–68). London: Academic Press.

Mowrer, O.H. (1952).Introduction. In Swami Akhilananda *Mental health and Hindu psychology.* London: Allen & Unwin.

Mukherjee, B.N. (1980). Psychological theory and research methods. In U. Pareek (ed.), *A survey of research in psychology (Vol I)* (pp. 1–135). Bombay: Popular Prakashan.

Müller, F. Max. (2013). *The six systems of Indian philosophy.* London: Forgotten Books (Original work published 1899).

Munn, N.L. (1946). *Psychology: The fundamentals of human adjustment.* London: George Harrap.

Murlidharan, R. (1969). Size of family and its relationship with behavior difficulties in children. *Journal of Psychological Researches, 13,* 94–100.

Murlidharan, R., & Kaur, B. (1987). A study of the relationship between physical development and language and cognitive development of tribal preschool children. *Bombay Psychologist, 9,* 7–17.

Murphy, L.B. (1953). Roots of tolerance and tensions in Indian child development. In G. Murphy (ed.), *In the minds of men* (pp. 146–158). New York: Basic Books.

Muthayya, B.C. (1971). *Farmers, and their aspirations.* Hyderabad : National Institute of Community Development.

Muthayya, B.C., & Prasad, H.C. (1982). Adult education in rural development: A study of the process of implementation in a block. *Journal of Rural Development, 1*(1), 72–113.

Myers, C. (1960). *Industrial relations in India* Bombay: Asia Publishing House.

Myers, R., & Hertenberg, P. (1987). *The eleven who survive: Toward a re-examination of early childhood development program options and costs.* Washington, DC: World Bank, Education & Training Development.

Myrdal, G. (1968). *Asian drama: An enquiry into poverty of nations.* Vol. 1. New York: Penguin Books.

Nagpal, R., & Sell, H. (1985). *Subjective well-being.* New Delhi: Regional WHO Office for South-East Asia.

Naidu, R.K. (1990). Academic self-respect vs. pseudo universalism: The travails of an Indian psychology teacher. *Indian Journal of Social Science, 3,* 569–574.

Naidu, R.K., Thapa, K., & Das, M.M. (1986). *On measuring detachment: An example of scientific analog of an indigenous concept.* Unpublished manuscript, Department of Psychology, University of Allahabad, Allahabad.

Nair, K. (1961). *Blossoms in the dust.* London: Duckworth.

Nandy, A. (1974). The non-paradigmatic crisis in psychology: Reflections on a recipient culture of science. *Indian Journal of Psychology, 49,* 1–20.

Narain, D. (1957). *Hindu character.* Bombay: University of Bombay.

Nehru, J. (1946/1981). *The discovery of India.* Bombay: Oxford University Press.

Neki, J.S. (1973). *Guru-Chela* relationship: The possibility of a therapeutic paradigm. *American Journal of Orthopsychiatry, 43,* 755–66.

Neki, J.S. (1976). An examination of the cultural relation of dependence as a dynamic of social and therapeutic relationships: I. Social development. *British Journal of Medical Psychology, 49,* 1–10.

Panda, K.C., & Behera, H.P. (1985). Perceived attitude of parents and teachers towards exceptional children. *Journal of Orissa Association of Educational Science and Research*, *2*, 6–18.

Panda, K.C., & Das, J.P. (1970). Acquisition and reversal in four subcultural groups generated by caste and class. *Canadian Journal of Behavioral Science*, *2*, 267–273.

Pande, N., & Naidu, R.K. (1986). Effort and outcome orientations as moderators of stress-strain relationship. *Psychological Studies*, *31*, 207–214.

Pande, N., & Naidu, R.K. (1992). *Anasakti* and health: A study of non-attachment. *Psychology and Developing Societies*, *4*, 89–104.

Pandey, J. (1980). *Social psychological study of ingratiation*. ICSSR Project Report. New Delhi: ICSSR.

Pandey, J. (ed.). (1988). *Psychology in India: The state-of-the-art*. New Delhi: SAGE.

Paranjpe, A.C. (1984). *Theoretical psychology: The meeting of east and west*. New York: Plenum.

Paranjpe, A.C. (1988). A personality theory according to Vedanta. In A.C. Paranjpe, D.Y.P. Ho, & R.W. Rieber (eds), *Asian contributions to psychology* (pp. 185–213). New York: Praeger.

Pareek, U. (1968). Motivational pattern and planned social change. *International Social Science Journal*, *20*(3), 464–473.

Pareek, U. (1970). Poverty and motivation: Figure and ground. In V.L. Allen (ed.), *Psychological factors in poverty*. New York: Academic Press.

Pareek, U. (ed.). (1980a). *A survey of research in psychology, 1971–76, Part-I*. Bombay: Popular Prakashan.

Pareek, U. (1980b), Preface. In U. Pareek (ed.), *A survey of research in psychology, 1971–76, Part-I*. Bombay: Popular Prakashan.

Pareek, U. (ed.). (1981). *A survey of research in psychology, 1971–76, Part-II*. Bombay: Popular Prakashan.

Poortinga, V.H., Van de Vijver, F.R.J., Joe, R.C., & Van de Koppel, J.M.H. (1987). Peeling the onion called culture: A synopsis. In C. Kagitcibasi (ed.), *Growth and progress in cross-cultural psychology* (pp. 22–34). Lisse: Swets & Zeitlinger.

Poortinga, Y.H. (1999). Different Psychologies? *Applied Psychology*, *48*(4), 419–432.

Poortinga, Y.H. (1992, January 3–7). *Indigenous psychology: Scientific ethnocentrism in a new guise*. Invited address to the IVth IACCP Asian Regional Congress, Kathmandu.

Prabhu, P.H. (1966). *Perception, personality and the Indian approach*. Special Lecture, Annamalai University.

Prasad, J. (1935). The psychology of rumour: A study relating to the great Indian earthquake of 1934. *British Journal of Psychology*, *26*, 1–151.

Prasad, M.B., & Prasad, A. (1975). Social and emotional development of pre-school children of employed mothers. *Journal of Social and Economic Studies*, *3*, 73–87.

Preale, I., Amir, Y., & Sharan, S. (1970). Perceptual articulation and task effectiveness in several Israel subcultures. *Journal of Personality and Social Psychology*, *15*, 190–195.

Price-Williams, D.R. (1980). Towards the idea of cultural psychology. *Journal of Cross-cultural Psychology*, *11*, 75–88.

Puhan, B. (1979). *Assessment of psychometric invariance of Wechsler Adult Intelligence Scales across two age groups*. New Delhi: Allied Publishers.

Puhan, B. (1982). *Issues in psychological measurement*. Agra: National Psychological Corporation.

Puhan, B.N., & Sahoo, P.M. (1991). Indigenization of psychological studies: Research agenda. *Indian Journal of Current Psychological Research*, *6*, 101–107.

Radhakrishnan, S. (1968). *Hindu view of life.* London: Allen & Unwin.

Radhamani (1975). Interactional patterns in the families of anxiety patients. Unpublished D.P.S.W. dissertation, National Institute of Mental Health and Neurosciences Bangalore.

Ramalingaswami, P. (1980). *Psychology in India: Challenge and opportunities.* New Delhi: Prachi Prakashan.

Ramanujam, B.K. (1972). The Indian family in transition. In *The Indian family in the change and challenge of the seventies* (pp. 22–34). New Delhi: Sterling.

Ramanujam, B.K. (1978). Studies of change. Unpublished manuscript, B.M. Institute of Mental Health, Ahmedabad.

Ramanujam, B.K. (1979). Towards maturity: problems of identity seen in the Indian clinical setting In S. Kakar (ed.), *Identity and adulthood* (pp. 37–45). Bombay: Oxford University Press.

Ramirez, M., & Price-Williams, D. (1974). Cognitive styles in children: Two Mexican communities. *International Journal of Psychology*, 8, 93–101.

Rand, Y. (1971). Styles Cognitifs et personnalité dans une situation de rencontre interculturelle: ētūde comparative et analitique. Unpublished doctoral dissertation, Sorbone, Paris.

Rao, C., & Murthy, H.M. (1975). *Comparison of different techniques of relaxation.* Proceedings of the VIth All India Convention of Clinical Psychologists, Banaras Hindu University, Varanasi.

Rao, S.N. (1977). *Concept development in children* (Monograph 1). Tirupathi, India: Sri Venkateswara University.

Rath, R. (1973, December 27–29). *Teaching and learning problem of primary school children: A challenge to Indian psychologists and educationists.* Presidential address, 14th Annual Conference of the Indian Academy of Applied Psychology, University of Calcutta.

Rath, R., Dash, A.S., & Dash, U.N. (1979). *Cognitive abilities and school achievements of the socially disadvantaged children in primary schools.* Bombay: Allied Publishers.

Ray, A. (1970). Indian managers of the 1980s. *Economic and Political Weekly*, 5, 105–106.

Ricciuti, H.N. (1977). Adverse social and biological influences on early development. In H. McGurk (ed.), *Ecological factors in human development.* Amsterdam. North-Holland.

Ricciuti, H.N. (1980, May 5–7). *Effects of adverse environmental and nutritional influences on mental development.* A working paper prepared for P.A.H.O. Conference.

Ricciuti, H.N. (1981). Developmental consequences of malnutrition in early childhood. In M. Lewis & L. Rosenblum (eds), *The uncommon child: The genesis of behavior* (Vol. 3). New York: Plenum.

Richardson, S.A. (1976). The relation of severe malnutrition in infancy to intelligence of school children with differing life histories. *Pediatric Research, 10,* 57–61.

Roland, A. (1980). Psychoanalytic perspective on personality development in India. *International Review of Psychoanalysis, 7,* 73.

Roland, A. (1980). *Towards a psychoanalytic psychology of hierarchical relationships in Hindu India.* Paper presented to the Indian Psychoanalytic Society, Bombay.

Rosenham, D.L. (1966). Effects of social class and race on responsiveness to approval and disapproval. *Journal of Personality & Social Psychology, 4,* 253–259.

Rosenthal, R., & Jacobson, L. (1968). *Pygmalion in the classroom.* New York: Holt, Rinehart & Winston.

Rostow, W.W. (1952). *The process of economic growth.* New York: Norton.

Roy, P., Fliegel, F.C., Kivlin, I.E., & Sen, L.K. (1968). *Agricultural innovations among Indian farmers.* Hyderabad: National Institute of Community Development.

Ruch, F.L. (1956). *Psychology and life.* Chicago: Scott, Foresman & Co.

Rudmin, F. (1987). Should the IACCP expand its mandate? Three specific proposals. *Cross-Cultural Psychology Bulletin, 21*, 1–2.

Russell, B. (1927). *An outline of philosophy.* London: Allen & Unwin.

Ryckman, D.B. (1966). Psychological processes of disadvantaged children. Unpublished doctoral dissertation, University of Illinois (University Microfilms No. 66–12, 417).

Sachchidananda. (1970). *Social dimensions of intensive agricultural district programme,* ICSSR Research Abstract, New Delhi.

Safaya, R. (1976). *Hindu psychology.* Delhi: Munshiram Manoharlal Publishers.

Sahu, S., & Mahanta, J. (1977). Socio-cultural factors, intelligence and mediational abilities. *Indian Journal of Psychology, 52*, 164–168.

Salazar, J.M. (1984). The use and impact of psychology in Venezuela: Two examples. *International Journal of Psychology, 19*, 113–122.

Salazar, J.M. (1989). Psychology and social change in Latin America. *Psychology & Developing Societies, 1*, 91–104.

Saraswati, T.S., Takkar, D., & Kaur, I. (1979). Perceived maternal disciplinary practices and their relation to development of moral judgement in 10–13 year-old Indian children. In L. Echkensberger, W. Lonner, & Y.H. Poortinga (eds), *Cross-cultural contributions to psychology* (pp. 345–352). Lisse: Swets & Zeitlinger.

Schulberg, L. (1968). *Historic India.* Great Ages of Man: A History of the World Cultures Series. Nederlands, N.V.: Time-Life International.

Seal, B.N. (1958). *Positive sciences of the ancient Hindus.* Delhi. Motilal Banarasi Das.

Sears, R.R. (1942). *Survey of the objective studies of psychoanalytic concepts.* New York: Social Science Research Council.

Sears, R.R. (1944). Experimental analysis of psychoanalytical phenomena. *Personality and behavior disorders* (J. McV. Hunt, ed.). New York: Ronald.

Seder, J.A. (1957). The origin of differences in extent of independence in children: Developmental factors in perceptual field dependence. Unpublished Bachelor's Thesis, Radcliffe College.

Segal, R. (1966). *The crisis of India.* New York: New York Library Publishers.

Segall, M.H. (1984). More than we need to know about culture but are afraid not to *ask. Journal of Cross-cultural Psychology, 15*, 153–162.

Segall, M.H., Campbell, D.T., & Herskovits, M.J. (1963). Cultural differences in perception of geometric illusions. *Science, 139*, 769–771.

Segall, M.H., Campbell, D.T., & Herskoyits, M.J. (1966). *The influence of culture on visual perception.* New York: Bobbs-Merrill.

Sethi, B.B., & Manchanda, R. (1978). Family structure and psychiatric disorders. *Indian Journal of Psychiatry, 20*, 283.

Sethi, B.B., & Sharma, M. (1982). Family factors in psychiatric illness. In A. Kiev & A. Venkoba Rao. (eds), *Readings in transcultural psychiatry.* Madras: Higginbotham.

Sethi, B.B., Gupta, S.C., Mahendru, R.K., & Kumari, P. (1974). Mental health and urban life: A study of 850 families. *British Journal of Psychiatry, 124*, 243–246.

Sethi, B.B., Gupta, S.C., Raj Kumar, & Promila (1972). A psychiatric survey of 500 rural families. *Indian Journal of Psychiatry, 14*, 183–196.

Shaffer, G.W., & Lazarus, R.S. (1952). *Fundamental concepts in clinical psychology.* New York: McGraw-Hill.

Shanmugam, T.E. (1972). Personality: A trend report. In S.K. Mitra (ed.), *A survey of research in psychology* (pp. 226–337). Bombay: Popular Prakashan.

Sharma, M. (1986). The effects of types of reward on performance of deprived and non-deprived children. *Journal of Psychological Researches, 30,* 40–44.

Sharma, M., Sethi, B.B., & Bhiman, A. (1984). Family jointness, social interaction and neurosis: A rural-urban comparison. *Indian Journal of Psychiatry, 26,* 357.

Sharma, M., Sethi, B.B., & Bhiman, A. (1985). Social interaction and family patterns in a rural urban-community. *Indian Journal of Social Psychiatry, 1,* 66–74.

Sharma, P. (1981). *Charaka Samhita* (English translation). Varanasi: Chaukhambha Orientalia.

Sharma, R., & Tripathi, R.C. (1988). Teachers' expectations and attributions: The self-fulfilling prophesy cycle. In A.K. Dalal (ed.), *Attribution theory and research* (pp. 33–59). New Delhi: Wiley Eastern.

Sharma, R.K., & Dash, B. (1976). *Charaka Samhita.* Varanasi: Choukhambha Sanskrit Series Office.

Shetty, G. (1975). Hysteria in childhood: A study of phenomenology, personality and family interaction. Unpublished M.D. thesis, National Institute of Mental Health and Neuroscience, Bangalore.

Shils, E. (1961). *The Intellectual between tradition and modernity: The Indian situation.* The Hague: Mouton & Co.

Shweder, R.A., & Bourne, R.J. (1984). Does the concept of the person vary crossculturally? In R.A. Shweder & R.A. LeVine (eds), *Culture theory* (pp. 158–199). Cambridge: Cambridge University Press.

Shweder, R.A., Mahapatha, R.A., & Miller, J.G. (1990). Culture and moral development. In J. Stigler, R.A. Shweder, & G. Herdt (eds), *Cultural psychology: Essay in comparative human development* (pp. 130–204). New York: Cambridge University Press.

Singer, M. (1956). Cultural values in India's economic development. *The Annals of the American Academy of Political and Social Science,* 81–91.

Singer, M. (1966). The modernization of religious beliefs. In M. Weiner (ed.), *Modernisation: The dynamics of growth* (pp. 59–70). New York: Basic Books.

Singh, A. (1987). Certain deprivational factors in language development in children. Unpublished doctoral dissertation, University of Allahabad, Allahabad, India.

Singh, A.K. (1975). Hindu culture and economic development in India. *Indian Social and Psychological Studies Publication, 1,* 89–108.

Singh, A.K. (1976). *Social disadvantage, intelligence and scholastic achievement.* New Delhi: NCERT.

Singh, A.K. (1980). Social disadvantage and academic achievement. *Social Change, 10,* 15–18.

Singh, A.K. (1983). Parental support and scholastic achievement. *Social Change, 13,* 9–14.

Singh, N.P. (1970). Risk-taking and anxiety among successful and unsuccessful, traditional and progressive agricultural entrepreneurs of Delhi. *British Journal of Social and Clinical Psychology, 9,* 301–308.

Singh, R., & Oberhummer, I. (1980). Behaviour therapy within a setting of Karm yoga. *Journal of Behavior Therapy and Experimental Psychiatry, 11,* 135–141.

Singh, R.B. (1972). A comparative study of western and Indian thoughts and concepts of personality. Unpublished doctoral dissertation, Jodhpur University, Jodhpur.

Singh, R.N. (1975). *Effects of transcendental meditation on personality pattern.* Proceedings of the VIth All India Convention of Clinical Psychology, Varanasi.

Singh, S. (1976). Achievement motivation and success in farming. *British Journal of Projective Psychology, 21,* 17–20.

Singh, S. (1978). *Achievement motivation, decision making, orientation and work values of brothers with contrasting farm output*. New Delhi: UGC Research Report.

Singh, S., & Gupta, B.S. (1977). Motives and agricultural growth. *British Journal of Social and Clinical Psychology, 16*, 189–190.

Singh, Y. (1977). *Modernization of Indian tradition*. Faridabad: Thomson Press.

Singh, Y. (1986). *Indian sociology: Social conditioning and emerging concerns*. New Delhi: Vistaar Publications.

Singhal, R., & Mishra, G. (1989). Variations in achievement cognition: Role of ecology, age and gender. *International Journal of Inter cultural Relations, 13*, 93–107.

Sinha, A.K.P. (1960a). Stereotypes of male and female university students in India towards the different ethnic groups. *Journal of Social Psychology, 51*, 93–102.

Sinha, A.K.P., & Upadhyay, O.P. (1960b). Change and persistence in stereotypes of university students towards different ethnic groups during Sino Indian border dispute. *Journal of Social Psychology, 52*, 31–39.

Sinha, J. (1958). *Indian psychology: 2 Vol*. Calcutta: Sinha Publishing House.

Sinha, J.B.P. (1968). The *n-Ach* and *n-*cooperation under limited/unlimited resource condition. *Journal of Experimental Social Psychology, 4*, 233–246.

Sinha, J.B.P. (1970). *Development through behavior modification*. Bombay: Allied Publishers.

Sinha, J.B.P. (1973). Methodology of problem-oriented research in India. *Journal of Social and Economic Studies, 1*, 93–110.

Sinha, J.B.P. (1974). A case of research in participative management. *Indian Journal of Industrial Relations, 10*, 179–187.

Sinha, J.B.P. (1976). Outgrowing the frame. *Vikalpa, 1*, 63–67.

Sinha, J.B.P. (1980). *The nurturant task master*. New Delhi: Concept.

Sinha, J.B.P. (1982a). The Hindu (Indian) identity. *Dynamic Psychiatry, 15*(74/75), 148–160.

Sinha, J.B.P. (1982b). Power structure, perceptual frame and behavioural strategies in a dyadic relationship. In R. Rath, H.S. Asthana, D. Sinha and J.B.P. Sinha (eds), *Diversity and unity in cross-cultural psychology* (pp. 308–316). Lisse: Swets & Zeitlinger.

Sinha, J.B.P., & Pandey, P. (1970). Strategics of high *n-Ach* persons. *Psychologia, 13*, 210–216.

Sinha, P. (1981). Determinants of role-conflict among female teachers. Doctoral dissertation, Patna University, Patna.

Sinha, Y. (1988). Subjective explanations of poverty. In A.K. Dalal (ed.), *Attribution theory and research* (pp. 115–128). New Delhi: Wiley Eastern.

Sood, R.K. (1971). A comparative study of families of hysterics and obsessionals. Unpublished M.D. thesis, National Institute of Mental Health and Neuroscience, Bangalore.

Soudijn, K.A., Hutschemaekers, G.J.M., & Van de Vijver, F.R.J. (1990). Culture conceptualizations. In J.R. Fans, Van de Vijver, & Giel J.M. Hutschemaekers (eds), *The conceptualisation of culture* (pp. 19–39). Tilburg: Tilburg University Press.

Sovani, N.V. (1963). Non-economic aspects of India's economic development. In R.J. Braibanti & J.J. Spengler (eds), *Administration and economic development in India*. Durham: Duke University Press.

Spear, P. (1968). Preface. In Lucille Schulberg, *Historic India*. Great Ages of Man: A History of the World Cultures Series. Nederland, N.V.: Time-Life International.

Spielberger, C.D., & Iscoe, I. (1970). The current status of training in community psychology. In I. Iscoe & C.D. Spielberger (eds), *Community psychology: Perspectives in training and research*. New York: Appleton-Century-Crofts.

Spratt, P. (1966). *Hindu culture and personality*. Bombay: Manaktala.

Sua, V.D. (1980). Familial and sociocultural antecedents of psychopathology. In H.D. Triandis & J.G. Draguns (eds), *Handbook of cross-cultural psychology* (Vol. 6). Boston: Allyn & Bacon.

Super, C.M., & Harkness, S. (1986). The developmental niche: A conceptualization at the interface of child and culture. *International Journal of Behavioral Development, 9*, 545–569.

Suresh, J. (1984). *Language socialization of scheduled caste children in India*. Paper presented at the National Seminar on Psycholinguistics in a Multi-Lingual Society, CAS in Psychology, Utkal University, Bhubaneshwar, India.

Suua, V.D. (1961). Socio-cultural factors of families of schizophrenics: A review of the literature. *Psychiatry, 24*, 246–265.

Tart, C.T. (1972). *Altered states of consciousness*. New York: Anchor.

Tart, C.T. (1975). *States of consciousness*. New York: Dutton.

Taylor, W.S. (1948). Basic personality in orthodox Hindu cultural patterns. *Journal of Abnormal and Social Psychology, 43*, 3–12.

Thacore, V.R. (1973). *Mental illness in an urban community*. Allahabad: United Publishers.

Thapa, K., & Murthy, V.N. (1985). Experiential characteristics of certain altered states of consciousness. *Journal of Transpersonal Psychology, 17*(1), 77–86.

Thapa, K., & Murthy, V.N. (1985). *Experimental characteristics of certain altered states of consciousness*. Unpublished manuscript, Department of Psychology, University of Allahabad, Allahabad.

Thompson, D.D. (1965). *Child psychology*. Bombay: Times of India Press.

Tiwari, P.S.N. (1983). Psychological study of motivation and change-proneness among farmers. Doctoral dissertation. Allahabad University, Allahabad.

Triandis, H.C. (1971). Some psychological dimensions of modernisation. *Proceedings of the 17th International Congress of Applied Psychology* (Vol. 2, pp. 1257–1265). Brussels: Editest.

Triandis, H.C. (1984). *Functional and dysfunctional aspects of collectivism for development*. Paper presented at the 7th International Conference of Cross-Cultural Psychology, Acapulco, Mexico, August.

Tripathi, R.C. (1988). Aligning development to values in India. In D. Sinha & H.S.R. Kao (eds), *Social values and development: Asian perspectives* (pp. 315–333). New Delhi: SAGE Publications.

Turtle, A.M. (1987). Introduction: A silk road for psychology. In G.H. Blowers & A.M. Turtle (eds), *Psychology moving east* (pp. 1–21). Boulder: Westview Press.

Tylor, E.B. (1871/1958). *The origins of culture*. New York: Harper & Row.

Udupa, K.N., Sinoh, R.H., & Yadav, R.A. (1973). Certain studies of psychological and bio-chemical responses to the practice of *hatha* yoga in young normal volunteers. *Indian Journal of Medical Research*, 61–62.

Udy, S.H. (1970). *Work in traditional and modern society*. Englewood Cliffs, N.J.: Prentice-Hall.

UGC. (1979). *Reorientation of teaching and research in psychology in Indian universities*. New Delhi: University Grants Commission.

United Nations. (1961). *International definition of measurement of levels of living*. An Interim Guide. U.N. Publication 61, IV. 7.

Vahia, N.S., Doongaji, D.R., Deshmukh, O.K., Vinekar, S.L., Parekh, H.C., & Kapoor, S.N. (1972). A deconditioning therapy based on the concepts of Patanjali. *International Journal of Social Psychiatry, 18*, 61–66.

Vahia, N.S., Doongaji, D.R., Jeste, D.V., Ravindranath, S., Kapoor, S.N., & Ardha Purkar, I. (1973). Psychophysiologic therapy based on the concepts of Patanjali in the treatment of psychiatric disorders. *Indian Journal of Psychiatry, 15,* 32–37.

Van den Ban, A.W., & Thorat, S.S. (1961). *Administrative relationships influencing the effectiveness of community development organisations in India.* Working Paper, Wageningen, Netherlands. University of Agriculture.

Vazir, S., Bhogle, S., & Naidu, N. (1988). Influence of psycho-social factors on the nutritional status of preschool children. *Journal of the Indian Academy of Applied Psychology, 14,* 1–8.

Verghese, A., Beig, A., Senseman, S.A., Rao, S.S.S., & Benjamin, V. (1973). A social and psychiatric study of a representative group of families in Vellore town. *Indian Journal of Medical Research, 61,* 609–620.

Verma, A., & Poffenberger, T. (1970). Social change and perception of change in child rearing practices in a suburban Indian village. Unpublished report, Department of Child Development, M.S. University, Baroda.

Vernon, P.E. (1933). The American *vs.* the German method of approach to the study of temperament and personality. *British Journal of Psychology, 24,* 156–177.

Vernon, P.E. (1965). Ability factors and environmental influences. *American Psychologist, 20,* 723–733.

Vivekananda, S. (1945). The powers of the mind. In *The complete works of Swami Vivekananda* (Mayawati Memorial Edition). Part II. Almora: Advaita Ashram.

Ward, C. (1987). The historical development and current status of psychology in Malaysia. In G.H. Blowers & A.M. Turtle (eds), *Psychology moving east* (pp. 201–222). Boulder: Westview Press.

Warwick, D.P. (1980). The politics and ethics of cross-cultural research. In H.C. Triandis (ed.), *Handbook of cross-cultural psychology* (Vols. I–IV). New York: Allyn and Bacon.

Weber, Max. (1958a) *The Protestant ethic and the spirit of capitalism* (trs. T. Parsons). New York: Charles, Scribner.

Weber, Max. (1958b). *The religion of India: The sociology of Hinduism and Buddhism* (trs. and ed. H.H. Gerth and D. Martindale). Glencoe: Free Press.

Weiner, B. (1986). *An attribution of motivation and emotion.* London: Springer-Verlag.

Weller, L., & Sharan, S. (1971). Articulation of the body concept among first-grade Israeli children. *Child Development, 42,* 1553–1559.

Werner, E., & Murlidharan, R. (1970). Nutrition, cognitive status and achievement motivation of New Delhi nursery school children. *Journal of Cross-Cultural Psychology, 3,* 271–181.

White, R.W. (1957). *The abnormal personality.* New York: Ronald.

Whitehead, A.N. (1926). *Religion in the making.* New York: Macmillan.

Whiteman, M., & Deutsch, M. (1968). Social disadvantage as related to intellective and language development. In M. Deutsch, I. Katz, & A.R. Jensen (eds), *Social class, race, and psychological development.* New York: Holt, Rinehart & Winston.

Whiting, B.B. (1976). The problem of packaged variable. In K. Riegel & J. Meacham (eds), *The developing individual in a changing world* (Vol. 1, pp. 693–728). Reading, M.A.: Addison-Wesley.

Whiting, J.W.M. (1961). Socialization process and personality. In F.L.K. Hsu (ed.), *Psychological anthropology: Approaches to culture and personality.* Homewood, Ill.: The Dorsey Press.

Whiting, J.W.M., & Child, I.L. (1953). *Child training and personality: A cross-cultural study.* New Haven: Yale University Press.

Wig, N.N., Pershad, D., & Verma, S.K. (1974). The use of psychological tests in Indian psychiatric research: A reappraisal. *Indian Journal of Clinical Psychology, 1,* 8–14.

Winter, D.G., & McClelland, D.C. (1975). Need for achievement and Hindu culture. *Indian Social and Psychological Studies, 1,* 109–127.

Witkin, H.A. (1965). Psychological differentiation and forms of pathology. *Journal of Abnormal Psychology, 70,* 317–336.

Witkin, H.A. (1977). *Cognitive styles in personal and cultural adaptation.* Vol. XI, 1977 Hoinz Werner Lecture Series, Clark University Press, 1978.

Witkin, H.A., & Berry, J.W. (1975). Psychological differentiation in cross-cultural perspective. *Journal of Cross-Cultural Psychology, 6,* 14–87.

Witkin, H.A., Dyk, R.B., Faterson, H.F., Goodenough, D.R., & Karp, S.A. (1974). *Psychological differentiation.* Potomac, Md: Erlbaum, 1974 (Originally published, Wiley, 1962).

Witkin, H.A., Price-Williams, D., Bertini, M., Christiansen, B., Oltman, P.K., Ramirez, M., & Van-Meel, J. (1974). Social conformity and psychological differentiation. *International Journal of Psychology, 9,* 11–29.

Wober, M. (1974). Towards an understanding of the Kiganda concept of intelligence. In J.W. Berry & P.R. Dasen (eds), *Culture and cognition* (pp. 261–280). London: Methuen.

Wolman, B.B. (ed.). (1973). *Dictionary of behavioral sciences.* New York: Van Nostrand Reinhold.

Zadik, B. (1968). Field dependence independence among Oriental and Western School children. *Mogamot: Behavioral Science Quarterly, 16,* 51–58.

Zimmerman, I.L., & Bernstein, M. (1983). Parental work patterns in alternative families: Influence on child development. *American Journal of Orthopsychiatry, 53,* 418–435.

# Complete Works of Durganand Sinha

## Books

Sinha, D., & Kao, H.S.R. (eds). (1997). *Asian perspectives on psychology*. New Delhi: SAGE.

Pandey, J., Sinha, D., & Bhawuk, D.P.S. (eds). (1996). *Asian contributions to cross-cultural psychology*. New Delhi: SAGE.

Mishra, R.C., Sinha, D., & Berry, J.W. (1996). *Ecology, acculturation and psychological adaptation*. New Delhi: SAGE.

Kao, H.S.R., Sinha, D., & Hong, N.S. (eds). (1995). *Effective organizations and social values*. New Delhi: SAGE.

Sinha, D., & Kao, H.S.R. (eds). (1988). *Social values and development: Asian perspectives*. New Delhi: SAGE.

Sinha, D, (1986). *Psychology in a third world country: The Indian experience*. New Delhi: SAGE.

Sinha, D., Tripathi, R.C., & Misra, G. (eds). (1982). *Deprivation: Its social roots and psychological consequences*. New Delhi: Concept.

Rath, R., Asthana, H.S., Sinha, D., & SINHA, J.B.P. (eds). (1982). *Diversity and unity in cross-cultural psychology*. Lisse, Holland: Swets & Zeitlinger, B.V.

Sinha, D., & Misra, G. (eds). (1980). *Samanya manovigyan*. Varanasi: Rupa Psychological Corporation (in Hindi).

Sinha, D. (ed.) (1980). *Socialization of the Indian child*. New Delhi: Concept.

De, B., & Sinha, D. (eds) (1977). *A perspective on psychology in India: Dr. SM Mohsin falicitation volume*. Allahabad: Authors.

Sinha, D. (1974a). *Motivation and rural development*. Calcutta: Minerva Associates

Sinha, D. (1974b). *The Mughal syndrome*. New Delhi: Tata McGraw Hill.

Sinha, D. (1972). *Studies in industrial psychology*. Agra: Sri Ram Mehra Publishers.

Sinha, D. (1970). *Academic achievers and non-achievers*. Allahabad: United Publishers.

Sinha, D. (1969). *Indian villages in transition: A motivational analysis*. Delhi: Associated Publishing House.

## Editing of Journals

*Indian Journal of Psychology*
*Psychology & Developing Societies*

*Social and Economic Studies*
*International Journal of Psychology (Special Issues)*

# Book Review

*Culture and social behavior* by H.C. Triandis, IACCP Bulletin/Journal of Cross-cultural Psychology, 1996/1997.

# Psychological Tests

Sinha, D. (1984). *Manual for story-pictorial EFT and Indo-African EFT.* Varanasi: Rupa Psychological Corporation.

Verma, M., & Sinha, D. (1971). *Test of moral Judgment for children.* Agra: National Psychological Corporation.

Sinha, D. (1968). *Manual for Sinha W.A. Self-analysis form (Anxiety Scale)* (in Hindi), Varanasi: Rupa Psychological Corporation.

# Book Chapters

Sinha, D. (1999). Social psychology of health behavior. In G. Misra (Ed.) *Psychological perspectives on health and stress* (pp. 55–65). New Delhi: Concept.

Sinha, D. (1997). Indigenizing psychology. In J. W. Berry, Y. H., Poortinga & J. Pandey (eds), *Handbook of cross-cultural psychology (2nd ed.), Vol. I. Theory and Method* (pp. 129–169). Boston: Allyn and Bacon.

Sinha, D., & Sinha, M. (1997). Orientations of psychology: East-west perspectives. In D. Sinha, & H.S.R. Kao (eds), *Asian perspectives on psychology* (pp. 25–39). New Delhi: SAGE.

Sinha, D. (1996). Cross-cultural psychology: The Asian scenario. In J. Pandey, D. Sinha, & Dharm P.S. Bhawuk (eds), *Asian contributions to cross-cultural psychology* (pp. 20–41). New Delhi: SAGE.

Sinha, D. (1996). Measurement in the fields of family and marriage: Its relevance and some issues involved. In S. Bharat (ed.), *Family measurement in India* (pp. 51–65). New Delhi: SAGE.

Sinha, D., & Tripathi, R.C. (1994). Individualism in a collective culture: A case of coexistence of opposites. In U. Kim, H.C. Triandis, C. Kagitcibasi, S. Choi, & G. Yoon (eds), *Individualism and collectivism: Theory, method and applications* (pp. 123–136). Thousand Oaks, CA: SAGE.

Sinha, D., & Naidu, R.K. (1994). Multilayered hierarchical structure of self and not-self: The Indian perspective. In A.M. Bouvy, F.J.R. van de Vijver, P. Boski, & P. Schmitz (eds), *Journey into cross-cultural psychology* (pp. 41–49). Lisse: Swets & Zeitlinger.

Sinha, D. (1993). Indigenization of psychology in India and its relevance. In U. Kim & J.W. Berry (eds), *Indigenous psychologies: Research and experience in cultural context* (pp. 30–43). Newbury Park, CA: SAGE.

Sinha, D. (1993). Research–policy interface: An uneasy partnership. In T.S. Saraswathi & B. Kaur (eds), *Human development and family studies in India an agenda for research and policy*. New Delhi: SAGE.

Mishra, R.C., & Sinha, D. (1993). Some methodological issues related to research in developmental psychology in the context of policy and intervention programmes. In T.S. Saraswathi & B. Kaur (eds), *Human development and family studies in India an agenda for research and policy*. New Delhi: SAGE.

Sinha, D. (1990). Applied social psychology in India. In G. Misra (ed.), *Applied social psychology in India* (pp. 28–40). New Delhi: SAGE.

Sinha, D., & Sinha, M. (1990). Dissonance in work culture in India. In D. Moddie (ed.), *The concept of work in Indian society* (pp. 206–219). New Delhi: Indian Institute of Advanced Study and Manohar Publications.

Sinha, D. (1990). Intervention for development out of poverty. In R.W. Brislin (ed.), *Applied cross-cultural psychology* (pp. 77–97). Newbury Park: SAGE.

Sinha, D. (1988). Basic Indian values and behavior dispositions in the context of national development: An appraisal. In D. Sinha & H.S.R. Kao (eds), *Social values and development: Asian perspectives* (pp. 31–55). New Delhi: SAGE.

Sinha, D. (1988). The family scenario of a developing country and its implications for mental health: The case of India. In P.R. Dasan, J.W. Berry, & N. Sartorius (eds), *Health and cross-cultural psychology: Toward applications* (pp. 48–70). Newbury Park, CA: SAGE.

Sinha, D. (1987). Psychology in India: A historical perspective. In G.H. Blowers & A.M. Turtle (eds), *Psychology moving east*. London: West View Press/Sydney: Sydney University Press.

Sinha, D. (1985). A plea for macro-psychology. In R. Diaz-Guerrero (ed.), *Cross-cultural and national studies in social psychology* (pp. 277–283). Amsterdam: North-Holland.

Sinha, D. (1985). Psychology in rural areas: The case of a developing country. In R. Diaz-Guerrero (ed.), *Cross-Cultural and national studies in social psychology*. Amsterdam: North-Holland.

Sinha, D. (1984). Community as target: A new perspective to research on prosocial behaviour. In E. Staub, D. Bar-Tal, J. Karylowski, & J. Reykowski (eds), *Development and maintenance of prosocial behavior* (pp. 445–455). New York: Plenum Press.

Sinha, D. (1983). Applied social psychology and the problems of national development. In F. Blackler (ed.), *Social psychology and developing countries* (pp. 7–20). Chickester: Wiley.

Sinha, D. (1983). Cross-cultural psychology: A view from the third world. In J.B. Degregowski, S. Dziurewil, & R.C. Annis (eds), *Explorations in cross-cultural psychology*. Lisse: Swets & Zeithlinger B.V.

Sinha, D. (1983). Human assessment in Indian context. In S.H. Irvine & J.W. Berry (eds), *Human assessment and cultural factors* (pp. 17–34). New York: Plenum Press.

Sinha, D., & Misra, G. (1982). Deprivation: Its motivational and personality correlates. In D. Sinha, R.C. Tripathi, & G. Misra (eds), *Deprivation: Its social roots and psychological consequences*. New Delhi: Concept Publishing Company.

Sinha, D. (with Ng, S.N., Akhtar Hossain, A.B.M., Bali, P., Bond, M.H.. Hayashi, K., Lim, S.P., O'Driscoll, M.P., & Young, K.S.) (1982). Human values in nine countries. In R. Rath, H.S. Asthana, D. Sinha, & J.B.P. Sinha (eds), *Diversity and unity in cross-cultural psychology*. Lisse, Holland: Swets & Zeitlinger, B.V.

Punetha, D., & Sinha, D. (1982). Sex role differentiation and cultural differences in the socialization of aggression. In R. Rath, H.S. Asthana, D. Sinha & J.B.P. Sinha (eds),

*Diversity and unity in cross-cultural psychology* (pp. 339–445). Lisse, Holland: Swets & Zeitlinger, B.V.

Sinha, D. (1982). Socio-cultural factors and the development of perceptual and cognitive skills. In W.W. Hartup (ed.), *Review of child development research* (pp. 441–472). Chicago: University of Chicago Press.

Sinha, D. (1982). Toward an ecological framework of deprivation. In D. Sinha, R.C. Tripathi & G. Misra (eds), *Deprivation: Its social roots and psychological consequences.* New Delhi: Concept Publishing Company.

Sinha, D. (1981). Experimental social psychology: Verbal or real? In J. Pandey (ed.), *Perspectives on experimental social psychology in India.* New Delhi: Concept Publishing Company.

Bisht, S., & Sinha, D. (1981). Socialization, family and psychological differentiation. In D. Sinha (ed.) *Socialization of the Indian Child.* New Delhi: Concept Publishing Co.

Sinha, D. (1981). Social psychology in India: A historical perspective. In J. Pandey (ed.), *Perspectives on experimental social psychology in India.* New Delhi: Concept Publishing Company.

Sinha, D. (1979). Perceptual style among nomadic and transitional agricultural Birhors. In Eckensherger, W.J. Lonner, & Y.H. Poortinga (eds), *Cross-cultural contributions to psychology* (pp. 83–93). Lisse, Netherlands: Swets and Zeitlinger, B.V.

Sinha, D. (1979). The young and the old: Ambiguity of role models and values among Indian youth. In S. Kakar (ed.), *Identity and adulthood* (pp. 56–64). Delhi: Oxford University Press.

Sinha, D. (1974). A note on student perception. In A. Singh, & P.G. Altbach (eds), *Higher learning in India.* Delhi: Vikas Publishing House.

Sinha, D. (1974). Job satisfaction and job behavior. In S.K. Roy & A. Sreekumar Menon (eds), *Motivation and organization effectiveness.* New Delhi: SRC for Industrial Relations and Human Resources.

Sinha, D. (1974). Motivation and economic development. In *Dictionnaric de la Psychologie.* Norbert Sillamy (ed ) Paris: Editorial Board.

Sinha, D. (1974). The Mughal syndrome: A psychological study of inter-generational difference. In Norbert Sillamy (ed.), *Dictionaire De la Psychologie.* Pasis: Editorial Board.

Sinha, D. (1972). Industrial psychology. In S.K. Mitra (ed.), *A survey of research in psychology in India,* ICSSR, Chapter 5 (pp. 175–237). Bombay: Popular Prakashan.

Sinha, D. (1970). Psychological researches on industrial labour in India. In V.B. Singh (ed.), *Labour research in India.* Bombay: Popular Prakashan.

Sinha, D. (1965). Integration of modern psychology with Indian thought. In A.J. Sutchi & M.A. Vick (eds), *Readings in humanistic psychology* (pp. 265–279). New York: Free Press.

Sinha, D. (1964). Development of interests, attitudes, ideals and character. In B. Kuppuswamy (ed.) *Advanced Educational Psychology.* Jullunder: University Publishers.

Sinha, D. (1962). Group morale, army and industry. *Article in Kannada Encyclopedia.* Government of Mysore.

Sinha, D. (1962). Psychology of thinking. *Article in Kannada Encyclopedia.* Government of Mysore.

Sinha, D. (1961). Frustration in industrial work. In Baker (ed.) *Industrial Organization and Health.* U.K.: Tavistock Publication.

Sinha, D. (1961). Psychology in the service of technology. In T.K.N. Menon (ed.), *Recent Trends in Psychology.* Calcutta: Longman.

# Journal Papers

Sinha, D. (2002). Culture and psychology: Perspectives from cross-cultural psychology. *Psychology and Developing Societies, 14*, 11–25.

Sinha, D. (1998). Changing perspectives in social psychology in India: A journey towards indigenization. *Asian Journal of Social Psychology, 1*, 17–31.

Sinha, D. (1997). Evading the challenge: A commentary on the research culture of psychologists in India. *Trends in Social Science Research, 4*, 141–147.

Sinha, D. (1996). Culture as the target and culture as the source: A review of cross-cultural psychology in Asia. *Psychology and Developing Societies, 8*, 83–105.

Sinha, D. (1994). Indigenous psychology: Need and potentiality. *Journal of Indian Psychology, 12*, 1–7.

Sinha, D. (1991). Rise in the population of the elderly, familial changes and their psychological implications of the scenarios of the developing countries. *International Journal of Psychology, 26*, 636–647.

Sinha, D. (1990). Concept of psychological well-being: Western and Indian perspectives. *NIMHANS Journal, 8*, 1–11.

Sinha, D., & Bharat, S. (1985). Three types of family structures and psychological differentiation. *International Journal of Psychology, 20*, 693–708.

Sinha, D. (1984). Psychology in the context of third world development. *International Journal of Psychology, 19*, 17–29.

Pawlik, K., & Sinha, D. (1984). Psychology of global change in 3rd-World Countries-Findings from The Iupsys Network Workshop. *Malaysia. International Journal of Psychology, 27*(3–4).

Sinha, D. (1981). Non-western perspectives in psychology: Why, what and whither? *Journal of Indian Psychology, 3*, 1–9.

Sinha, D., & Praharaj, G.S. (1980). Leadership patterns in developed and underdeveloped villages. *Behavioral Sciences and Rural Development, 3*, 133–139.

Sinha, D. (1980). Sex differences in psychological differentiation among different cultural groups. *International Journal of Behavioral Development, 3*, 455–456.

Sinha, D. (1980). Social psychology in India: A historical perspective. *Psychological Studies, 25*(2), 157–163.

Sinha, D. (1980). Some cognitive and motivational concomitants of poverty. *Bombay Psychologist, 2*(2), 8–14.

Sinha, D. (1980). Some cognitive and motivational concomitants of poverty. *Social Change, 10*, 3–8.

Sinha, D. (1980). Student unrest: A general cross-cultural perspective. *Journal of Social and Economic Studies, 8*, 73–78.

Sinha, D. (1980). Student unrest: Emergency and post-emergency phases. *Journal of Social and Economic Review, 8*(2), 303–321.

Sinha, D. (1980). Toward outgrowing alien model: A review of some recent trends in psychological research in India. Paper presented at the Symposium on History of Psychology in various countries, XXII International Congress of Psychology (5–12 July), Leipzig, Germany.

Sinha, D. (1979). Cognitive and psychomotor, skills in India: A review of research. *Journal of Cross-Cultural Psychology, 10*, 324–355.

Sinha, D. (1978). Story-pictorial EFT: A culturally appropriate test for pictorial disembedding. *Indian Journal of Psychology, 53*(A), 160–171.

Sinha, D., & Saatchi (1977). A comparative study of supervisory orientation among Indian and Iranian students. *Indian Journal of Psychology, 52,* 228–239.

Sinha, D., & Naidu, R.K. (1977). Defence phenomenon in perception learning and memory: An experimental study of cognitive consistency. *Journal of General Psychology, 97,* 219–226.

Sinha, D. (1977). Orientation and attitude of the social psychologist in a developing country: The Indian case. *International Review of Applied Psychology, 26,* 1–10.

Sinha, D. (1977). Scientist professional model in problem-oriented applied social psychology research. *Journal of Social and Economic Studies, 5,* 219–233.

Sinha, D. (1977). Some social disadvantage and development of some perceptual skills. *Indian Journal of Psychology, 52,* 115–132.

Sinha, D. (1976). Study of psychological dimensions of poverty. *Journal of Social and Economic Studies, 4,* 167–200.

Jahoda, G., Cheyne, W.M., Deregowski, J.B., Sinha, D., & Collingbourne, R. (1976). Utilization of pictorial information in classroom learning: A cross-cultural study. *AV Communication Review, 24,* 295–315.

Sinha, D. (1975). Dimensions of student agitation in India. *Journal of Social and Economic Studies, 3*(2), 193–211.

Sinha, D., & Shukla, P. (1974). A developmental study of relative efficacy of different cues in pictorial depth perception. *Indian Journal of Psychology, 49,* 220–230.

Sinha, D. (1974). Deprivation and development on skill for pictorial depth perception. *Journal of Cross-Cultural psychology, 5*(4), 434–450.

Sinha, D. (1974). Interpersonal peacemaking: Confrontation and third party consultation. *Indian Journal of Industrial Relations, 10*(1), 137–139.

Sinha, D., & Gupta, N. (1974). Need satisfaction and absenteeism. *Indian Journal of Industrial Relations, 10*(1), 1–14.

Sinha, D., & Naidu, R.K. (1974). Reciprocal facilitations and impairment in perception learning and memory. *Indian Journal of Psychology, 49*(4), 279–284.

Sinha, D., & Chaubey, N.P. (1974). Risk taking and economic development. *International Review of Applied Psychology, 23,* 55–61.

Chaubey, N.P, & Sinha, D. (1972). Risk-taking, risk-avoidance and fear of failure in villagers. *Psychologia, 15,* 112–121.

Jahoda, G., Deregowski, J.B., & Sinha, D. (1974). Topological and Euclidean spatial features noted by children. *International Journal of Psychology, 19,* 159–72.

Sinha, D. (1973). A reinforcement model of student agitation: Analysis of factors involved in handling student agitations. *LBS National Academy of Administration Journal, 184,* 536–547.

Sinha, D., & Sidana, U.R. (1973). Child rearing practices and the development of fears in children. *Psychological Studies, 18*(2), 50–60.

Sinha, D. (1973). Priorities and programme of research in the field of psychology. *Journal of Psychological Researches, 17,* 22–27.

Sinha, D. (1973). Psychology and the problems of developing countries: A general overview. *International Review of Applied Psychology, 22*(1), 5–27.

Sinha, D., & Chaubey, N.P. (1972). Achievement motive and rural economic development. *International Journal of Psychology, 7,* 267–272.

Sinha, D., & Naidu, R.K. (1972). Anxiety and conformity behaviour. *Journal of Psychological Researches, 16,* 40–45.

Sinha, D., & Verma, A.K. (1972). Anxiety and perceptual construction. *Indian Journal of Psychology, 47,* 377–383.

Sinha, D., & Verma, M. (1972). Knowledge of moral values in children. *Psychological Studies, 17,* 1–6.

Sinha, D., & Verma, M. (1972). Pattern of moral values in children. *Psychological Studies, 17,* 42–50.

Sinha, D., & Chaubey, N.P. (1972). Risk-taking, risk-avoidance and fear of failure in villagers. *Psychologia, 15,* 112–121.

Sinha, D. (1972). Transitional villages re-visited: An analysis of motivational changes after five years. *Behavioural Science and Community Development, 6*(2).

Sinha, D., & Ghosh, E.S.K. (1971). A peer rating form for assessment of adjustment in children. *Indian Journal of Psychology, 46,* 289–295.

Sinha, D., & Agarwal, U.N. (1971). Job satisfaction and adjustment of Indian workers. *Indian Journal of Industrial Relations, 6,* 357–367.

Sinha, D. (1971). Problems of innovations in examinations in higher education. *Inter-University Board of India and Ceylon,* New Delhi.

Sinha, D. (1969). Level of aspiration of villagers in certain community development areas. *Journal of General and Applied Psychology, 11,* 50–56.

Sinha, D. (1969). Study of motivation in a developing country: Concept of happy life among Indian farmers. *Journal of Social Psychology, 79,* 89–97.

Sinha, D. (1968). Badania and motywacja spolocznosci wiejskiej Kraju rozwijajacyuesic. Studia socjologiczne (Instytut Filozofit isocjologii, Polskiej, Academii Nauk, Warszawa, Poland), *7*(28), 59–82.

Sinha, D., & Singh, U.P. (1968). The self-concept of the criminals. *Psychological Studies, 13.*

Sinha, D. (1967). Behaviour ratings as an index of motivation: A study of human motivation of rural population in a developing country. *Psychologia, 10,* 167–176.

Sinha, D. (1966). A psychological analysis of some factors associated with success and failure in university education. *The Indian Educational Review, 1*(1), 34–47.

Sinha, D. (1966). A psychological analysis of some factors associated with success and failure in university education: Intelligence, anxiety and adjustment of academic achievers and non-achievers. *Psychological Studies, 11*(2), 69–88.

Sinha, D., & Kumar, P. (1966). A study of certain personality variables in student leadership. *Psychological Studies, 11,* 1–8.

Ghosh, E.S.K., & Sinha, D. (1966). A study of parental role perception in siblings. *Journal of Psychological Researches, 1,* 8–18.

Sinha, D. (1966). *Psychologist in the arena of social change.* Presidential address to the Section of Psychology and Educational Sciences, 53rd Indian Science Congress, Chandigarh.

Sinha, D. (1965). An analysis of anxiety areas and manifestation: A factorial study. *Journal of Psychological Researches, 9,* 55–62.

Sinha, D., & Nair, R.R. (1965). A study of job satisfaction in factory workers. *Indian Journal of Social Work, 26,* 1–9.

Sinha, D., & Kumar, P. (1965). Differential perception of student leadership. *Psychologia, 5,* 99–105.

Sinha, D. (1965). Integration of modern psychology with Indian thought, *Journal of Humanistic Psychology, 5,* 6–17.

Sinha, D. (1965). Job satisfaction and absenteeism. *Indian Journal of Industrial Relations, 1,* 1–10.

Sinha, D. (1965). Validation of an anxiety scale. *Journal of Psychological Researches, 9*(1), 19–27.

Sinha, D. (1964). A psychological analysis of caste tension. *Indian Psychological Review*, *1*, 25–32.

Sinha, D. (1964). Position effect in the re-administration of an anxiety scale. *Journal of General Psychology*, *70*, 305–309.

Sinha, D. (1963). Manifest anxiety on an Indian sample. *Journal of General Psychology*, *69*, 261–265.

Sinha, D., & Pai, M.U. (1963). Motivational analysis of union membership. *Indian Journal of Social Work*, *23*, 343–349.

Sinha, D., & Misra, C.H.K. (1963). Qualities desirable for engineering students and profession: Part III: Comparison of the teachers and students samples. *Journal of Psychological Researches*, *7*(1).

Sinha, D. (1962). Cultural factors in the emergence of anxiety. *Eastern Anthropologist*, *15*, 21–37.

Sinha, D. (1962). Reliability and norms of an anxiety scale. *Manas*, 2, 37–42.

Sinha, D. (with Sharma, J.C.). (1962). Union attitudes and job satisfaction in Indian works. *Journal of Applied Psychology*, *46*, 247–251.

Sinha, D. (1961). Controlling industrial absenteeism. *Indian Journal of Labour Economics*. *4*(2).

Sinha, D. (1961). Developments of two anxiety scales, *Manas*, *1*, 1–10.

Sinha, D. (with Singh, P.) (1961). Job satisfaction and absenteeism. *Indian Journal of Social Work*, *21*, 337–843.

Sinha, D. (1961). Manifest anxiety and academic performance. *Psychologia*, *4*, 119–122.

Sinha, D., & Misra, C.H.K. (1961). Qualities desirable for engineering students and profession. Part I: Teacher's sample. *Journal of Psychological Researches*, *5*(2), 53–62.

Sinha, D., & Misra, C.H.K. (1961). Qualities desirable for engineering students and profession. Part II: Student's sample. *Journal of Psychological Researches*, *5*, 1–12.

Sinha, D. (1960). Caste dynamics: A psychological analysis. *Eastern Anthropologist*, *13*(4), 159–171.

Sinha, D. (1960). Social and behavioural problems in industry. *Indian Journal of Social Work*, *21*, 233–245.

Sinha, D., & Singh, T.R. (1959). Manifest anxiety and performance on problem solving tasks. *Journal of Consulting Psychology*, *23*(5), 469.

Sinha, D (1958). Job satisfaction in office and manual workers. *Indian Journal of Social Work*, *19*, 39–46.

Sinha, D., & Sinha, N.K. (1957). Affective reactions and perceptual judgments. *Social Study*, *2*, 13–19.

Sinha, D. (1956). Personal factors in absenteeism. *Indian Journal of Social Work*, *17*(2), 1–8.

Sinha, D. (1952). An experimental study of social factor in perception: The influence of an arbitrary group standard. *Patna University Journal*, 1–10.

Sinha, D. (1952). Behaviour in a catastrophic situation: A psychological study of reports and rumours. *British Journal of Psychology*, *43*, 200–209.

Davis, D.R., & Sinha, D. (1950). Effect of an experience upon the recall of author. *Quarterly Journal of Experimental Psychology*, *2*, 43–52.

Davis, D.R., & Sinha, D. (1950). The influence of an interpolated experience upon recognition. *Quarterly Journal of Experimental Psychology*, *2*, 132–137.

# Index

# About the Authors

**Durganand Sinha** (Born: 23 September 1922; Died: 23 March 1998) did his B.A. and M.A. in Philosophy (with specialization in Psychology) from Patna University. Subsequently, he went to Cambridge University where he was awarded the M.Sc. degree. On his return to India in 1949, Professor Sinha joined as the faculty of Psychology at Patna University. His research article 'Behavior in a catastrophic situation: A psychological study of reports and rumors' published in the *British Journal of Psychology* showed his scientific creativity and responsiveness to the problems of his immediate surroundings. He left Patna in 1958 and joined the newly established Indian Institute of Technology, Kharagpur.

Professor Sinha came to Allahabad University in 1961 as a professor to chair the newly created Department of Psychology. In the mid-1980s, he also served as the Director of the A.N. Sinha Institute of Social Studies, Patna. The present status of the Department of Psychology at Allahabad as a Centre of Advanced Study owes much to his vision and dedication.

In a career spanning half a century, Professor Sinha made significant contributions as a researcher in diverse areas. It encompassed the role of socio-cultural factors in perception and cognition; changes in the Indian family and the implications for the socialization process; larger applied social psychological issues such as motivation and rural development, deprivation and poverty; and social change. His books (listed in the section 'Complete Works of Durganand Sinha' in this volume) have left his name permanently in the field of psychology of social sciences. In India, he was a central figure of the psychological profession. He served as the President of the Indian Psychological Association, the Indian Academy of Applied Psychology and Psychology Section of the Indian Science Congress.

**Girishwar Misra** is Professor of Psychology and currently Vice Chancellor of Mahatma Gandhi International Hindi University, Wardha. Some of his recent publications are: *Psychological Perspectives on Stress and Health* (2000), *Rethinking Intelligence* (with A.K. Srivastava, 2007),

*Psychology and Societal Development, Foundations of Indian Psychology* (with Matthijs R. Cornellison and S. Varma, 2011), *Psychology in India: Advances in Research, Handbook of Psychology in India* (2011), *New Directions in Health Psychology* (Ajit Dalal, 2012) and *Psychology and Psychoanalysis* (2013). He is the editor-in-chief of the journal *Psychological Studies*. He is currently coordinating the Sixth ICSSR Survey of Psychological Research in India as its Chief Editor.

**Ajit K Dalal** is Professor of Psychology at the University of Allahabad, Allahabad. He had obtained his Doctor of Philosophy degree (1978) from the Indian Institute of Technology, Kanpur. Some of his major publications include *Handbook of Indian Psychology* (with K.R. Rao and A.C. Paranjpe, 2008), *New Directions in Health Psychology* (with G. Misra, 2012), *Qualitative Research on Well-Being and Self-Growth: Contemporary Indian Perspectives* (with R. Priya, 2014) and *Health Beliefs and Coping with Chronic Diseases* (2015).